THE THREE GREAT CHURCHES

A comparison of of Catholic, Protestant and Orthodox beliefs

Prayer for the dead, purgatory, the apocrypha, holy fools, infant baptism, Mary, icons, the pope, the ecumenical councils, the filioque, holy places, candles, relics, priests, confession, hesychasm, Eucharist, salvation, prayer to saints, sign of the cross, celibacy, tradition, mystery, sacraments, theosis, chrismation, the liturgy, confirmation, church fathers, and more.

BY KERBY RIALS

I08898323

SPECIAL THANKS TO the following persons who offered help and encouragement in writing this book:

Tonya Eschelmann, Betty Rials, Robert Hosken, Tom Tulinsky, Bruce Edwards, Svetlana Reznichenko

The Three Great Churches:
A comparison of Catholic, Protestant and Orthodox beliefs
Copyright 2006 Kerby Rials
Revised and updated Sept. 2007, July 2008, April 2010, October 2012, October 2015

ISBN-10: 0-9786918-0-6
ISBN-13: 978-0-9786918-0-6

ABOUT THE AUTHOR: Kerby Rials is a missionary with the Assemblies of God to Belgium. He has pastored churches in Russia, the United States, and Belgium, and was an assistant pastor in Switzerland. He is a graduate of Michigan State University and Mount Hope Bible Training Institute. He and his wife, Sheila, served as missionaries in Russia for 14 years. They have two adult sons, Luke and Daniel, of whom they are very proud.

ORDERING INFORMATION: Looking Glass River Publishing, 524 Riverwalk Dr., Mason MI 48854, USA. TEL: 1 877-885-9781. E-MAIL: kerbyrials@aol.com

TABLE OF CONTENTS

PREFACE
Why to read this book

They say you should never discuss religion or politics.

And so we avoid certain controversial questions, about which we all would like to know more.

When it comes to Christianity, some of those questions are:

How do you get to heaven? Can you pay money to do so?

Can you pray someone else into heaven after they have died?

Should you pray to saints? Can priests forgive sins?

Do relics and icons have supernatural power, or are they spiritual traps that harm Christians who rely upon them?

Must we baptize infants to save them from hell?

Since Catholic and Eastern Orthodox churches are older, does that mean that they are right and Protestants wrong?

This book, however, jumps into these controversial mud puddles with both feet.

What makes it even more difficult for us Protestants, is that just asking these questions opens us up to the charge of being anti-Catholic or religious bigots. We are taught not to discuss them in polite company.

And in the rare times when we are able to discuss these things, it may be with people who really are religious bigots, or with people who simply don't know the answers, or (worse) both!

The books that are available seem themselves to be bigoted — either boldly promoting Catholic or Orthodox teaching and condemning Protestants, or condemning Catholics and Orthodox.

Other authors, desiring to please all Christian groups, leave out controversial subjects and information that might offend their readers. This book, however, jumps into these controversial mud puddles with both feet.

While it presents all sides of these controversial issues, it explains and defends Bible-based Protestant Christianity.

It meets an increasing need. Fewer and fewer Protestants know why they are Protestant. Some of the lines have been blurred. This is not all bad, of course, but nonethelesss, what we believe makes a big difference. Certainly there must be teachings that are critically important, that we cannot ignore or compromise.

While it presents all sides of these controversial questions, it explains and defends Bible-based Protestant Christianity.

As the apostle Paul said: "Watch your life and doctrine closely. Persevere in them, because if you do, you will save both yourself and your hearers." (1 Tim. 4:16)

Here the apostle says that what we believe affects our salvation and those we influence. No clearer statement can be given about the importance of truly understanding the word of God.

May God bless your reading of this book.

— *Kerby Rials*

1. THE THREE CHURCHES:
Compared and contrasted

Christianity is the largest religion in the world. One out of every three people walking the planet is a Christian — almost 2 billion people.[1]

It's the dominant faith in 164 of the world's 237 countries, where it is divided into three churches (or branches) — Catholic, Protestant and Eastern Orthodox .

Catholicism — largest of the three

The Roman Catholic Church is the largest of these churches. Almost one billion people belong to it — one sixth of the world's population. Headquartered in Rome, Italy, and led by an elected pope, it is the largest Christian church in France, Italy, Spain, Switzerland, Austria, Hungary, Poland, Slovakia, Czech Republic, Slovenia, Croatia, Lithuania, Tanzania, Angola, Rwanda, Congo, Canada and most of South America (except Guyana and some islands).

The Catholic Church considers itself to be the true church of Christ on the earth, and the oldest. Catholics are united by their belief in the pope as the representative of Christ on the earth, a belief that is not shared by the other two Christian churches. Numbers of adherents of the Catholic church, although increasing slightly, are gradually declining as a percentage of the world population. [2]

Protestants take second place

The second largest group of churches is Protestant.

Approximately 720 million people[1] call themselves Protestants. Some of the countries where most Christians are Protestant are Germany, Finland, Sweden, Great Britain, the United States, the Netherlands, Norway, Latvia, Greenland, Denmark, Australia, New Zealand, Iceland, South Africa, Nigeria, Kenya, South Korea, Zimbabwe, Estonia, Botswana, Malawi, Mozambique, Cote d'Ivoire, Ghana, Liberia, Namibia, and Uganda.

Protestant churches include Lutherans, Baptists, Anglicans, Pentecostals, Reformed, Methodists, Presbyterians, independent charismatics, Adventists, and others (but not Mormons or Jehovah's Witnesses).[3]

These churches, although administered separately, are generally united by belief in salvation by faith alone, and by belief in scripture over tradition. These and several other beliefs set them apart from Catholics and Orthodox, as shown further in this book. Protestant churches are generally considered to

PRE-DOMINANT CHURCH BY COUNTRY

CATHOLIC

PROTESTANT

ORTHODOX

NON-CHRISTIAN

have started with the Reformation of Martin Luther in 1517 A.D.

Protestants are the only one of the three great churches to be growing as a percentage of the world population, increasing roughly three percent annually. Most of this growth, by far, is in evangelical churches. Evangelicals are defined by *Operation World*[1] as those who emphasize salvation by faith in Christ alone, personal conversion, the Bible as the ultimate authority, and a commitment to evangelism. Some Catholics and Orthodox are evangelical, but the great majority are Protestant

The Eastern Orthodox

Approximately 211 million people belong to the Orthodox churches. The largest group is an association of 19 independent churches, mostly in Eastern Europe but with members worldwide. These churches have the same beliefs and share communion. Countries that are predominantly Eastern Orthodox are Russia, Greece, Romania, Moldova, Bulgaria, Serbia, Albania, Macedonia, Montenegro, Ukraine, Belarus, Georgia, and Cyprus. Also predominantly Orthodox are the nations of Eritrea, Ethiopia and Armenia, but their churches are not included in the main association of Orthodox churches, nor are other smaller Nestorian, Coptic and breakaway Orthodox groups. They are counted in the total of Orthodox churches by *Operation World* [1] as they share the same doctrinal foundation except for the council of Chalcedon. [4] Numbers of Orthodox believers, like Catholic, are increasing slightly but not growing as fast as the world's population.

Orthodoxy holds doctrines that are similar to Catholic teaching, but it rejects the pope, and believes it is the only church organization that has remained true to the teaching of the apostles. It also believes it is the oldest.

A word of caution

This book compares the official beliefs of the three churches but does not presume to say what individual Catholics, Protestants or Orthodox believe. Few people believe exactly what their church teaches. Many people, for instance, call themselves Catholics but still use contraceptives and don't believe the pope is infallible. For that reason, when comparing beliefs this book takes care to refer to "official" doctrine, meaning what the churches officially proclaim, not what individuals may believe.

Comparing apples and oranges

Counting who is Catholic, Orthodox or Protestant is also not simple. For instance, there is a major difference between religious preference and religious practice. Most people have a preference for one religion or the other, but that does not mean that they practice that religion, or believe all that it teaches. To measure religious preference, a survey is all that is needed.

Identifying practicing Christians is much more difficult. One method is to count everyone who has been baptized as a member. The problem with this approach, which is used by Catholic, Orthodox and some Protestant churches, is that many baptized as infants are in fact not Christians nor church members as adults. For instance, Lenin, Stalin, Hitler, Joseph Goebbels, and Friedrich Nietzsche were all baptized as infants in the Orthodox, Catholic and Lutheran churches, but were certainly not Christians, even though by this method they were counted as church members. This

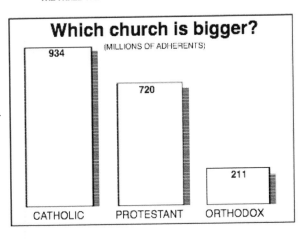

Which church is bigger?

(MILLIONS OF ADHERENTS)

CATHOLIC	PROTESTANT	ORTHODOX
934	720	211

problem is also illustrated by church attendance. In France, 67 percent are listed as Catholic, but only 8 percent attend church regularly. In Russia, 50 percent of the population are counted as members of the Orthodox Church, but only 7 percent attend church monthly.[1] In Sweden, almost 90 percent are baptized as Lutheran Protestants but only 1 percent attend church.[5]

Most evangelical churches, by contrast, only count a person as a member if they regularly attend and are living a holy life. Accordingly, comparing evangelical Protestant church numbers with other churches may be like comparing apples with oranges.

What the three churches have in common

Regardless of numbers, Protestants, Catholics and Orthodox share the same fundamental beliefs about Christianity. For instance, all three accept the Nicene Creed, adopted by the first church council in 325 A.D. (With one minor difference — see p. 173 regarding the filioque.) All three believe in the death, burial and resurrection of Jesus Christ, in his divinity and in his return. All three accept the Bible as the word of God, and all three agree that repentance and faith are necessary to have eternal life and escape hell.

All agree with Christ's prayer in John 17: "I pray also for those who will believe in me through their message, that all of them may be one..."

Because Christian churches have so much in common, some may believe that a book on differences is misguided. But when the apostles Paul and Barnabas were confronted with fellow Christians who had different doctrines, they had a "sharp dispute and debate with them" (Acts 15:2). This shows that it is indeed permissible to have disagreements over doctrine. True unity does not mean ignoring differences, but it does mean loving our brothers in the midst of those differences. It then says "the apostles and elders met to consider this question" and had "much discussion." That wonderful word, "discussion," shows that the church, divided as it was and with strong feelings on both sides, was able still to resolve the question. A thorough examination of the truth is not something to be feared. Truth can take the most rigorous inspection, and still come up shining. The Bible says, "Seek and ye shall find." Let us seek the truth without being afraid of finding it.

PLEASE NOTE: In order to facilitate a comparison, this book primarily uses evangelical Protestant theology instead of liberal Protestant, when these differ. While it is difficult sometimes to separate one from the other, in general it can be said that evangelical Protestants:

1) Believe the Bible to be the literally true, inspired word of God, that is still relevant today.

2) Believe in a real heaven, a real hell and a real devil.

3) Consider basic doctrines such as the death and resurrection of Christ as foundational and not open to serious questioning.

Many liberal Protestants do not accept these three premises, while (officially at least) Catholics, Orthodox and evangelical Protestants do. A comparison, therefore, that included the liberal Protestant point of view, differing foundationally as it does from the other churches, is beyond the scope of this book.

Secondly, regarding Catholic and Orthodox theology, please note that care has been taken to quote recognized sources, and to document those well. Yet it is entirely possible to find other Catholic and Orthodox sources who may contradict what is presented here, and of course individual believers may differ greatly from the official position of their church. Such is the diversity in Christianity. In choosing which sources to quote, effort has been made to choose those that represent the mainstream of Orthodoxy/Catholicism/evangelical Protestantism, and those that have the approval of the pope, bishops or patriarchs, when appropriate.

---

1) Johnstone, Patrick, *Operation World,* Paternoster Publishing, Carlisle, U.K. (2001)

2) Churches that are considered Catholic include all those that swear allegiance to the pope. This includes Uniate, Maronite, Chaldean, Melkite, Armenian and Syrian Catholic churches.

3) As defined by *Operation World.* Mormons and Jehovah's Witnesses are not included because their beliefs differ significantly from traditional Christianity. For instance, Mormonism teaches that there are many gods, and we may become gods ourselves, and Jehovah's Witnesses say that Jesus was a created being and was not God. See http://www.watchman.org/.

4) Orthodox numbers in this book include all Eastern, Oriental and Nestorian groups, Armenian (Gregorian), Old Believers, Old Calendarists, Syriac and most Ukrainian.

5) *Christianity Today,* February 7, 2000, Vol. 44, No. 2, p. 29, also at http://www.christianitytoday.com/ct/2000/002/22.29.html

2. THE THREE CHURCHES:
Which is oldest?

It is not uncommon for Catholic, Orthodox and Protestant churches to each claim to be the most ancient Christian faith, and therefore the only correct one.

This argument of antiquity is a powerful one. Whichever church can prove that it is the oldest can then argue that it is the right church, and all those that came after it are imposters. This "oldest" church can say that it is the closest to the apostles and to Jesus, since it has been around longer than other "new" churches. It can say that its doctrines are therefore correct, and any  churches that differ from it, differ also with the teaching of the apostles.

So which is oldest? Catholic? Protestant? Orthodox?

At first glance, one would naturally rule out the Protestant churches, since most people know that the Protestant Reformation traditionally started when Martin Luther nailed his 95 theses on the Wittenburg door in Germany almost 500 years ago. The history of the Catholic and Orthodox churches can be traced back at least a thousand years earlier.

The Catholic and Orthodox churches accordingly refer to themselves as the churches of the apostles, faithfully keeping the traditions as handed down to them by the first century church. Protestant churches, however, say that there are two kinds of "old" — older teaching, and older organizations. A church that has existed longer than others has organizational antiquity. A church that has older doctrine has doctrinal antiquity.

Therefore, an older church that has changed in what it believes, can be "newer" in teaching than a younger organization that holds to the ancient teaching of the apostles.

It is similar, by way of illustration, to an ancient library founded to promote Shakespeare's writings, but that over the centuries has replaced many of Shakespeare's books with more popular ones. This old library has had the same organization for centuries. It is in the same place, and has the same name. However, the books have changed. Shakespeare's books have been joined by several others. The library has departed from the goal of the founder. It has changed with the times. At the same time a new library has opened in a different building, but dedicated wholly to Shakespeare. All it has inside are books by and about Shakespeare. Although it is newer, does not have the same history as the first library, and is in a different building, it nonetheless has fulfilled the founder's intention to honor Shakespeare. It is more true to the founder's intentions than the older library. It has doctrinal antiquity, but not organizational antiquity.

This story illustrates the Protestant point of view. They feel that it doesn't matter if one church has been around longer than other churches. A long history is no guarantee that a church's teaching has not changed.

But how can one know if a church has drifted from the teaching of the apostles over the centuries? The simplest answer is to look at the teaching of the apostles and compare it with what is being taught today.

Protestants take the New Testament as the purest evidence of what Jesus and the apostles actually taught. They use it as the rule to measure the doctrinal antiquity of all churches. In this book this rule is used over and over again as we look at controversial issues.

Another help is the record of the early churches. If we can find evidence that certain traditions arose hundreds of years after the apostles, then we know that this is "new" teaching. This second method of determining doctrinal antiquity is not as easy to use as the New Testament.

One can always say that a certain practice was a tradition of the apostles, but proving that objectively is not as easy.

After all, we are talking about events that occurred 2,000 years ago.

But most if not all agree that the writings of the early church fathers are accurate records of their times. Catholic, Orthodox and Protestant authorities usually accept them as proof of the opinions of ancient church leaders. Protestant theologians therefore use these two methods (the New Testament and the writings of the church fathers) in evaluating ancient practices. One such example would be mandatory priestly celibacy. It is absent in the New Testament, as Peter and many of the other apostles were married. The earliest reference to the practice was in 315 A.D, and it was not formally accepted as a requirement until 692 A.D. in the Eastern (Orthodox) churches, and 1123 in the Catholic churches. (See the chapter on celibacy.)

In conclusion, Protestant leaders agree that their churches are not as old organizationally as Catholic or Orthodox churches, but feel their doctrines are older, or closer to the teaching of the apostles.

3. THE CHURCH:
Can it be wrong?

It is sometimes argued that it is impossible for the true church of God to fall into error. However, if one accepts that the church cannot make a mistake, then there is an immediate dilemma.

Since there are many differences between churches, it's impossible for them all to be right. And if they have made mistakes, they cannot be the true church, according to this theory.

The implications of such teaching are mind-boggling. If there is only one true church, will those outside it all go to hell? How can one know which church is right?

If, on the other hand, it is possible for the churches to be wrong, then we must know which ones are right. We also must be careful of what teaching we accept from churches, since it could be wrong. So a careful look at both sides of this argument is warranted.

The Orthodox/Catholic viewpoint

Orthodox and Catholic leaders say the church as a whole cannot make a mistake. They base this on Jesus' statement, "I will build my church, and the gates of hell shall not prevail against it" (Matt. 16:18).

The Catholic Catechism (889) says Christ gave to the church "a share in his own infallibility." Orthodox theology professor Eusebius Stephanou writes, "Of course the Church as the Body of Christ, is holy and unerring...."[1]

The Protestant viewpoint

Protestants believe there is no scripture that shows the church can't be wrong. In fact, many scriptures show church mistakes.

Proof that the church can have doctrinal error is in Revelation. There the Lord rebuked several churches for doctrinal error:

"I have a few things against you: You have people there who hold to the teaching of Balaam.. Likewise you also have those who hold to the teaching of the Nicolaitans." (Rev. 2:14-15) "You tolerate that woman Jezebel... By her teaching she misleads my servants into sexual immorality... To you who do not hold to her teaching ...I will not impose any other burden on you." (Rev. 2:20,24)

Notice the word "teaching," which is translated in the King James as "doctrine." It was wrong doctrine. The church was in error, and God rebuked it for that.

The apostle Paul also prophesied that wrong doctrine would be found in the heart of the church, coming from its own leaders: "I know that after I leave, savage wolves will come in among you and will not spare the flock. Even from your own number men will arise and distort the truth in order to draw away disciples after them." (Acts 20:29-30).

The apostle Peter prophesied that false teaching would afflict the church: "But there were also false prophets among the people, just as there will be false teachers among you. They will secretly introduce destructive heresies, even denying the sovereign Lord who bought them— bringing swift destruction on themselves" (2 Peter 2:1).

In Jesus' day and in the Old Testament, the experts in Bible teaching were called scribes. Even they were guilty of false teaching, as the prophet Jeremiah wrote: "How can you say, 'We are wise, for we have the law of the LORD,' when actually the lying pen of the scribes has handled it falsely?" (Jer. 8:8).

For more on error in the church, see the chapter, "The Bible: Who has the right to interpret it?"

As to the argument that the church cannot fall into error because of Matt. 16:18 ("...I will build my church, and the gates of Hades will not overcome it."), Protestants note that in biblical times the courts and leaders of a city met at the city gates to make decisions and get counsel (Gen. 23:10, Ruth 4:1-11, 1 Kings 22:10, Job 29:7-12). Accordingly, the verse doesn't say that the church will always be free from error -- just that it will overcome the plots, counsel, strategies and defenses of hell.

---

1) *The Challenge of the Ecumenical Movement for the Orthodox Church*, p.. 7.

4. THE CHURCH:
Can it be divided?

Some Christians argue that it is impossible to divide the true church into separate denominations and organizations. This view is most often put forth by Orthodox or Catholic churches, which compare their relative unity with the many Protestant churches. Many Catholic and Orthodox leaders say there is only one true church, and theirs is it. Most Protestants feel that unity is more of the Spirit than of organization, and that it is possible to be unified even if in different organizations.

The Orthodox/Catholic viewpoint

Orthodox and Catholic leaders base their argument on Eph. 4:5, where the apostle Paul says there is "one Lord, one faith, one baptism." Therefore, since there is "one faith" it cannot be divided.

Accordingly, Catholic and Orthodox leaders don't use the word "denomination" to describe themselves, since that would be imply that they are just one of many Christian groups. Instead, they refer to themselves as the "Church," implying that all other denominations are outside the church and have fallen away. The argument is that by rejecting church tradition and authority, Protestants have fallen into disunity and heresy.

The very fact that there are so many Protestant churches, each proclaiming different things, is proof that they cannot all be right, they say.

The Protestant viewpoint

Protestants agree that the church cannot be divided spiritually. God knows all who are his, and there is no division with him. There is indeed only one church redeemed from sin and called to serve God. But that unified heavenly church is organized in different ways on the earth, based upon varying beliefs, cultural traits and preferences. The members of this one church may not agree on every point, but that does not divide them in God's eyes.

For instance, the New Testament shows divisions between believers from the very beginning. They disagreed on many nonessential doctrines and even on who their leaders should be, and yet the Bible still calls them Christians.

For instance, Rom. 14:1 says: "Accept him whose faith is weak, without passing judgment on disputable matters." Here Paul is saying that there are indeed "disputable matters" that divide Christians doctrinally, yet he stresses that this should not be a reason to divide Christians spiritually ("Accept him..."). Christians do not have to agree on every doctrine to be unified. Paul says accept them anyway.

Divisions in the early church

The New Testament shows the early Christians were divided into the circumcision group and the non-circumcision group: "So when Peter went up to Jerusalem, the circumcised believers criticized him." (Acts 11:2)

"Then some of the believers who belonged to the party of the Pharisees stood up and said, 'The Gentiles must be circumcised and required to obey the law of Moses'" (Acts 15:5).

Notice the phrases "the circumcised believers" and "some of the believers who belonged to the party of the Pharisees."

Two things can be found here: first, that these people were divided and distinct from other Christians, and second, that they were still called believers. This party of the Pharisees had strong opinions and influence. Even the Apostle Peter was afraid of them. "Before certain men came from James, he used to eat with the Gentiles. But when they arrived, he began to draw back and separate himself from the Gentiles because he was afraid of those who belonged to the circumcision group" (Gal. 2:12).

Paul had "sharp dispute and debate with them" as Acts 15:2 says. An apostle of God strongly disagreed with them, yet they were still Christians.

The Corinthian church was also divided into at least two groups, the Bible tells us (1 Cor. 3:3-4): the followers of Paul and the followers of Apollos. "You are still worldly. For since there is jealousy and quarreling among you, are you not worldly? Are you not acting like mere men? For when one says, 'I follow Paul,' and another, 'I follow Apollos,' are you not mere men?"

Paul said what was important was their allegiance to God, and not to their human leaders: "I planted the seed, Apollos watered it, but God made it grow. So neither he who plants nor he who waters is anything, but only God, who makes things grow" (1 Cor. 3:6-7).

The early history of the church (after the New Testament was completed) also shows many divisions and splits, many of which continue today. Accordingly, the argument that the church was unified until 1054 A.D. (when the Catholic and Orthodox churches divided) is not borne out by history or scripture. For instance:

1) In 172 A.D. the Montanists split off from other churches, surviving until the fifth century.[1] They could be defined as more Pentecostal than the churches of the times.

2) In 251 A.D. the Novationists broke off from the other churches,

advocating a more strict discipline of fallen church members than that of most other churches. They established a network of their own churches and continued as a separate movement until the 7th century, being attacked in the writings of Eulogius, patriarch of Alexandria (580-607 A.D.) [2]

3) In 451 the Nestorian churches split off, and later the Monophysite churches, disagreeing with the Council of Chalcedon's report on the nature of Jesus. Monophysite churches still exist today in India, Armenia, Syria, Egypt, Eritrea, and Ethiopia. Encyclopedia Britannica states: "In modern times those churches usually classified as Monophysite (the Coptic, the Syrian, and the Armenian) are generally accepted by Roman Catholic, Eastern Orthodox, and Protestant Christendom as essentially orthodox in their doctrine of the person of Jesus Christ." [3] The Nestorian churches exist today primarily in Iraq, Syria and Iran.

Subsequent splits that continue to the present day include, of course, the Catholic/Orthodox split (1054 A.D.), the Protestant/Catholic split (16th century), the Orthodox/Old Believer split (17th century) and many others.

What is clear is that the Christian church — meaning all Christians — began with the pouring out of the Holy Spirit at Pentecost. After that, differences emerged little by little between the churches. The actual dates that mark the birth of the individual churches is often hard to place. For instance, there is no specific time when one can say, "This was the day the Orthodox church was formed." The distinctive characteristics of the Orthodox church appeared gradually, as did the characteristics of the Catholic church.

Icons, for instance, gradually appeared from the fourth century until the sixth. (See the chapter on icons.) The Catholic church approved new doctrines as late as 1950, when it approved the bodily ascension of Mary into heaven as an official teaching of the Catholic church.[4]

These changes in doctrine, Protestants believe, are evidence that the church was at its most perfect state in the first century when the apostles lived, just after Christ's ascension to heaven. Since that time the church has struggled to return to that level of miraculous power and holiness.

Is unity organizational or spiritual?

Despite the many divisions in the churches today — Catholic, Protestant and Orthodox — many Christians today maintain that the church is still unified spiritually if not organizationally. They believe in a unity in Christ that supersedes organizational structures and minor differences in doctrine. Protestants believe that there is a unity that crosses denominational boundaries. For instance, Protestants share foundational doctrines about the divinity of Christ, repentance and faith in God, the inspiration of the scriptures, heaven, hell and eternal judgment. Protestant churches have different views on church government and other minor issues. But their essential unity in Christ and devotion to him is unchanged. This creates a unity that supersedes organizational diversity.

The proof of this unity is evidenced by cooperation with other denominations in evangelistic outreaches, mission organizations and joint projects.

Examples of this interdenominational cooperation include broadcasts such as 700 Club and Focus on the Family, missions such as Campus Crusade and Youth with a Mission, publications such as Christianity Today, and organizations such as the National Association of Evangelicals and the Billy Graham Evangelistic Association, to name a few.

All of these unite primarily evangelical Protestant Christians.

Lastly, Protestants note that theological and organizational divisions exist not only in Protestant churches, but also in Orthodox and Catholic churches. A list of seven Catholic and 13 Orthodox breakaway groups and churches is below:

SEPARATE CATHOLIC CHURCHES AND GROUPS

OLD CATHOLIC CHURCH

The Old Catholic church broke off from Rome in the 1870s, opposing the First Vatican Council's new doctrine of papal infallibility. Catholic churches who broke away were primarily in Germany, Austria and Switzerland, but today exist in many other countries as well, including the US. Members say they follow a more authentic Catholic tradition than that of Rome. They claim apostolic succession stemming from the bishop of Utrecht in Holland.[5]

SOCIETY OF ST. PIUS X

This international breakaway Catholic group was founded by French Archbishop Marcel Lefebvre in 1970 to "maintain the traditional Catholic priesthood and all the works related to it" as they say on their web site. They hold masses in Latin and reject Vatican II reforms. The society is active in 31 countries, and has six seminaries and 453 priests. The group was excommunicated by the Catholic church, but after the death of Archbishop Lefebvre the excommunications were lifted in 2009. Doctrinal discussions continue with the Catholic church.[6]

SOCIETY OF ST. PIUS V

This Catholic breakaway group describes itself as "an organization of traditional Catholic priests dedicated to the preservation of the Traditional Latin Mass." It has its own seminary and convent in Round Top, New York. It argues that the change of the mass in 1962 left the church without a true priesthood and brought the effectiveness of the sacraments into question. They are opposed to what they call liberal tendencies in the Catholic church.[7]

LATIN TRIDENTINE CHURCHES – UNA VOCE

This is an association of Catholics and Catholic churches in 24 countries that advocate the mass in Latin. Founded in 1964, the group, called Una Voce, is opposed to the decision of the Vatican II decision to do the mass in the language of the people. It, however, is still submitted to the authority of the pope, who permits Latin masses in most cases.[8]

CATHOLIC TRADITIONALIST MOVEMENT

Formed by Priest Gommar DePauw, J.C.D., of Westbury, New York in 1965 to counteract what he called "hootenanny Masses." They base their support for a traditional Latin mass on a statement establishing the Latin mass by Pope Pius V in 1570:

"By this our decree, to be valid in perpetuity, we determine and order that never shall anything be added to, omitted from, or changed in this Missal..." [9]

ONE HOLY CATHOLIC APOSTOLIC CHURCH (The Vatican in Exile)
This small traditionalist Catholic group in Kansas (USA) elected their own pope in 1990. Pope Michael was the subject of a documentary (http://popemichaelfilm.com) [10]

SPIRITUS CHRISTI
This breakaway Catholic parish in Rochester, New York, USA, was organized in 1999 after its leaders were excommunicated for using women clergy, offering communion to non-Catholics and celebrating gay marriages. It continues to expand.[11]

SEPARATE ORTHODOX CHURCHES

The churches below are all Eastern Orthodox in that they use icons, reject the pope*, and reject the filioque, but they aren't united for various reasons. *(excepting the Uniate churches)

TRUE ORTHODOX CHURCH
This is a group of about 100 Orthodox parishes in Russia and Russian-speaking regions of Ukraine which rebelled against the Russian Orthodox Church and formed the True Russian Orthodox Church (TROC). [12]

RUSSIAN ORTHODOX CHURCH OUTSIDE OF RUSSIA
ROCOR was founded by refugee Russian Orthodox bishops and priests in Yugoslavia in 1923, and is headquartered in New York. A few TROC churches are affiliated with ROCOR. Church leaders were cut off from the Russian Orthodox Church by the Soviet government in the 1920s after they refused to sign a pledge of loyalty. ROCOR today has 15 dioceses worldwide, and has legal control of some of the holy sites in Jerusalem. It has monasteries and convents in several countries, and parishes in most U.S. states. A 2006 proposal to accept ROCOR as a self-governing part of the Russian Orthodox Church was accepted by both groups.[13]

OLD BELIEVERS
One of the largest groups out of fellowship with other Orthodox is the Old Brethren, with approximately two million members. They broke away from the Russian Orthodox Church in 1666-67 during the Roskol dispute over how to make the sign of the cross. There are approximately 250 parishes of Old Believers in Russia and many more in Asia, Brazil, Canada and the United States. In 1971 the Council of the Russian Orthodox Church completely rescinded all the anathemas of the 17th century and recognized the validity of the old rites; however, the two groups are still separated. [14]

THE RUSSIAN ORTHODOX/UKRAINIAN ORTHODOX CHURCH
The Moscow Patriarchate is of course the largest of the four traditional Orthodox churches in Russia. Membership estimates vary depending upon how that is defined. Roughly half of Russians say they are Orthodox, but only three percent attend the liturgy weekly. Affiliated with the Russian Orthodox Church – Moscow Patriarchate is the Ukrainian Orthodox Church of the Moscow Patriarchate. It is the largest church in Ukraine, with 34 bishops, and 6,500 parishes.
It is the only Orthodox church in Ukraine recognized by the rest of the Orthodox

world. The Moscow Patriarchate gave it semi-autonomous status in 1991.

THE UKRAINIAN ORTHODOX CHURCH, KYIVAN PATRIARCHATE

The Ukrainian Orthodox Church of the Kyivan Patriarchate (UOC-KP) is the second largest Ukrainian Orthodox church with 1,300 parishes and 1,600 priests. It is rooted in the eastern and central Ukraine and in the region of Volhynia. The popular denomination was formed in 1992 when the Ukrainian Autocephalous Orthodox Church (UAOC) joined a breakaway faction of the Moscow Patriarch Church. The denomination has had much disunity. Five of its bishops left in 1993 to form a new UAOC in 1993. Five others rejoined the Moscow-supported Ukrainian Orthodox church in 1994.[15]

THE UKRAINIAN AUTOCEPHALOUS ORTHODOX CHURCH

As mentioned above, the Ukrainian Autocephalous Orthodox Church (UAOC) was formed when several bishops left other Ukrainian Orthodox churches. It claims some 1,200 parishes, but others estimate 550 parishes and 220 priests. In 1996 the UAOC split into two factions, the breakaway portion being led by Metropolitan Vasili Bodnarshchuk. In November 1996 UAOC bishops dismissed Patriarch Dymitri. His successor, Bishop John (Boichuk), subsequently transferred his allegiance to the Ukrainian Orthodox-Kyiv Patriarchate .[16]

THE UKRAINIAN EASTERN-RITE CATHOLIC CHURCH

The Ukrainian Eastern Rite Catholics are composed of 5 million members (17 percent of Ukrainians) in 3,000 parishes served by 1,700 priests. It was formed more than 400 years ago in an attempt to lead Orthodox Christians into the Catholic church. They use Orthodox rituals, icons and liturgy, but swear allegiance to the pope.[17]

MACEDONIAN/MONTENEGRIN ORTHODOX CHURCH

The Macedonian Orthodox Church broke away from the Serbian Orthodox church in 1967. This church has never been recognized by other Orthodox churches. In 1995, the Serbian Orthodox Church declared the Macedonian Orthodox Church schismatic. The Serbian Orthodox Church also refuses recognition of the Montenegrin Orthodox Church, created in 1993.[18]

COPTIC CHURCHES

The Egyptian Coptic Orthodox Church (8 million), the Eritrean Coptic Orthodox Church (1.6 million) and the Ethiopian Orthodox Coptic Church (36 million) have many of the same beliefs as other Orthodox but are separated from them by their rejection of the Council of Chalcedon's rulings about the nature of Christ.[19]

ARMENIAN ORTHODOX CHURCH

The 2.7 million members of the Armenian Orthodox Church are non-Chalcedonian, like the Coptic Churches, and as such are not accepted by the rest of Orthodoxy.[20]

SYRIAN ORTHODOX CHURCH

Three Orthodox denominations in Syria are non-Chalcedonian: Syrian Orthodox (90,000), the Assyrian Church of the East (48,000), and the Armenian Apostolic Church (118,000).[21]

INDIAN ORTHODOX CHURCH

The 1.9 million believers in the Malankara Orthodox Syrian Church in India claim spiritual descent from the Apostle Thomas who came to India 2,000 years ago. They hold to Nestorian (non-Chalcedonian) Christianity. They have links to the Syrian Jacobite Church.[22]

---

1) *Eerdman's Handbook to the History of Christianity*, p.74.

2) Ibid p.78.

3) Vol. 8, p. 264.

4) *Catechism of the Catholic Church*, p. 274.

5) http://members.tripod.com/Old_Catholic/history.html, accessed Nov. 1, 2015.

6) http://www.fsspx.org/fr/node/7151, accessed Nov. 1, 2015 (in French)

7) http://www.sspv.org, accessed Nov. 1, 2015.

8) http://www.unavoce.org, accessed Nov. 1, 2015.

9) http://www.latinmass-ctm.org, accessed Nov. 1, 2015.

10) http://popemichael.vaticaninexile.com, accessed Nov. 1, 2015.

11) http://www.spirituschristi.org/#/welcome/history, accessed Nov. 1, 2015.

12) Janice Broun, "Jurisdictional Conflicts Among Orthodox and Eastern-Rite Catholics in Russia and Ukraine," *East-West Church & Ministry Report*, Summer 1997, and http://theorthodox.org./true_orthodox_church2.htm and http://www.trueorthodox.org, accessed Nov. 1, 2015

13) http://www.russianorthodoxchurch.ws/synod/enrt07/enakt.html, accessed Nov. 1, 2015.

14) https://sites.google.com/a/lclark.edu/rsco/immigrant-communities/old-believers, accessed Nov. 1, 2015.

15) http://www.cerkva.info/en.html, accessed Nov. 1, 2015.

16) http://uaoc.blago.org/home/index.html, accessed Nov. 1, 2015.

17) http://www.cin.org/rite.html, accessed Nov. 1, 2015.

18) http://www.mpc.org.mk/english, accessed Nov. 1, 2015.

19) http://www.copticcentre.com/the-coptic-orthodox-church, accessed Nov. 1, 2015.

20) http://i-cias.com/e.o/arm_orth.htm, accessed Nov. 1, 2015.

21) http://www.syrianorthodoxchurch.org, accessed Nov. 1, 2015.

22) http://malankaraorthodoxchurch.in, accessed Nov. 1, 2015.

5. MYSTERY:
Can we understand God?

Author Daniel Clendenin once got complaints from Russian students that his course on Christianity was "too logical and rational" and that "problems relating to God transcend human logic." [1]

Such comments show one of the hallmarks of Eastern Orthodoxy: its teaching about mystery. Catholic and Protestant churches do not have the same emphasis on mystery. "Orthodox theology is essentially mystical and thus does not depend on scholarship and academic pursuit, though these are valuable for an articulation of mystical experience," according to Orthodox theologian Eusebius Stephanou. [2] The Orthodox view of western theology is that it is too intellect-oriented. Some say Protestants have replaced the priest with a professor. Orthodox writer John of Damascus (655-749 A.D.) said, "It is plain, then, that there is a God. But what he is in his essence and nature is absolutely incomprehensible and unknowable.... All that is comprehensible about him is his incomprehensibility." [3]

(Clendenin points to this as a good example of apophatic theology — from the Greek apophasis or "denial." Apophatic theology describes God by saying what he is not.)

Few of those acquainted with Protestant theology (or even Catholic) will deny that it is sometimes too intellectual. The dry atmosphere in many churches is only too evident, and certainly needs to become more a heartfelt worship than an exercise in logic. The greatest commandment, after all, is to love God, Jesus said.

However, most Protestants, while admitting the excesses in an intellect-centered Christianity, would say that God does want us to understand him as much as we are able.

Eph. 5:17 says, "Therefore do not be unwise, but understand what the will of the Lord is." The apostle Paul prayed for the Philippians (1:9) that they would "abound yet more and more in full knowledge and in all perception." He also prayed for the Colossians (1:9-10) that they "might be filled with the knowledge of his will in all wisdom and spiritual understanding..., increasing in the knowledge of God."

Col. 2:2-3 calls for "the full knowledge of the mystery of God, and of the Father, and of Christ; in whom are hidden all the treasures of wisdom and knowledge." Eph. 3:4 tells us to read Paul's epistles "so that you may understand my knowledge in the mystery of Christ."

The apostle Peter advises us (2 Peter 3:18) not to be satisfied with what little knowledge we have, but to "grow in grace and in knowledge of our Lord and Savior Jesus Christ..."

Jesus says his disciples will understand mysteries (Mark 4:11): "And he said to them, To you it is given to know the mystery of the kingdom of God. But to those outside, all these things are given in parables."

The apostle Paul wants us to understand mysteries (Rom. 11:25): "For I do not want you to be ignorant of this mystery, brothers..." Eph. 1:9 says God has "made known to us the mystery of his will..." Paul asks for prayer (Eph. 6:19, Col. 4:3) "that I may open my mouth boldly to make known the mystery of the gospel." Col. 1:26 says "the mystery which has been hidden from ages and from generations.... now has been revealed to his saints."

Protestants believe these scriptures show that we are to seek to understand God and his will for our lives. This is not to say that we as Christians will always understand everything or that it is even possible to understand everything. Jesus did not understand everything on the cross, for he said, "My God, my God, why have you forsaken me?"

Accordingly, Protestants consider the argument that God is infinite and therefore unknowable to be partly true, and partly false. It is true that a finite man cannot fully understand an infinite God. Yet God has revealed Himself to us in a way that we can know him — in Jesus. "For in Christ all the fullness of the Deity lives in bodily form" (Col. 2:9).

Mystery, rather than being something we should cherish, instead is seen in the Bible as something we should seek to understand.

The elevation of mystery beyond what is called for in the Bible has often left Christians with nothing to defend themselves when challenged intellectually by the world. It has seemed that the church has championed ignorance instead of knowledge. The apostle Peter advocated a ready defense: "... Always be prepared to give an answer to everyone who asks you to give the reason for the hope that you have" (1 Peter 3:15).

1) Clendenin, Daniel, "What the Orthodox Believe: Four Key Differences between the Orthodox and Protestants," *Christian History*, Issue 54, p. 33

2) *The Challenge of the Ecumenical Movement for the Orthodox Church*, Rev. Eusebius A. Stephanou, p. 5

3) Book 1, chap. 4, Nicene and Post-Nicene Fathers, series 2, vol. 9, (CD — p. 641-642)

6. THE BIBLE:
More important than tradition?

Among the many differences between Protestants, Catholics and Orthodox there is one foundational disagreement from which almost all others stem — sola scriptura.

"Sola scriptura" is Latin for "only scripture." It is the belief that the Bible is the final authority in matters of doctrine, and is superior to tradition. It is a foundational doctrine that all Protestant churches share. They believe that all traditions must agree with what is taught in the Bible. Church reformer Martin Luther championed this almost 500 years ago.

The Orthodox and Catholic viewpoint

Orthodox and Catholic churches, by contrast, argue that tradition, especially as determined by the church fathers and the seven church councils, are more important than scripture when it comes to interpreting scripture, developing doctrine, and answering difficult questions. Scripture is part of that tradition, but not superior to it, they say.

The Catholic Church considers unwritten tradition to be part of God's word: "...the Word of God, whether in its written form or in the form of Tradition..."[1]

Orthodox writer George Florovsky said preferring the Bible over church tradition is "the sin of the Reformation." [2] Orthodox theologian John Meyendorff simply said that sola scriptura was incompatible with Christianity.[2] The Orthodox view is that church tradition should determine the truth. The sources for church tradition are the Bible, the seven ecumenical councils, writings of the church fathers, the liturgy, canon law, and icons.

The Catholic church also says it does not rely on scripture alone, but uses tradition to determine doctrine.[3]

Orthodox and Catholic leaders find support for tradition in the apostle Paul's comments. He wrote "I praise you because you remember me in everything and hold fast to the traditions just as I handed them on to you" (1 Cor. 11:2). He commanded the Thessalonians to "keep aloof from every brother who leads an unruly life and not according to the tradition which you received from us...." (2 Thes. 3:6-7, NASB). He also told them to "stand firm and hold fast to the traditions that you were taught, either by an oral statement or by a letter of ours" (2 Thes. 2:15).

Catholic and Orthodox writers say these oral statements of the apostles that Paul referred to are the basis of some of their traditions.

The Protestant viewpoint

However, Protestants believe there's no proof that the traditions referred to by Paul are those that the Orthodox or Catholic churches practice.

First, it should be noted that any tradition which began after Paul lived could not have been one of those to which he was referring.

Indeed, research shows that many traditions started hundreds of years after the apostles. (See the chapters on icons and infant baptism.)

There is no evidence for them in the Bible, nor in the history of the early church. Accordingly, they could not have been the ones to which Paul was referring, since Paul had been dead for many years before these traditions came into being.

Second, Paul certainly would have known of Jesus' statements that scripture is more important than tradition. Accordingly, it doesn't seem likely that he would have passed on traditions that contradict scripture.

In Mark 7:8 Jesus said, "You have let go of the commands of God and are holding on to the traditions of men." In Matt. 15:3 and 6 he said, "Why do you break the command of God for the sake of your tradition? You nullify the word of God for the sake of your tradition."

In other words, Jesus pointed out that it was wrong to accept human traditions that violate the word of God.

Paul said the same in 1 Cor. 4:6, when he warned: "Do not go beyond what is written." This principle allows oral traditions, but limits them to the boundaries written in scripture.

Third, the fact that Paul only mentions oral traditions, but not which ones, means it is difficult to support any tradition from his statement.

Who can say, based on such scriptures, whether their traditions are the ones of which Paul spoke, or if he was referring to others? We can only say that he was not referring to traditions that arose later, nor was he referring to traditions that contradict scripture.

For instance, in Col. 2:8 Paul warns us against false traditions: "See to it that no one takes you captive through philosophy and empty deception, according to the tradition of men, according to the elementary principles of the world, rather than according to Christ." Christ's statements on sola scriptura, of course, are the most authoritative of any.

Similarly, Paul wrote that scripture is the basis for correct doctrine: "All scripture is given by inspiration of God, and is profitable for doctrine, for reproof, for correction, for instruction in righteousness: That the man of God may be perfect, thoroughly furnished unto all good works." (2 Tim. 3:16-17).

Paul is saying that the scripture is the source for making doctrines. He goes on to say that it will result in a "perfect" man of God, ready to do good works. No mention is made of tradition here.

Similarly, when questioned, Jesus never answered argument with a tradition, but instead referred to the scripture by saying, "it is written" (Matt. 4:4-10, 21:13, 26:31; Mark 7:6, 9:12; Luke 4:4-12, 10:26; John 8:17, 10:34).

Other problems with tradition

As mentioned above, Orthodox derive their traditions from seven sources that make up what is called Holy Tradition: the Bible, the seven ecumenical councils, later councils, church fathers, the liturgy, canon law and icons.

Protestants note that interpreting these seven sources consistently is not possible. For instance, the Catholic and Orthodox churches consider the seven ecumenical councils to be infallible, but these councils contradict other similar councils. (See the chapter on the seven ecumenical councils.)

Later councils are sometimes accepted as sources of tradition and sometimes not. These may be modified. Traditions may also be based on local councils or bishops' letters, but, of course, not all.

The liturgy is also accepted as a source of doctrine for church tradition, including not only its words but the actions performed during the liturgy. But some liturgies contradict the Bible, such as the statement in Chrysostom's liturgy that communion grants eternal life. (See the chapter on communion.)

Canon law (church law) is accepted as a source of tradition, but Orthodox Bishop Ware concedes that some of rulings are out of date.

Icons (paintings) are also an official source of teaching for Orthodoxy, but are not very specific. Orthodox and Catholic doctrine also accepts the church fathers as a source of tradition, while conceding that individual writers have at times fallen into error and at times contradicted each other. (See the chapter on church fathers.) But many of these church fathers speak out for the Protestant position on sola scriptura, as shown below.

John Chrysostom: "All things are plain and simple in the Holy Scriptures; all things necessary are evident."[4] *(NOTE: Here the great church father makes the statement that all things necessary are in the scripture. This of course means traditions are not necessary.)* "For from this it is that our countless evils have arisen — from ignorance of the Scriptures; from this it is that the plague of heresies has broken out; from this that there are negligent lives; from this labors without advantage."[5] *(NOTE: In effect, he is saying that scripture should be used to determine the truth — he makes no mention of church tradition.)*

Irenaeus: "We have learned the plan of our salvation from ... those through whom the gospel has come down to us ... At a later period, by the will of God, they handed the gospel down to us in the Scriptures, to be the ground and pillar of our faith."[6] *(NOTE: Irenaeus says the scriptures are the ground and pillar of our faith — in other words, the source from which we determine what is true and what isn't. This is a Protestant viewpoint as well.)*

Gregory of Nyssa: "We make the Holy Scriptures the rule and the measure of every tenet; we necessarily fix our eyes upon that, and approve that alone which may be made to harmonize with the intention of those writings."[7] *(NOTE: Gregory is especially respected in Orthodox circles. He says they accept only those teachings and traditions "which may be made to harmonize" with the Bible. This is an excellent summation of Protestant teaching.)*

Augustine: "This mediator (Jesus Christ)... inspired the Scripture, which is regarded as canonical and of supreme authority and to which we give credence concerning all those truths we ought to know and yet, of ourselves, are unable to learn." [8] *(NOTE: Augustine says scripture has "supreme authority" in determining what is true.)*

Cyril of Jerusalem: "For concerning the divine and sacred mysteries of the faith, we ought not to deliver even the most casual remark without the holy scriptures: nor be drawn aside by mere probabilities and the artifices of argument. Do not then believe me because I tell you these things, unless you receive from the Holy Scriptures the proof of what is set forth: for this salvation, which is of our faith, is not by ingenious reasonings but by proof from the Holy Scriptures."

Jerome: "As we accept those things that are written, so we reject those things that are not written (in Scripture)" [10]

Basil: "I do not consider it fair that the custom which obtains among them should be regarded as a law and rule of orthodoxy..... Therefore let God-inspired Scripture decide between us; and on whichever side be found doctrines in harmony with the word of God, in favor of that side will be cast the vote of truth." [11]

Athanasius: "...The sacred and inspired Scriptures are sufficient to declare the truth..."[12]

---

1) Catechism of the Catholic Church, 85

2) Clendenin, Daniel, "What the Orthodox Believe: Four Key Differences between the Orthodox and Protestants," *Christian History*, Issue 54, p. 35

3) Catechism of the Catholic Church, 82.

4) II Thes., Homily III, Nicene & Post-Nicene Fathers

5) Homilies on Paul, The Argument, Nicene & Post-Nicene Fathers

6) Nicene & Post-Nicene Fathers, quoted in *A Dictionary of Early Christian Beliefs*, p. 414

7) Ibid, On the Soul and the Resurrection, p. 439 (p. 859*)

8) Ibid, p. 454 (or *City of God*, book 11, chap. 3)

9) *The Catechetical Lectures of St. Cyril, Lecture 4.17; A Library of the Fathers of the Holy Catholic Church*, Oxford, Parker, 1845 (p. 149)

10) *Treatises*, Perpetual Virginity, Against Helvidius, p. 746

11) Basil, Letter 189, 3

12) *Against the Heathen* (Contra Gentes 1) , p. 209, Book 1

7. THE BIBLE:
Who has the right to interpret it?

Can you, a solitary individual, interpret scripture by yourself?

Or can only the church leadership do that? This question causes many disagreements between Orthodox, Catholic and Protestant leaders.

Official Orthodox and Catholic doctrine says only the church has the right to interpret scripture, through councils and decisions of its leaders. Individuals, they say, have no right to do this and will likely fall into error if they try.

The Orthodox/Catholic viewpoint

Orthodox Bishop Timothy Ware writes, "Orthodox, when they read the Scripture, accept the guidance of the Church. When received into the Orthodox Church, a convert promises, 'I will accept and understand Holy Scripture in accordance with the interpretation which was and is held by the Holy Orthodox Catholic Church of the East, our Mother.'" [1]

Similarly, Orthodox theologian Bulgakov says: "No reader of the Word of God can comprehend for himself the inspired character of that which he reads, for to the individual there is not given an organ of such comprehension. Such an organ is available to the reader only when he finds himself in union with all in the Church." [2]

The Catholic church disagrees and says that only it can interpret scripture: "The task of giving an authentic interpretation of the Word of God, whether in its written form or in the form of Tradition, has been entrusted to the ... (Catholic) church alone." [3] Both churches base their belief on 2 Peter 1:20: "Above all, you must understand that no prophecy of Scripture came about by the prophet's own interpretation." They believe that the phrase "no prophecy of scripture came about by the prophet's own interpretation" means we should not individually interpret the Bible — that only the church collectively may do that.

In addition, 1 Tim. 3:14-15 (NAS) is quoted: "...the church of the living God, the pillar and support of the truth." If the church is the "pillar and support of the truth" then, it is argued, only it has the right to interpret the truth. Also, it's often said that there are so many Protestant churches because they interpret the scriptures themselves, leading to disunity and division.

The Protestant viewpoint

Protestants believe individual believers can interpret scripture with the help of the Holy Spirit. They believe this for several reasons.

First, the Bible says individuals can and should interpret scripture.

Second, the Bible says that God himself teaches us to interpret scripture.

Third, Protestants believe the Orthodox/Catholic interpretation of 2 Peter 1:20 and 1 Tim. 3:14-15 is incorrect.

Fourth, church leaders can make mistakes in interpreting scripture just as individuals can.

Fifth, if only the church can interpret scripture, then we must decide which church, since there are many, each with its own views.

1) Many scriptures show that individuals can and should interpret scripture. Probably the most well-known scripture supporting individual interpretation of scripture is Acts 17:11: "Now the Bereans ... examined the Scriptures every day to see if what Paul said was true."

Note that the Bereans were not yet even Christians, yet God's word commends them for double-checking in the Bible to confirm what Paul was saying. These people did not believe Paul simply because he said he was a leader of the church. They checked what he said against what was written in the Bible, and made up their own minds. The Bible commends them for this, as is shown in the full verse: "Now the Bereans were of more noble character than the Thessalonians, for they received the message with great eagerness and examined the Scriptures every day to see if what Paul said was true."

The Bible says that individual believers have the responsibility to discern the truth themselves — they cannot just rely on their teachers.

For instance, Rev. 2:14-15 says the Lord criticizes some "who hold to the teaching of Balaam" and "those who hold to the teaching of the Nicolaitans."

The Lord was angry with them because they had accepted false teaching. Accordingly, if individual believers accept false teaching from their leaders, they are to blame for it. This means that individual believers not only may, but should decide for themselves if what they are being taught is true.

Heb. 5:14 says we should sharpen our senses "to distinguish good from evil" by training ourselves constantly. King Josiah, who was not a priest, interpreted scripture himself just from the plain reading of the word, and God commended him for it (2 Chron. 34:19-27).

Jesus warns us not to put our trust in church leaders to interpret scripture (Mark 12:38-40): "...Watch out for the teachers of the law..."

In Mark 13:5-6 Jesus issued a similar warning: "Watch out that no one deceives you. Many will come in my name, claiming, 'I am he,' and will deceive many." Jesus concluded this discourse on deception and the end times by warning all individual believers (verse 37): "What I say to you, I say to everyone: 'Watch!'"

In other words, the responsibility to avoid deception and wait for the Lord is for everyone, not just the apostles, priests and church leaders.

God even warns us about trusting prophets (Deut. 13:1-3): "If a prophet, or one who foretells by dreams, appears among you and announces to you a miraculous sign or wonder, and if the sign or wonder of which he has spoken takes place, and he says, 'Let us follow other gods' (gods you have not known) 'and let us worship them,' you must not listen to the words of that prophet or dreamer. The LORD your God is testing you to find out whether you love him with all your heart and with all your soul."

Note that this warning was given to the whole congregation — not just to the spiritual leaders of Israel.

The Bible says we are to judge what people say by the word of God (Is. 8:20): "To the law and to the testimony! If they do not speak according to this word, they have no light of dawn."

The importance of knowing and interpreting the scriptures for ourselves is also shown in Acts 20:29-30. Paul, speaking to the elders of a church, said: "Even from your own number men will arise and distort the truth in order to draw away disciples after them."

Protestants therefore believe that those who give away their right to interpret scripture to others will be easy prey for such deceivers.

Jesus said that believers should know the Bible [4] in several passages: In Matt. 21:42 he said, "Have you never read in the Scriptures: 'The stone the builders rejected has become the capstone?...'" In the same way, Jesus said in Matt. 22:31: "...have you not read what God said to you..."

Note how he says, "Have you never read" and "what God said to you." Apparently Jesus considers the scriptures to be a personal letter from God to us. As such, it is obligatory for us to read them and to know them.

This same thought is echoed in Hosea 8:12, "I wrote for them the many things of my law, but they regarded them as something alien."

Jesus even said the source of errors is due (at least in part) to ignorance of the Bible (Matt: 22:29, Mark 12:24): "You are in error because you do not know the Scriptures or the power of God."

Note that Jesus did not say "you are in error because you have departed from the teaching of the church," nor did he make any reliance upon tradition. Rather, in Mark 7:8, he spoke against those persons who place men's traditions ahead of the word of God: "You have let go of the commands of God and are holding on to the traditions of men."

Our own weaknesses and desires sometimes lead us to accept false teaching, the Bible says. "If a liar and deceiver comes and says, 'I will prophesy for you plenty of wine and beer,' he would be just the prophet for this people!" (Micah 2:11).

"For the time will come when men will not put up with sound doctrine. Instead, to suit their own desires, they will gather around them a great number of teachers to say what their itching ears want to hear" (2 Tim. 4:3).

How can we avoid being deceived? Paul says as we grow into Christian maturity, we will be able to resist the lies of men (Eph. 4:14): "Then we will no longer be infants, tossed back and forth by the waves, and blown here and there by every wind of teaching and by the cunning and craftiness of men in their deceitful scheming."

For all these reasons Protestants believe the responsibility lies with us to identify liars and deceivers and mistaken doctrine, as is clear in this warning to all the members of the Colossian church (Col. 2:8): "See to it that no one takes you captive through hollow and deceptive philosophy, which depends on human tradition and the basic principles of this world rather than on Christ."

Lastly, some say the Bible is too difficult to understand — that only trained theologians can interpret it. But the Bible says, "we do not write to you anything you cannot read or understand" (2 Cor. 1:13).

2) The Bible says that God himself teaches us how to interpret scripture. Protestants believe it is possible for individual believers to interpret scripture because the Holy Spirit is our teacher.

Jesus said the Holy Spirit "will teach you all things" (John 14:26).

The Holy Spirit will use what means he desires to teach us, including church leaders, but the ultimate source is God.

For instance, the Ethiopian eunuch did not understand and needed someone to teach him (Acts 8:26-39). The Holy Spirit sent Philip to him for this purpose, miraculously moved Philip to the desert and told him to go to the eunuch (v. 29). Note also that Philip was not an elder, priest, apostle or pastor, but only a deacon in charge of feeding widows (Acts 6:2-5).

In the same way, God taught Paul the gospel, not any man, as he says in Gal. 1:11-12: "I want you to know, brothers, that the gospel I preached is not something that man made up. I did not receive it from any man, nor was I taught it; rather, I received it by revelation from Jesus Christ."

Jesus echoed this in John 6:45: "It is written in the Prophets: 'They will all be taught by God.' Everyone who listens to the Father and learns from him comes to me."

"But when he, the Spirit of truth, comes, he will guide you into all truth. He will not speak on his own; he will speak only what he hears, and he will tell you what is yet to come" (John 16:13).

The Lord says the same in the Book of Psalms:

"I will instruct you and teach you in the way you should go; I will counsel you and watch over you" (Ps. 32:8). "Who, then, is the man that fears the LORD? He will instruct him in the way chosen for him" (Ps. 25:12). "The LORD confides in those who fear him; he makes his covenant known to them" (Ps. 25:14). This time of teaching by God is prophesied in Jer. 31:33-34: "... I will put my law in their minds and write it on their hearts....No longer will a man teach his neighbor, or a man his brother, saying, 'Know the LORD,' because they will all know me, from the least of them to the greatest, declares the LORD." The prophet Isaiah wrote: "All your sons will be taught by the LORD...." (Is. 54:13).

The fulfillment of these prophecies is shown in 1 John 2:27: "As for you, the anointing you received from him remains in you, and you do not need anyone to teach you... His anointing teaches you about all things..."

The Holy Spirit helps all believers understand the deep things of God.

"We have not received the spirit of the world but the Spirit who is from God, that we may understand what God has freely given us" (1 Cor. 2:12).

"I keep asking that the God of our Lord Jesus Christ, the glorious Father, may give you the Spirit of wisdom and revelation, so that you may know him better" (Eph. 1:17).

But some may also ask, "Doesn't the Bible say that there are teachers that God has given to the church to teach his word? Don't these teachers have a better understanding of the scripture than do other people?"

Yes, that is true, but we cannot rely upon them as we do God, because all of us make mistakes, even church leaders (see below).

James 3:1-2 says, "Not many of you should presume to be teachers, my brothers, because you know that we who teach will be judged more strictly. We all stumble in many ways." God holds us responsible for the teaching or doctrines we accept.

3) Protestants believe the Orthodox/Catholic interpretation of 2 Peter 1:20 and 1 Tim. 3:14-15 is incorrect.

A careful reading of 2 Peter 1:20 shows that the verse is not saying that only the church can interpret scripture. It just says that the Holy Spirit inspires scripture, not man: "Above all, you must understand that no prophecy of Scripture came about by the prophet's own interpretation. For prophecy never had its origin in the will of man, but men spoke from God as they were carried along by the Holy Spirit."

Nothing is said in this verse about the church interpreting scripture, nor does it say that only church leaders may interpret scripture. It simply says that scripture came by revelation of the Holy Spirit.

As to 1 Tim. 3:14-15, Protestants note that the verse simply says the church (meaning all Christians) is a pillar of the truth on the earth. The verses don't say that only church leaders can interpret scripture. To say they do is to force the verse to mean something that is not evident from the plain reading of the text.

Noted Bible commentator Matthew Henry, commenting on 1 Tim. 3:14-15, said church leaders can misinterpret scripture. "The church holds forth the Scripture and the doctrine of Christ, as a pillar holds forth a proclamation. When a church ceases to be the pillar and ground of truth, we may and ought to forsake her; for our regard to truth should be first and greatest."

The essence of the Orthodox and Catholic argument, however, is that the church is infallible — it cannot err in the matter of holding and proclaiming the truth. Scriptures show, however, that churches can indeed err. All but two of the seven churches of Revelation were rebuked for error, including doctrinal error. (See below, and also the chapter, "THE CHURCH: Can it be wrong?")

4) Church leaders can make mistakes just as individuals can.

The apostle Peter said false teachers will be in the church (2 Peter 2:1): "But there were also false prophets among the people, just as there will be false teachers among you. They will secretly introduce destructive heresies, even denying the sovereign Lord who bought them— bringing swift destruction on themselves."

Is. 9:15-16 refers to "prophets who teach lies" and says, "Those who guide this people mislead them, and those who are guided are led astray."

Note what the prophet Jeremiah wrote (Jer. 8:8): "'How can you say, 'We are wise, for we have the law of the LORD,' when actually the lying pen of the scribes has handled it falsely?"

Here is an example of a people who had relied on their spiritual teachers, but these very leaders had misled them by teaching the word incorrectly.

And yet Protestants agree that it's possible for a believer who is not willing to listen to the Holy Spirit to deceive himself as to the interpretation of a scripture. But it is also possible for entire churches to be deceived, as is evident from the many different Catholic, Orthodox and Protestant beliefs — they can't all be right.

Having only the church leadership interpret scripture is no guarantee that it will be free of error, Protestants believe. The only guarantee is a pure heart and the Holy Spirit. Where these two things do not exist, error can occur, whether it is in a church council or in a single individual, as the following scriptures show:

"For this people's heart has become calloused; they hardly hear with their ears, and they have closed their eyes. Otherwise they might see with their eyes, hear with their ears, understand with their hearts and turn, and I would heal them'" (Mat. 13:15). (Note: An impure heart hindered understanding.)

"...Give me discernment that I may understand your statutes" (Ps. 119:125). (Note: discernment comes from God.)

"None of the wicked will understand, but those who are wise will understand" (Dan. 12:10). (Note: impurity hindered understanding.)

"Then he opened their minds so they could understand the Scriptures" (Luke 24:45). (Note: God is the one who gives understanding.)

"We have not received the spirit of the world but the Spirit who is from God, that we may understand what God has freely given us.... The man without the Spirit does not accept the things that come from the Spirit of God, for they are foolishness to him, and he cannot understand them, because they are spiritually discerned" (1 Cor. 2:12, 14). (Note: Again we see it is the Holy Spirit who gives understanding of the scriptures.)

5) If only the church can interpret scripture, then we must decide which church.

There are many, each with their own views — Catholic, Orthodox, Baptist, Pentecostal, Methodist, etc.

It is not enough to say "the oldest church" as being old is no guarantee that the church's doctrine has not changed over the centuries. *(See the chapter, "THE CHURCH: Which is oldest?")*

1) Ware, Timothy, *The Orthodox Church,* p. 200
2) Bulgakov, Sergei, *The Orthodox Church,* p. 13
3) Catechism of the Catholic Church, 85
4) It is interesting to note that the New Testament was written in Koine Greek — the language of the street, not classical (literary) Greek. This shows that it was intended for the common man to read, not the educated elite.

8. THE BIBLE:
Who gave it to us?

A recurring argument between some Orthodox, Catholic and Protestant leaders is the source of the Bible.

Orthodox or Catholic writers sometimes say that their churches determined which books make up the Bible. They believe that each time Protestants quote from the Bible they unwittingly acknowledge their trust in the infallible divine guidance given to the Catholic or Orthodox church, because it was a church council that first approved the canon of scripture that we know of today as the New Testament. They further argue that if Protestants accept their canon of scripture, then Protestants should also trust the Catholic or Orthodox churches to teach them about other essential Christian doctrine.

Accordingly, it is essential to understand how the Bible came to be. Was it given to Christianity by the Orthodox or Catholic church?

The Protestant viewpoint

First of all, Protestants respond that they trust the Bible, but not because a church gathering 1,600 years ago said they should.

Church councils are subject to error as we all are. There is no biblical guarantee of infallibility to church councils. Church councils have contradicted each other, such as the councils in 754 A.D. and 787 A.D. on icons (see the chapters on icons and the seven church councils), and the six conflicting synods on hesychasm in the 14th century. (See the chapter on Hesychasm).

Church councils can, at best, simply confirm what is already accepted by the Christian church.

Second, the council only confirmed the practice of Christians, who had been using the New Testament scriptures for more than 300 years already. The council's decision was quite late, accordingly, and helped only by adding its authority to the common practice of the churches.

In the first century, the Apostle Peter already considered Paul's letters to be scripture, as he wrote in 2 Peter 3:15-16, "...Our dear brother Paul also wrote you with the wisdom that God gave him.... His letters contain some things that are hard to understand, which ignorant and unstable people distort, as they do the other Scriptures..." Paul's letters make up about half of the New Testament. In addition, citations of almost all the New Testament books have been found in writings from the first and second century church fathers, who treated them as scripture (70-120 A.D.), according to *Unger's Bible Dictionary* (p. 177-178).

Third, no single denomination can claim authorship of the Bible. The Orthodox and Catholic churches were not fully developed into the churches that we know today until they approved icons, relics and prayer to saints in 787 A.D., and split from each other in 1054 A.D. The development of the churches into denominations was a gradual process that took hundreds of years. The Bible was established by common usage long before this occurred.

How, then, did the early Christians know which scriptures were from God? And how can we know today?

First and foremost is the testimony of the Holy Spirit in our hearts. Paul referred to this in Rom. 2:15, "their consciences also bearing witness", in Rom. 9:1: "...my conscience confirms it in the Holy Spirit," and in 2 Cor. 1:12 "our conscience testifies..." God is able to show us the truth as it says in Rom. 1:19: "...what may be known about God is plain to them, because God has made it plain to them."

On a more objective basis, Christians accept certain writings as biblical because of the prophecies in them that have come true, such as Is. 53 (about the coming of the Messiah), and Is. 11:11 (about the restoration of Israel). Christians also find support for the Bible in archeology and history, which confirm the things written in them.

Christians also accept these books as the word of God because Christ and the apostles testified to them. Jesus repeatedly used scripture as sufficient proof to settle controversial issues, such as the resurrection (Matt. 22:31-32). Thus when one part of the Bible, which has been established as from God, confirms another part of the Bible, then we can be sure of it.

Lastly, Christians also accept certain writings as biblical because of the witness of reliable sources. It is in this latter category that we can place the men at the church council, alongside many thousands of others who testify that the Bible is the life-changing and true word of God.

9. BAPTISM:
Does it save us?

Baptism is without doubt one of the areas in which there are marked differences between Orthodox, Catholics and Protestants. Even Protestants are divided on how it should be done and on its significance.

Orthodox and Catholics believe that without proper baptism, a person will likely go to hell. Evangelical Protestants believe baptism is not essential to salvation although it is important.

Obviously, with one's eternal destiny at stake, it's important to understand exactly what God expects of us when it comes to baptism.

The Orthodox/Catholic viewpoint

The official Orthodox and Catholic position is that a person is saved, at least in part, at the very moment they are baptized.[1]

Called "baptismal regeneration," this view is also held by some Protestants. Orthodox theologian Karmiris writes: "By means of holy baptism, the 'bath of regeneration' and renewing of the Holy Spirit, believers shed the sinful garments of the old man and are clothed in Christ.... According to Chrysostom, 'It is through baptism that we received remission of sins, sanctification, communion of the Spirit, adoption, and life eternal.' And according to Basil the Great, baptism is 'the ransoming of captives, the forgiving of their debts, the regeneration of the soul, the bright garment, the unassailable seal, chariot to heaven, the cause of the kingdom, the gift of adoption.'"[2]

The Orthodox Study Bible note on 1 Peter 1:3 says believers are born again through water baptism. "As Jesus told Nicodemus, we enter the Kingdom of God by being 'born of water and the Spirit' (John 3:5). This new birth in baptism unites us with Christ and his resurrection (Rom. 6:3)." Orthodox Bishop Ware writes similarly: "At baptism the Christian undergoes an out-

ward washing in water and is at the same time cleansed inwardly from sin…
Through baptism we receive a full forgiveness of all sin, whether original or
actual; we 'put on Christ', becoming members of his body the church." [3]

Orthodox writer John Karmiris notes, "Baptism and chrismation transmit
justifying and regenerating grace." [4]

The Catholic Catechism (1263) says similarly: "By baptism all sins are
forgiven, original sin as well as all personal sins, as well as all punishment for
sin. Baptism not only purifies us from all sin, but also makes the neophyte
'a new creature,' an adopted son of God, who has become a 'partaker of the
divine nature,' member of Christ and coheir with him, and a temple of the
Holy Spirit" (1265). "The Lord himself affirms that baptism is necessary for
salvation" (1257).

However, the Catechism states that when baptism is not possible, repentance makes one acceptable to God: "Those who die for the faith, those who
are catechumens, and all those who, without knowing of the Church but acting under the inspiration of grace, seek God sincerely and strive to fulfill his
will, are saved even if they have not been baptized" (Catechism, 1281,1259).
The Council of Trent, which is considered infallible by Catholic leaders, ruled
that those who disagree with Catholic teaching on baptism will go to hell: "If
any one saith, that in the Roman church…there is not the true doctrine concerning the sacrament of baptism; let him be anathema." [5]

The Protestant viewpoint

Believing that the act of baptism grants eternal life or forgiveness of sins
is understandable, as in the scripture the relationship between repentance and
baptism is so close that they seem to be the same thing.

For instance, baptisms recorded in the New Testament show that as soon
as a person repented, they were baptized. The Phillippian jailer was baptized
in the middle of the night after he repented (Acts 16:33) and the Ethiopian
eunuch was baptized immediately on the side of the road (Acts 8:36-39). The
3,000 who repented on the day of Pentecost were also baptized that very same
day — no small achievement (Acts 2:41).

However closely baptism may follow repentance, Protestants believe it is
still important to realize that salvation comes when a person trusts Christ and
repents, and not at baptism. Protestants point to the apostle Peter's recognition of this in Acts 10:46-47.

Here an entire household was filled with the Holy Spirit and began to
speak in tongues before they were baptized. Peter recognized this as evidence
of salvation and the baptism of the Holy Spirit, and ordered that they be baptized in water. "For they heard them speaking in tongues and praising God.
Then Peter said, 'Can anyone keep these people from being baptized with
water? They have received the Holy Spirit just as we have.'"

Peter's logic is clear: God does not give the baptism of the Holy Spirit to
an unrepentant sinner. He gives it to those who are saved and in union with
Christ. It is clear then that Cornelius and his household were saved before
their baptism in water. In just the same way, Abraham was righteous before

he got the external symbol of circumcision, as the apostle Paul said in Rom. 4:11: "He received the sign of circumcision, a seal of the righteousness that he had by faith while he was still uncircumcised." In other words, he had internal righteousness before he got external circumcision.

Confusing externals with the inner state

Confusing the external rite with the reality of the internal state is easy to do, according to Robert Haldane's Exposition on Romans (p. 331-332):

"The figure of baptism was very early mistaken for a reality, and accordingly some of the fathers speak of the baptized person as truly born again in the water. They supposed him to go into the water with all his sins upon him, and to come out of it without them. This indeed is the case with baptism figuratively. But the carnal mind soon turned the figure into a reality. It appears to the impatience of man too tedious and ineffectual a way to wait on God's method of converting sinners by his Holy Spirit through the truth, and therefore they have effected this much more extensively by the performance of external rites."

In Rom. 2:28-29 the apostle Paul says an external ritual is ineffective without a corresponding inner state: "A man is not a Jew if he is only one outwardly, nor is circumcision merely outward and physical. No, a man is a Jew if he is one inwardly; and circumcision is circumcision of the heart, by the Spirit, not by the written code..." Accordingly, baptism is meaningless if it is merely physical and lacks a corresponding action of the heart.

Rom. 6:5 says baptism is a symbol or likeness of the death of Christ: "For if we have become united with him in the likeness of his death (e.g., through baptism, which symbolizes his death), we will also be part of his resurrection."

The Apostle Peter describes baptism as a symbol of repentance in 1 Peter 3:21: "this water symbolizes baptism that now saves you also — not the removal of dirt from the body but the pledge of a good conscience toward God." Here Peter is saying it is not the physical act of baptism that saves us ("the removal of dirt"), but the mental repentance ("pledge of a good conscience") to live right before God with a good conscience. That is simply what repentance is.

Even the church father Origen, often cited by Orthodox writers, contends that baptism without repentance is meaningless: "Matthew alone adds the words, 'to repentance,' teaching us that the benefit of baptism is connected with the intention of the baptized person. To him who repents, it is saving. However, to him who comes to it without repentance, it will produce greater condemnation." [6]

Solving John 3:5

Nonetheless, Protestants must answer Orthodox and Catholic references to John 3:5, where Jesus seems to say that water baptism is essential to salvation: "I tell you the truth, no one can enter the kingdom of God unless he is born of water and the Spirit." This scripture seems to teach that baptism is essential to salvation, assuming that "born of water" means water baptism. Supreme importance is therefore placed on this ritual by some churches.

However, the phrase "born of water" in John 3:5 may refer to the water sac that surrounds all unborn children. Under this interpretation, the point that Jesus is making is that physical birth (born of water) is not enough for salvation, but spiritual birth (born of the Spirit) is needed.

For instance, in verse 3 Jesus is speaking about spiritual birth. In verse 4 Nicodemus assumes Jesus is speaking about physical birth. Accordingly, in John 3:5 Jesus contrasts physical birth with spiritual birth. This is made even more clear by verse six: "The flesh gives birth to flesh" (physical birth, born of water) "but the Spirit gives birth to Spirit" (spiritual birth, or born of the Spirit)." Another possible understanding of John 3:5 is that it refers to water baptism (born of water) as meaningless without the presence of the Holy Spirit in our hearts (born of the Spirit): "Having believed, you were marked in him with a seal, the promised Holy Spirit..." (Eph. 1:13). In this interpretation, it is important to realize that the emphasis is on the participation of the Holy Spirit, and not on water baptism,which is powerless to save anyone.

So is baptism a meaningless ritual?

But if baptism is not essential for our salvation, is it therefore unimportant? Just a symbol?

No. Baptism is important because it lets us prove our faith is genuine by obeying God's command to be baptized. It provides the person with the chance to publicly confess Christ, as the Lord said in Luke 12:8-9: "I tell you, whoever acknowledges me before men, the Son of Man will also acknowledge him before the angels of God. But he who disowns me before men will be disowned before the angels of God."

If a person cannot be baptized, they can still be saved, since the thief on the cross (Luke 23:40-43) died before he could be baptized but Jesus clearly said he went to heaven (v. 43). However, a person who refuses to be baptized when it is possible to be baptized is in rebellion against God's command to repent and be baptized (Mark 16:16).

One can truly question such a person's salvation because he has not really repented and made Christ the Lord of his life. If he had, he would have obeyed Christ's command to be baptized.

So baptism is indeed important. We should be baptized because God commanded us to be, and when he said to be: after repentance.

Other differences

These include the methods of baptism: Catholic priests baptize by sprinkling water, while Orthodox and many Protestants usually baptize by immersion. Which is right?

Most say that what matters is not the method of baptism, but the intent of the heart. A sincere faith and repentance is what justifies us to God — not the method of baptism. Nonetheless, scripture does seem to indicate that the apostles baptized by immersion. According to Thayer's Greek-English

Lexicon, the word "baptize" in the original Greek (baptizo) literally means to immerse ("to dip repeatedly, to immerse, to submerge, to cleanse by dipping or submerging... to overwhelm.")

Other scriptures imply baptism by immersion: "As soon as Jesus was baptized, he went up out of the water." (Matt. 3:16). "Then both Philip and the eunuch went down into the water and Philip baptized him. When they came up out of the water..." (Acts 8:38-29). [7]

"Now John also was baptizing at Aenon near Salim, because there was plenty of water..." (John 3:23). [8]

---

1) Two Protestant groups that often teach baptismal regeneration are the Churches of Christ and "Oneness" Pentecostals (United Pentecostal Church, apostolic, etc.).

2) Karmiris, John. "Concerning the Sacraments", p. 24, as cited in *Eastern Orthodox Theology: A Contemporary Reader*, edited by Daniel B. Clendenin. Grand Rapids: Baker, 1995.

3) Ware, *The Orthodox Church*, 274, 278

4) Karmiris, John. "Concerning the Sacraments.", as cited in *Eastern Orthodox Theology: A Contemporary Reader*, edited by Daniel B. Clendenin. Grand Rapids: Baker, 1995.

5) On Baptism, Canon III, The Seventh Session. Also at http://history.hanover.edu/texts/trent/ct07.html

6) Commentary on the Gospel of John, Book 6.17. Ante-Nicene Fathers

7) Note that with Jesus' baptism and the eunuch's, they had to come out of the water and apparently went down into it. If sprinkling were done this would not have been necessary. They could have done it anywhere.

8) If sprinkling were the method, not much water can baptize many hundreds of people. Immersion, however, requires more water.

10. BAPTISM:
Should we baptize infants?

Many people — Catholic, Orthodox and some Protestants — have been baptized as infants. Catholic and Orthodox churches both baptize infants. Protestant churches that practice infant baptism include Lutheran, Presbyterian, Methodist, Episcopalian, Anglican and Reformed. Most evangelical Protestant churches, however, baptize only after a person has repented.

The Catholic/Orthodox viewpoint

The Catholic and Orthodox positions on baptism are closely linked to baptismal regeneration, the belief that it is the ritual of baptism that saves a person. Accordingly, a child that has not been baptized is at risk of going to hell. Orthodox leaders make no definite statements about the fate of unbaptized infants, although they urge parents to have their children baptized.

The Catholic church says we can only "hope that there is a way of salvation for children who have died without baptism" (1261). If a child has died without baptism, it says we are to "trust in God's mercy and to pray for their salvation" (1283).

The Orthodox theologian Meyendorff wrote that infant baptism saves a child even if he is unaware of it: "Considering baptism as 'new birth' implies also that it is a free gift from God, and is in no sense dependent upon human choice, consent, or even consciousness: 'Just as in the case of physical birth we do not even contribute willingness to all the blessings derived from baptism.' In the East, therefore, there was never any serious doubt or controversy about the legitimacy of infant baptism." [1]

Similarly the Catholic church says children don't have to do anything to be baptized: "Since the earliest times, baptism has been administered to children, for it is a grace and a gift of God that does not presuppose any human merit..." (Catechism, 1282). Those that practice infant baptism sometimes contend that it is a sign of our covenant with God, and replaces the Old Testament practice of circumcision, which was given to all male infants eight days old. For that reason, water baptism occurs in the Orthodox church usually on the eighth day, when circumcision was performed.

Lastly, the Catholic church officially ruled at the Council of Trent in the 16th century that those who speak against infant baptism will not go to heaven: "If any one saith...that it is better that the baptism of [infants] be omitted ... [until] believing by their own act... let him be anathema" (Canon 13).

The Evangelical Protestant viewpoint

Many Protestant churches have a different view.

They believe that God accepts young children into heaven without baptism. Accordingly, they only baptize adults or older children who have repented. These churches include Baptist, Nazarene, Wesleyan, Church of God, Assembly of God, independent charismatic/pentecostal, and Adventist.

Evangelical Protestants base their belief that infant baptism is not necessary on several scriptures.

First, they note that there is no verse in the Bible showing an infant being baptized, or requiring that.[2] (It is true, nonetheless, that in Acts 10:24-44, 16:15, 16:33 and 18:8 entire households were baptized, but no one knows if infants were included. Accordingly these scriptures don't prove or disprove infant baptism. To argue that there probably were infants in those households is an "argument from silence.")

Second, an infant conceived in adultery who went to heaven is described in 2 Sam. 12:23. After the death of King David's infant son that he had with Bathsheba, David said confidently that he would see his son in heaven. "...I will go to him, but he will not return to me," he said. David was forgiven his sin (2 Sam. 12:13, Ps. 32:1) and went to heaven, so his words mean his son went to heaven also. Original sin, accordingly, did not keep the infant out of heaven. Infant baptism, further, was not practiced by the Jews.

Third, the Bible shows that salvation without baptism for young children is possible because they are not conscious of good or evil ("your children who do not yet know good from bad," Deut. 1:39). Rom. 5:13 says, "Sin is not taken into account where there is no law."

Jesus confirmed God's acceptance of children when he said, "Let the little children come to me, for of such is the Kingdom of God" (Matt. 19:14). Jesus' statement in Mark 16:16 that, "whoever does not believe will be condemned," shows that it is not the lack of water baptism, but the lack of faith that causes condemnation. Protestants note that even Jesus waited until he was 30 to be baptized.

Fourth, in the Bible the word "baptize" always follows repentance or belief ("Repent and be baptized," Acts 2:38, "believes and is baptized," Mark 16:16). Accordingly, when people were baptized in the Bible it always followed their repentance or belief. Most Protestants therefore believe that baptism confirms our decision to repent. Since young children are not able to understand repentance, it is premature to baptize them, and unnecessary.

If a person has not repented, then their baptism confirms nothing and is invalid. This is what John the Baptist was apparently referring to when a crowd of unrepentant persons came to him seeking baptism, in Matt. 3:7-8. He refused them baptism, stating that they first must, "bring forth fruit in keeping with repentance." The apostle Peter also linked baptism with repentance in 1 Peter 3:21, defining baptism as "a pledge of a good conscience toward God." It is a pledge to do what? To repent, of course, and live for God. Infants, being unaware, can make no such pledge or repentance, nor do they need to. Since they are unaware of right and wrong, they have nothing of which to repent.

Fifth, many Protestants believe infant baptism results from a misunderstanding about original sin. Protestants accept the doctrine of original sin, just as it is stated in Ps. 51:5: "Surely I was sinful at birth, sinful from the time my mother conceived me." However, they don't believe this means an infant will be condemned by God for this, or that an infant must be baptized.

Those who believe that may be confusing imperfection with guilt. All babies are born with an imperfect sinful nature, but are not judged as guilty by God because they have had no opportunity to do anything about it. It is when we are older, when we have had a chance to accept or reject Christ, that our guilt becomes a factor.

Jesus said the basis of our judgment is not our original sin, but failure to repent. "Unless you repent, you too will all perish" (Luke 13:3).

Lastly, baptizing infants, Protestants believe, shows ignorance of the kindness of God, who would not send innocent children to hell. It also shows ignorance of the biblical teaching about the age of responsibility or accountability. Children before that age are innocent before God and go to heaven. This is shown in Is. 7:14-16, where it speaks of the age when a young child "knows how to refuse the evil and choose the good."

As already mentioned, Deut. 1:39 shows this age, too: "your children who do not yet know good from bad..." Children who die before the age of accountability are not judged as guilty before God. After that age they need to make a decision to trust Christ for forgiveness of their sins.

What about those baptized as infants?

What then shall we say of those who were baptized as infants? Do they need another baptism? The answer is found in Acts 19:1-7 where the apostle Paul baptized 12 men who had previously been baptized.

Most evangelical Protestants therefore rebaptize persons who were baptized as infants, for the reasons cited below. This is not to say that infant baptism is without value, if the parents intend it as a dedication of the child to God. It does not, nonetheless, grant salvation.

Infant dedication is good and scriptural. Samuel, for instance, was dedicated to God and the Bible indicates that it made a major difference in his life.

(See 1 Samuel.)

But most evangelical Protestants do not believe that such a dedication justifies us to God. A person who has been baptized as an infant but is living without repentance does not have salvation. Unfortunately, they may not seek after that salvation if they mistakenly believe that infant baptism is a guarantee of eternal life. (No baptism — adult or infant — is a guarantee of eternal life, if it is not followed by truth faith and repentance.) Accordingly, most evangelical Protestants are concerned that infant baptism provides a false assurance and is deceptive. It is not uncommon for persons to consider themselves Christian because they were baptized, yet they may live an immoral life. Paul addressed this kind of deception in 1 Cor. 6:9: "Do you not know that the wicked will not inherit the kingdom of God? Do not be deceived: Neither the sexually immoral nor idolaters nor adulterers nor male prostitutes nor homosexual offenders nor thieves nor the greedy nor drunkards nor slanderers nor swindlers will inherit the kingdom of God."

Does baptism replace circumcision?

One of the main arguments for infant baptism is that it is the replacement of the Old Testament ritual of circumcision, which was a sign of the Jewish covenant with God. The ritual is done for male infants by parents.

Some base this argument on Col. 2:11-12: "In him you were also circumcised, in the putting off of the sinful nature, not with a circumcision done by the hands of men but with the circumcision done by Christ, having been buried with him in baptism and raised with him through your faith in the power of God, who raised him from the dead."

Most Protestants do not accept this argument.

First, Protestants say this verse cannot refer to infant baptism, because it says baptism occurs "through your faith." Infant baptism requires no faith. Accordingly, this verse cannot be speaking about infant baptism. Similarly, Peter defines baptism as a pledge of a good conscience (1 Pet. 3:21). Infants cannot make any such pledge, and don't need to.

Second, there is no verse saying baptism replaces circumcision. Col. 2 is speaking about a spiritual circumcision ("not...done by the hands of men"), not the physical one. It doesn't say the Old Testament physical ritual of circumcision has been replaced by the New Testament practice of baptism.

Third, if baptism simply takes the place of circumcision, then children should be baptized only on the eighth day and only boys should be baptized, since these were the rules of circumcision.

Fourth, if baptism is the same thing as circumcision, then there would be no need to baptize circumcised believers, but circumcised Jews were routinely baptized in the New Testament, including the 3,000 on the day of Pentecost (Acts 2). Jews continued to be circumcised, even after conversion to Christianity, as is shown by the dispute about circumcising Gentile converts in Acts 15. If baptism replaced circumcision, then Paul would not have had to circumcise Timothy, but in Acts 16:3 he did.

Fifth, the history of the early church shows that adult believer baptism was the norm until the fifth century. (See below.) If infant baptism had re-placed circumcision, this would not have been the case — people would have been baptized as infants. History therefore shows that the early church did not believe that circumcision had been replaced by infant baptism.

The history of infant baptism

Tracing the history of infant baptism isn't easy, since complete records of exactly what happened 2,000 years ago don't exist.

The best history of this time, however, is the New Testament, and it shows no case of infant baptism. The Encyclopedia Britannica[2] further notes: "There is no certain evidence of [infant baptism] earlier than the 3rd century, and the ancient baptismal liturgies are all intended for adults. The liturgy and the instructions clearly understand the acceptance of baptism as an independent adult decision; without this decision the sacrament cannot be received."

Earliest reference objected to infant baptism

The writings of the early church fathers confirm that the early church baptized adults, and not infants.

The earliest clear reference to infant baptism found among the church fathers objected to it. This shows that infant baptism was not a practice of the early church. Tertullian, writing in 198 A.D. said:

"And so according to the circumstances, disposition, and even the age of each individual, the delay of baptism is preferable. This is particularly true in the case of little children... Let them become Christians when they have become able to know Christ. Why does the innocent period of life hasten to the remission of sins? ...If anyone understands the weighty importance of baptism, he will fear its reception more than its delay. Sound faith is secure of salvation." [3]

First references to infant baptism:	*YEAR*
Tertullian (opposed)	198 A.D.
Cyprian (for)	256 A.D.

Less than sixty years later, however, north African bishop Cyprian wrote in favor of infant baptism, showing the beginnings of this new doctrine (see footnote 4 regarding Hippolytus and Origen).[4] The slow growth of this teaching is shown by the fact that 100 years after Cyprian issued his statement, most Christians still did not practice infant baptism, as is shown in the lives of the early church fathers (see chart below). In all known cases until the fifth century all the church fathers were baptized as adults, even when raised from infancy in Christian homes.

(NOTE: Origen allegedly made statements in support of infant baptism about 50 years after Tertullian. See footnote 4.)

The church fathers who were baptized as adults even though they were raised in Christian families were: St. John Chrysostom, St. Gregory Nazianzen, St. Basil the Great, St. Gregory of Nyssa, St. Ambrose, St. Jerome, St. Augustine and Rufinus. Perhaps the most interesting of these is Gregory Nazianzen, as he was the son of a priest. It is hard to imagine that the son of a priest, of all people, would not have been baptized as an infant if indeed this was the practice of the early church. The fact that he was not shows that infant baptism arrived at a later date. Gregory's mother was described as follows:

"Nonna, the mother of our Saint, was the daughter of Christian parents, and had been very carefully brought up. Like St. John Chrysostom and St. Augustine, Gregory had the inestimable advantage of being reared at the knee of a mother of conspicuous holiness....Gregory was certainly born at a late period of the life of his mother. He tells us that, like so many other holy men of whom we read both in the Bible and outside its pages, he was consecrated to God by his mother even before his birth." [5]

He himself was not baptized until he almost died on a sea voyage, according to his biography:

"Gregory, who was not yet baptized, was thrown into terrible distress at thus finding himself in peril of death while yet outside the covenant of God. In earnest prayer he renewed his self-dedication, and vowed to give himself wholly to the service of God, if his life might be spared to receive holy baptism."

Clearly, if infant baptism had been practiced at that time, Gregory would have been baptized long before this crisis — by his father the priest and his devout Christian mother. His case, however, was not an isolated one, as shown in the following chart:

Adult baptisms of church fathers raised from infancy in Christian homes:

NAME	AGE AT BAPTISM	YEAR
John Chrysostom	23	370 A.D.
Gregory Nazienzen	26* approximate	356 A.D.
Augustine	33	387 A.D
Basil the Great	28	357 A.D.
Gregory of Nyssa	30	361 A.D.
Ambrose	34* approximate	374 A.D.
Jerome	19	366 A.D.
Rufinus	28	344 A.D.

Chrysostom's case is also interesting. He was raised by a devout Christian mother, so one would expect that she had him baptized as an infant. Instead, he reports that he was not baptized until his conversion as an adult.

Below is a description of his mother showing that such a mother surely would have had her son baptized if that was the practice of the time.

"His mother, Anthusa, was a rare woman. Left a widow at the age of twenty, she refused all offers of marriage, and devoted herself exclusively to the education of her only son and his older sister. She was probably from principle averse to a second marriage, according to a prevailing view of the Fathers. She shines, with Nonna and Monica, among the most pious mothers of the fourth century... Anthusa gained general esteem by her exemplary life. The famous advocate of heathenism, Libanius, on hearing of her consistency and devotion, felt constrained to exclaim: 'Bless me! What wonderful women there are among the Christians.' She gave her son an admirable education, and early planted in his soul the germs of piety, which afterwards bore the richest fruits for himself and the church. By her admonitions and the teachings of the Bible, he was secured against the seductions of heathenism. Yet he was not baptized till he had reached the age of maturity." [6]

He was 23 when he was finally baptized in 370 A.D.

Basil the Great also had Christian parents who easily could have had him baptized. His father, also named Basil, was known "in the church for probity and piety..." His mother, Emmelia, was an orphan "whose father had suffered impoverishment and death for Christ's sake, and who was herself a conspicuous example of high-minded and gentle Christian womanhood. It would be quite consonant with the feelings of the times that pious parents like the elder Basil and Emmelia should shrink from admitting their boy to holy baptism before his encountering the temptations of school and university life." He was baptized at about the age of 28, in 357 A.D. [7]

Likewise, his brother Gregory of Nyssa, also a well-respected church father, and of course from the same Christian family, was baptized as an adult at the age of 30. [8]

Ambrose was also baptized as an adult about age 34. He was also from a Christian family, as noted in his biography. He was the bishop of Milan, descended from a distinguished Roman family which had been Christian for many years. It counted martyrs among the family members. After he was elected bishop against his will, he decided to get baptized.

"St. Ambrose did all in his power... to escape from the dignity laid upon him, but when his election was ratified by the Emperor Valentinian, he recognized his appointment as being the will of God, and insisted on being baptized by a Catholic priest. Eight days later, December 7, A.D. 374, he was consecrated bishop." [9]

Augustine was saved at the age of 33 and subsequently baptized by Ambrose in Milan on Easter Sunday, 387 A.D. His mother was also noted for her godliness and raised him in the faith. "...his Christian mother, Monica (was) one of the noblest woman in the history of Christianity, of a highly intellectual and spiritual cast, of fervent piety..." [10]

Jerome was also baptized as an adult, at the age of 19: "His father Eusebius and his mother were Catholic Christians, but he was not baptized in infancy." [11]

Rufinus' biographer said "both his parents were Christians. But he was not baptized till about his 28th year."[12]

Eusebius was also baptized as an adult. He may have been raised in a Christian home: "...He was taught the creed of the Caesarean church in his childhood, or at least at the beginning of his Christian life, and that he accepted it at baptism."[13]

There is no evidence of a church father who was baptized as an infant. The earliest evidence of infant baptism, also previously noted, was recorded in 256 A.D. It is an account of a meeting of 66 bishops in North Africa responding to a question about when to baptize infants, chaired by Cyprian. They decided that they should be baptized as soon as they were born. The fact that in all known cases the church fathers were baptized as adults for many years after this, shows that Cyprian's meeting was an isolated ruling that was not accepted in the rest of the empire.

Noted theologian Kurt Aland, a supporter of infant baptism, nonetheless writes that infant baptism wasn't practiced by the early church: "...the practice takes its rise at the end of the second century. For the time before this we do not possess a single piece of information that gives concrete testimony to the existence of infant baptism.... To this day nobody can prove an actual case of the baptism of an infant in the period before A.D. 200 on the basis of 'the sources.'"[14]

Many Protestants believe that the lack of New Testament support for infant baptism, the earliest writings of church fathers opposing it, and the example of church fathers baptized as adults show that infant baptism was not a practice of the early church, but took root gradually over several centuries.

How infant baptism began

How, then, one might ask, was such a practice finally adopted? Aland says it came primarily from the growth of the doctrine of original sin, which says all children are born with sin.

"So long as it is believed that children are without sin, infant baptism is not needed," Aland says. "As soon as the conviction becomes prevalent, however, that an infant participates in sin, even when born of Christian parents, infant baptism as a requirement to practice is unavoidable."[15]

The writings of the early church show that it did not believe children had sin. The Letter of Barnabas (6.11) says those baptized "have the soul of children" (implying that children are innocent of sin). In the Shepherd of Hermas, at the beginning of the second mandate, it says "Keep simplicity and be guileless, and thou shall be as little children, who do not know the wickedness that destroys the life of men." Tertullian also said that children are not guilty of sin (De. Bapt. 18:5).

But by Augustine's time, opinions had changed.

Church historian C.B. Hassell believes the catalyst for the widespread acceptance of infant baptism was a crisis in the fourth century:

"In the year 370 the Emperor Valens sent for Basil to baptize his dying son Galetes; the ground of the request was the illness of the youth. Basil refused to do it, and it was eventually done by an Arian bishop."[16]

The example of the emperor very likely set a precedent in the empire regarding infant baptism.

1) Meyendorff, *Byzantine Theology*, p. 193, as cited in *Eastern Orthodox Teachings in Comparison with The Doctrinal Position of Biola University*

2) Electronic edition, article on Roman Catholicism and Baptism, copyright 2000

4) Epistles of Cyprian, 58.5, Ante-Nicene Fathers, c. 250 A.D. There are serious doubts about the truthfulness of comments about infant baptism supposedly made by both Origen and Hippolytus. Origen allegedly said that infant baptism was a practice of the apostles in his commentary on Rom. 5:9. However, several commentators say it may have been forged. These include church father Jerome, theologian John Gill in *Antipaedobaptism*, Dr. Frederick Crombie, contemporaneous commentators Scultetus (Medulla Patrum, part 1. 1. 6. c. 2. p. 124) and Huetius (Huetii Origeniana, 1. 2. p. 116, 1. 3. c. 1. p. 233. p. 253. ,. 1. 2. p. 59. p. 35. p. 124.). Dr. Crombie, translator of Origen's works, on his introduction to the practical works of Origen, notes problems with De Principiis. "The work has come down to us in the Latin translation of his admirer Rufinus; but, from a comparison of the few fragments of the original Greek which have been preserved, we see that Rufinus was justly chargeable with altering many of Origen's expressions, in order to bring his doctrine on certain points more into harmony with the orthodox views of the time... There can be no doubt that he often took great liberties with his author. So much was this felt to be the case, that Jerome undertook a new translation of the work... (Jerome) strongly accuses Rufinus of unfaithfulness as an interpreter..." Hippolytus was the supposed author of the Apostolic Tradition. It is sometimes cited as proof that infant baptism was practiced by the early church (21:4). It has not been cited here for several reasons. First, the Apostolic Tradition cannot be used as a model for infant baptism, as it includes many other aberrant practices that are rejected today, such as baptism in the nude (21:11), a waiting period of three years to be baptized (17:1-2), and a refusal to baptize soldiers, mayors or governors (16:10-11). (http://www.bomb-axo.com/hippolytus.html) Second, there is considerable doubt about the Apostolic Tradition. The many versions appear to have been heavily edited in the fourth century rather than the third. As Catholic Jesuit scholar John F. Baldovin notes, "It cannot be attributed to Hippolytus... it is even doubtful whether the corpus of that writer can actually be attributed to a single writer. Finally, the document does not give us certain information about the liturgical practice of the early-third-century Roman Church....Bradshaw and his colleagues agree with the arguments of Wilhelm Kinzig and Markus Vinzent ... that [it] corresponds to a late-fourth-century situation." ...Bradshaw, Johnson, and Phillips also argue that the combination of pre-baptismal and post-baptismal anointings occur nowhere before the fourth century." (Hippolytus and the Apostolic Tradition: Recent Research and Commentary. John F. Baldovin S.J. - author. Journal Title: Theological Studies. Volume: 64. Issue: 3. Publication Year: 2003. Page Number: 520+)

5) Prolegomena, Division 1, Nicene and Post-Nicene Fathers, series 2, vol. 7, p. 371-373.

6) Prolegomena: Life & Work of Chrysostom, chap. 2-3, Nicene & Post-Nicene Fathers

7) Prolegomena: Life of St. Basil, series 2, vol. 8, p. 9-14.

8) Life and Writings of Gregory of Nyssa. Prolegomena, chap. 1, Nicene & Post-Nicene Fathers

9) Prolegomena: Life of St. Ambrose, Nicene & Post-Nicene Fathers, p. 16.

10) Prolegomena: St. Augustine's Life and Work, Nicene & Post-Nicene Fathers, p. 13-15.

11) Prolegomena: Life of Jerome, series 2, vol. 6, p. 24-25

12) Prolegomena: On the Life and Works of Rufinus, Nicene & Post-Nicene Fathers, p. 835

13) Prolegomena, chap. 1, series 2, vol. 1, p. 13.

14) Aland, Kurt, *Did the Early Church Baptize Infants?*, p. 101,107, Philadelphia, Westminster Press, 1963, Library of Congress card number 63-8863)

15) Ibid, p. 104

16) Hassell, C.B. and Sylvester, *History of the Church of God,* chap. 11, p. 27 (Wilson, North Carolina, 1886). Online edition.

11. <u>SALVATION</u>:
How do we get to heaven?

Four times in the New Testament we read the question, "What must I do to be saved?" (Mark 10:17, Luke 10:25, 18:18, Acts 16:30).

Unfortunately, even after 2,000 years there are still different answers to this question among Christians.

How does one get to heaven? Are certain rituals needed? Can a person be sure of going to heaven?

Obviously these questions are very important. If certain rituals are needed to get to heaven, we need to know. And if they aren't, then let's free ourselves from unnecessary worry and legalism.

For example, the belief that these rituals are essential is why many baptize newborns, at a time when most parents would rather stay home with them.

Finding the answers isn't easy, due to contradictory statements and lack of information. For example, Orthodox Bishop Timothy Ware writes, "The Orthodox Church has never formally endorsed any particular theory of atonement." [1]

With that said, let us look at the differences between the three great branches of Christianity on salvation (soteriology), followed by an explanation of the Catholic/Orthodox viewpoint, and then an explanation of the Protestant viewpoint.

First it should be noted that any short statement of differences is bound to be a distortion. Nonetheless, in order to help clarify these issues, below are short summations of the major differences: [2]

1) Catholic/Orthodox teaching says certain works (rituals or sacraments) are needed to be saved. Protestants say sincere faith is all that is needed.

2) Catholic/Orthodox teaching emphasizes the process of salvation. Protestants emphasize salvation as an event.

3) Catholic/Orthodox doctrine speaks little or not at all about assurance of salvation. Protestants teach that we can be sure we are saved.

4) Orthodox doctrine, and to some extent Catholic, often treats justification and sanctification as one thing, and little is said about justification. Protestants treat them separately, and put great emphasis on justification.

5) Catholic/Orthodox leaders say that other things may be required to be saved, such as membership in their churches, use of icons, priests, and gifts and prayers for the dead. Protestants don't believe these are required to be saved.

1) The Catholic/Orthodox view: Faith is not enough

As mentioned, Catholic/Orthodox teaching says that belief alone is not enough to be saved, based on James 2:14-26: "What good is it, my brothers, if a man claims to have faith but has no deeds? Can such faith save him? ...You see that a person is justified by what he does and not by faith alone... faith without deeds is dead."

The Catholic Council of Trent condemns those who say that faith alone justifies us to God: "If anyone says... that it is that trust alone by which we are justified: let him be anathema."[3]   The formula for anathema used by the Catholic church reads: "We judge him condemned to eternal fire with Satan and his angels and all the reprobate, so long as he will not... do penance and satisfy the Church."

Orthodox Bishop Timothy Ware says faith plus sacraments save us: "Our salvation is founded first and foremost on baptism and the Eucharist (communion). It also involves the sacrament of confession."[4]

Orthodox and Catholic leaders teach that these sacraments, or rituals, change the person, and contribute to his salvation. Without them, they both say, it is impossible to be saved.

"The Church affirms that for believers the sacraments of the New Covenant are necessary for salvation." (Catholic Catechism 1129)

Orthodox theologian John Meyendorff writes, "These sacraments are ... redeeming man from sin and death and bestowing upon him the glory of immortality."[5]

Catholic and Orthodox churches observe seven sacraments, although they differ somewhat from each other.

The Catholic sacraments are:
- Baptism.
- Confirmation/Chrismation.
- Communion (Eucharist).
- Repentance (penance).
- Ordination.
- Marriage.
- Anointing of the sick (formerly called last rites).

The Orthodox sacraments are the same as the Catholic except chrismation replaces confirmation. Chrismation (anointing with oil for receiving the Holy Spirit) occurs during infant baptism, after which the infant is given communion. Catholics do not offer communion, usually, until age 7. (See the chapters on communion and chrismation/confirmation.)

These sacraments, especially baptism, communion and confession, grant salvation: "...A human being ... is introduced to new life by partaking of baptism, chrismation, and holy communion."[6]

However, even though the Catholic church states that the sacraments and baptism "are necessary to salvation," (Catechism, 1277) they also say a person can be saved without baptism in exceptional situations (1281, 1258, 1259): "Those who die for the faith, those who are catechumens, and all those who, without knowing of the Church but acting under the inspiration of grace, seek God sincerely and strive to fulfill his will, are saved even if they have not been baptized." If a person willingly refuses baptism, however, they will not be saved (1257).

The Protestant view: Faith alone

Protestants accept the Bible as the final source of doctrine, and so one must accept James 2:24 at face value — that faith is not enough to be saved — we must also have works. So it would seem, from reading this verse.

But in fact, James is not contradicting the many other verses that show that we are saved by faith alone. (See further in this chapter.) Nor is this support for the Catholic/Orthodox position that faith plus sacraments save us, Protestants say. James is addressing persons who have mouthed empty religious phrases about believing, but who have not changed their lives — they have not repented. This is what he calls dead faith (James 2:17).

The subject of James 2:14-26, notes James McCarthy, "is the kind of faith that saves... The passage is talking about living faith as opposed to dead faith. It is about a faith which is evidenced by good works. James' challenge is: 'Show me your faith' (James 2:18) even as Abraham showed his."[14]

Real faith and trust in Christ, means a person will act accordingly — they will show their faith by their works. The works don't save them, but simply show that their faith is real.

Note that Abraham had been counted righteous by God 20 years before he offered his son Isaac in obedience to God.

"Abram believed the LORD, and he credited it to him as righteousness." (Gen. 15:6). His action in obeying God many years later was a confirmation of his genuine faith, but did not justify him. He was already justified, forgiven and accepted by God.

About the sacraments

Most Protestant churches also have a different view of ritual sacraments than that of Orthodox and Catholics.

First, most evangelical Protestants observe only two ordinances instead of the seven sacraments of the Orthodox and Catholic: baptism and communion.

Second, they don't believe the rituals themselves change people, but are symbolic of an inner change.

For instance, John the Baptist, when facing a group of religious leaders who wanted to be baptized, refused them because they had not repented:

"You brood of vipers! Who warned you to flee from the coming wrath?

Produce fruit in keeping with repentance" (Matt. 3:7-8). In other words, he felt the ritual alone was insufficient. They had not repented, so any baptism was meaningless.

This contrasts with the Orthodox/Catholic view that the sacrament of baptism confers forgiveness of sins. (See the chapters on baptism.)

The powerlessness of sacraments (such as confession) given to insincere people is also shown in Mark 7:6 when Jesus quoted the prophet Isaiah: "These people come near to me with their mouth and honor me with their lips, but their hearts are far from me. Their worship of me is made up only of rules taught by men" (Is. 29:13).

Repetitious prayers that are insincere are not effective, Jesus said:

"And when you pray, do not keep on babbling like pagans, for they think they will be heard because of their many words" (Matt. 6:7).

Rituals or sacraments cannot save us, Protestants believe, just as the Old Testament ritual of circumcision by itself could not save anyone: "Circumcision is nothing and uncircumcision is nothing. Keeping God's commands is what counts." (1 Cor. 7:19) "For in Christ Jesus neither circumcision nor uncircumcision has any value. The only thing that counts is faith expressing itself through love" (Gal. 5:6).

Faith and works

Protestants, Catholic and Orthodox agree that if a person says they have faith, but have no works to go with it, they are not saved.

Faith must show itself in our actions (works) if we are truly saved. However, Protestants believe that if we must perform works to be saved, then our salvation is partly our own doing, and is not fully of God. We therefore cannot be sure we are saved until our last breath, and even then we would be in doubt of it. Who can say if their works are sufficient to be saved? Only God can say.

For example, the Emperor Constantine, although apparently a lifelong believer, waited until moments before his death to be baptized, since he believed that the ritual of baptism washes away our sins ("baptismal regeneration"), and he wanted to make sure all his sins were washed away. [15]

He did not believe that faith alone was enough for salvation.

Many scriptures show that salvation is by faith alone: "You who are trying to be justified by law have been alienated from Christ; you have fallen away from grace" (Gal. 5:4). "So the law was put in charge to lead us to Christ that we might be justified by faith" (Gal. 3:24).

"Clearly no one is justified before God by the law, because, 'The righteous will live by faith" (Gal. 3:11).

"And are justified freely by his grace through the redemption that came by Christ Jesus" (Rom. 3:24).

"For we maintain that a man is justified by faith apart from observing the law" (Rom. 3:28).

"...To the man who does not work but trusts God who justifies the wicked, his faith is credited as righteousness" (Rom. 4:5).

A Mathematical Comparison

CATHOLIC/ORTHODOX: FAITH + WORKS = SALVATION
PROTESTANT: FAITH = SALVATION + WORKS

Catholic and Orthodox leaders say that faith and good works lead to salvation. They point to James 2:26 as support for this: "Faith without deeds is dead."The Protestant perspective is that sincere faith and trust in Christ leads to repentance, which results in salvation and good works. Good works don't cause our salvation, but are a result of the change in the person done by the Holy Spirit: "if anyone is in Christ, he is a new creation; the old has gone, the new has come!" (2 Cor. 5:17).

"For it is with your heart that you believe and are justified, and it is with your mouth that you confess and are saved" (Rom. 10:10).

"He saved us, not because of righteous things we had done, but because of his mercy" (Titus 3:5)

"A man is not justified by observing the law, but by faith in Jesus Christ. So we, too, have put our faith in Christ Jesus that we may be justified by faith in Christ and not by observing the law, because by observing the law no-one will be justified." (Gal. 2:16)

"...Who has saved us and called us to a holy life—not because of anything we have done but because of his own purpose and grace." (2 Tim. 1:9) "For it is by grace you have been saved, through faith—and this not from yourselves, it is the gift of God — not by works, so that no-one can boast" (Eph. 2:8,9). Phil. 3:9 says, "not having a righteousness of my own that comes from the law, but that which is through faith in Christ--the righteousness that comes from God and is by faith."

Protestants believe that obtaining salvation by a mixture of works and grace is not possible based on Rom. 11:6: "And if by grace, then it is no longer by works; if it were, grace would no longer be grace."

Paul is saying it is either one or the other — not both. Rom. 1: 17 says we are saved by faith alone: "For in the gospel a righteousness from God is revealed, a righteousness that is by faith from first to last, just as it is written: 'The righteous will live by faith.'"

This is also shown in Lev. 23: 28-32, describing the day of atonement (or justification). It is interesting that work was especially forbidden on this day: "Do no work on that day, because it is the Day of Atonement, when atonement is made for you before the LORD your God."

In these five verses, the Israelites are told five times not to do any work on that day, and those that worked would be destroyed by God himself. There was to be no mixing of work and justification.

Lev. 19:19 hints at this in a mysterious passage — it forbids wearing "a garment mingled of linen and woolen (sha'atnez). Strong's Exhaustive Concordance defines this as "linsey-woolsey, i.e. cloth of linen and wool carded and spun together:— garment of divers sorts, linen and woolen." What is the significance of this? Why was it forbidden?

Linen, of course, is from flax, a plant. Wool, of course, is sheared from sheep. So this forbidden fabric is a mixture of plant and animal.

Although this is conjecture, there may be a link between this strange passage and Adam and Eve, Cain and Abel, and faith and works.

For instance, Adam and Eve worked to clothe themselves with fig leaves (plants), which were rejected by God, who Himself freely clothed them with fur, which obviously came through the death of animals (Gen. 3:7, 21).

Clothing represents righteousness in scripture. Rev. 19:8 says, "Fine linen stands for the righteous acts of the saints." *(See also Ps. 132:9, Is. 61:10, 64:6.)* The parallel here is that we cannot by our own works obtain the righteousness of God. It is something God does for us when we repent and trust in Christ. This is also illustrated symbolically when Cain by the sweat of his brow (work) produced plants for sacrifice to God, which were rejected by God in favor of the bloody animal sacrifice Abel offered which he had not worked for (grace). (See Gen. 4:3-5.)

Shepherds don't hoe and plow under the hot sun. They sit in the shade and watch the flock multiply by itself. This is another illustration of human works (represented by Cain's vegetables) being unacceptable, and the unearned gift being accepted.

So the prohibition of mixing of linen and wool is likely a symbolic prohibition against the mixing of grace with works.

Similarly, Abram and Sarah by their own works agreed to use a slave woman (Hagar) to have an heir (Gen. 16). But their efforts were rejected by God in favor of the freewoman's son (Sarah's), whom she had birthed by believing God. So again we see human effort and work rejected in favor of the free grace obtained by faith. This is shown in the chart below:

WORKS:	*FAITH:*
FIG LEAVES (grown by man, sweat)	FUR (from God, blood)
CAIN (sweated over plants)	ABEL (rested watching sheep)
HAGAR (slave labor)	SARAH (free woman)
LINEN PLANT (labor intensive)	WOOL (unearned)

Gal. 4:30 echoes this: "Get rid of the slave woman and her son, for the slave woman's son will never share in the inheritance with the free woman's son." Notice several things here:

1) It says "get rid of the slave woman." This is strong wording, allowing no compromise. We must get rid of our reliance upon our own works — to drive it out as they did the slave woman.

2) Note the word "never" — not in purgatory or in any future event.

3) Note the word "share." Works don't have even a small part to play in our salvation. They don't share in it at all. Salvation is not works plus faith, or faith plus a few works. It is all faith, shown by our works.

Is. 64:6 reinforces the Protestant position: "All our righteous acts are like filthy rags." Our good deeds are not good enough.

What good, then, are good works?

What is the place of good works then? Good works are the result of our salvation and confirm that our faith is genuine. But those works do not save us — they just show that we are saved, like a gas gauge shows we have gasoline, but which in itself provides none.

Real "saving" faith will result in salvation and good works. One needs only look for the works to know that one is really saved.

For instance, to see if a house has electricity, one needs only to see if the lights are on. These lights don't bring electricity — they only prove that it is there. Just so, good works don't bring salvation, they only prove that it is there.

The benefit of rituals or sacraments to many, however, is that they can point to that ritual (such as baptism) and say that was when they were saved. If, however, the ritual does not technically save us, at what point are we saved? Protestants believe we are saved when we repent and begin to trust in God for our salvation. At that instant we are baptized BY the Holy Spirit into Christ supernaturally, as it says in 1 Cor. 12:13: "For we were all baptized by one Spirit into one body— whether Jews or Greeks, slave or free— and we were all given the one Spirit to drink." This baptism by the Holy Spirit into the body of Christ at salvation may be the "one baptism" described in Eph. 4:5.

(Note also that this should not be confused with the baptism in the Holy Spirit, which is done by Christ: (Matt. 3:11: "(Christ) will baptize you with the Holy Spirit..."), or the symbolic baptism in water, which is done by a minister.)

2) Catholics/Orthodox: Salvation is a process

Catholic and Orthodox doctrine emphasizes the process of salvation, while Protestant teaching more often refers to salvation as an event in time when we were forgiven (justification), followed by the process of becoming holy (sanctification).

Orthodox Bishop Ware says: "Our salvation is a process...and not a single event...I cannot speak as if its successful termination was already certain and secure, and for that reason.. I prefer to answer, not 'I am saved,' but 'I am being saved.'"[7]

Catholic doctrine shows this also, referring to baptism as the beginning of the process: "The faith required for baptism is not a perfect and mature faith, but a beginning that is called to develop... Preparation for baptism leads only to the threshold of new life." (Catechism 1253,1254).

In both Catholic and Orthodox writings, the concept of salvation as a process is often assumed more than it is spoken of doctrinally. This may be because salvation as a process naturally follows infant baptism — if the infant is already forgiven and justified before God by baptism, only the process of sanctification remains. Salvation as an event is rarely seen, as most rely upon their infant baptism and the other sacraments for making them acceptable to God. Most who were baptized as infants cannot look to a certain day (event) when they made a decision to follow Christ, as would be the case if they had made a conscious decision to repent later in life.

Key to the understanding of the Orthodox perspective is its teaching on "theosis" or deification. Orthodox define this as the process of becoming holy or becoming like God. *(See the chapter on theosis.)* It places more emphasis on the process of salvation than it does on salvation as an event; as a result it cannot be said that a person is saved, as the process is lifelong.

Protestants: Salvation is an event and a process

Protestants say our forgiveness (justification) is an event that occurs when we repent, followed by the process of becoming more holy (sanctification), which continues throughout our lives. By comparison, this event or "moment of decision" is often absent in Catholic and Orthodox practice, since it is assumed to occur with infant baptism.

The Greek word for repentance, metanoia, literally means "decision."

Thayer's Greek-English Lexicon defines it as "a change of mind,...of a purpose he has formed or of something he has done."

A person who repents, therefore, is one who has made a decision to follow Christ -- they can often point with certainty to that event, time and day, and the changes that resulted in their lives.

This is shown in the the Bible in the life of the apostle Paul (Saul), who was one day a vicious persecutor of the church, and a few days later, after his decision, was a humble worshipper of Christ (Acts 9:1-20):

"Saul was still breathing out murderous threats against the Lord's disciples... He got up and was baptised...He began to preach in the synagogues that Jesus is the Son of God."

The Bible also shows salvation as an event in the lives of the corrupt tax collector Zacchaeus (Luke 19:1-10), the 3,000 people who repented on the day of Pentecost (Acts 2:37-42), the household of Lydia (Acts 16:14-15), etc.

This decision for Christ and the resultant change is also shown in 1 Cor. 6: 9: "Do you not know that the wicked will not inherit the kingdom of God? ... And that is what some of you were. But you were washed, you were sanctified, you were justified in the name of the Lord Jesus Christ and by the Spirit of our God."

Evangelical Protestants feel the lack of a moment of decision in the life of a believer can lead him or her to assume that they are in right relationship to God, when in fact they are not. Giving of sacraments to persons who have never personally made a decision to make Christ Lord of their lives can create a false assurance of salvation. Such a system does not challenge them to make a life-changing decision to follow Christ.

One reason, perhaps, why there is confusion over this issue, is that scripture refers to salvation in three tenses — past, present and future. This shows salvation is both a completed deed (justification, past tense), an ongoing process (sanctification, present tense) and a future event (resurrection). (Note: italic emphasis is the author's.)

FUTURE TENSE (resurrection or glorification):

:   "He who stands firm to the end will be saved." (Matt. 10:22)

"Whoever believes and is baptized will be saved" (Mark 16:16)

"I am the gate; whoever enters through me will be saved" (John 10:9).

"Everyone who calls on the name of the Lord will be saved" (Acts 2:21).

"He will bring you a message through which you and all your household will be saved" (Acts 11:14).

"Since we have now been justified by his blood, how much more shall we be saved from God's wrath through him!" (Rom. 5:9).   (NOTE: This scripture shows two of the tenses of salvation: Already justified, but not yet saved.)

"That if you confess with your mouth, 'Jesus is Lord,' and believe in your heart that God raised him from the dead, you will be saved" (Rom. 10:9).

"Now there is in store for me the crown of righteousness, which the Lord, the righteous Judge, will award to me on that day..." (2 Tim. 4:8).

PRESENT TENSE (sanctification — becoming holy):

"For the message of the cross is foolishness to those who are perishing, but to us who are being saved it is the power of God" (1 Cor. 1:18).

"By this gospel you are saved, if you hold firmly to the word I preached to you" (1 Cor. 15:2).

"For we are to God the aroma of Christ among those who are being saved and those who are perishing" (2 Cor. 2:15).

"I write these things to you who believe in the name of the Son of God so that you may know that you have eternal life" (1 John 5:13).

"Whoever believes in the Son has eternal life, but whoever rejects the Son will not see life, for God's wrath remains on him" (John 3:36).

"I tell you the truth, whoever hears my word and believes him who sent me has eternal life and will not be condemned; he has crossed over from death to life" (John 5:24).

"For you are receiving the goal of your faith, the salvation of your souls" (1 Peter 1:9).

"I tell you the truth, he who believes has everlasting life" (John 6:47).

PAST TENSE (justification — forgiveness):

"Jesus said to him, "Today salvation has come to this house, because this man, too, is a son of Abraham..." (Luke 19:9).

"For it is by grace you have been saved, through faith—and this not from yourselves, it is the gift of God—" (Eph 2:8).

"Who has saved us and called us to a holy life" (2 Tim. 1:9).

"He saved us, not because of righteous things we had done, but because of his mercy. He saved us through the washing of rebirth and renewal by the Holy Spirit" (Tit. 3:5).

"I tell you the truth, whoever hears my word and believes him who sent me has eternal life and will not be condemned; he has crossed over from death to life" (John 5:24). (NOTE: This verse shows both present tense ("has") and past tense ("has crossed over").

3) Catholics/Orthodox: No assurance of salvation

Perhaps because of the emphasis on salvation as a process, Orthodox doctrine (and to a lesser extent Catholic) tends not to speak about assurance of salvation, until life is over. The Catholic Church says that no one will "obtain eternal life but he who endures to the end" (Catechism, 162).

Orthodox Bishop Timothy Ware, when asked about his salvation, wrote: "Twice in my life, once in a bus and once in a railway carriage, I have been asked by a stranger: 'Are you saved?' How should we reply to this question? For my own part, I hesitate to respond categorically, 'Yes, I am saved.'...The warning issued by the pagan Solon applies equally in a Christian context: 'Call no one blessed until he has died.' It is the one who endures to the end who will be saved. (Matt. 10:22, 24:13)." [1]

Protestants: Assurance of salvation

Protestants believe that we can be sure of our salvation before death because it is not based on our good deeds — which the Bible says are like filthy rags (Is. 64:6). Instead it is based by faith on the good deeds of Jesus Christ, who lived without sin and gave Himself for us. Our salvation is assured as long as we trust in him, for he said as he died, "It is finished."

According to Thayer's Greek-English Lexicon, this word for "finished" (teleo) is in the perfect past tense, and means "to bring to a close, complete, fulfill, to perform the last act which completes a process, and to pay." It is the word used when completely paying a debt.

Jesus assured us of our salvation when he said, ""I tell you the truth, whoever hears my word and believes him who sent me HAS eternal life and will not be condemned; he has crossed over from death to life" (John 5:24).

Those who believe in him, Jesus said, HAVE eternal life. They are assured of it and do not need to be in doubt of it, unless they turn away from the Lord (Heb. 6:4-6, Rom. 11:22).

The apostle John also assures us of our salvation: "I write these things to you who believe in the name of the Son of God so that you may know that you have eternal life" (1 John 5:13).

` The apostle Paul had assurance of his salvation. He said, "I desire to depart (die) and be with Christ" (Philippians 1:23). If he had no assurance of his salvation, he would have had to say, "I hope when I die, I will be with Christ."

4) Catholics/Orthodox: Justification + sanctification

Orthodox leaders teach that justification (forgiveness) and sanctification (becoming holy) are one process which they call theosis. (See the chapter on theosis.) Orthodox Bishop Ware says, "...When we Orthodox speak about salvation, we do not have in view any sharp differentiation between justification and sanctification. Indeed, Orthodox usually have little to say about justification as a distinct topic... Orthodoxy links sanctification and justification together, just as St. Paul does in 1 Cor. 6:11: 'You were washed, you were sanctified, you were justified in the name of the Lord Jesus Christ...'" [8]

Catholic teaching, while not as strongly stated, also mixes justification (forgiveness of sins) with sanctification (becoming holy): "Justification is not only the remission of sins, but also the sanctification and renewal of the interior man." (*Catechism*, 1989)

Protestants: Justification, sanctification are separate

Protestant theology primarily treats justification and sanctification separately. Unless this is done, many Protestants say, a believer may think that they must work to obtain justification (forgiveness) in the same way we work to be more sanctified (holy).

Sanctification in the Old and New Testaments most commonly means to set apart, or consecrate. All Christians are set apart to serve God, which occurs at the moment of our justification (forgiveness). Hence, it is understandable how the term can be confused with justification. But sanctification in common usage has two meanings -- one the setting apart for service to God of a believer or a thing, and the other the process of becoming more holy. It is the latter definition the Protestants usually have in mind when they refer to sanctification.

This process of sanctification is best shown in the following verses:

" May God...sanctify you through and through. May your whole spirit, soul and body be kept blameless at the coming of our Lord Jesus Christ" (1Thes. 5:23).

"Since we have these promises, dear friends, let us purify ourselves from everything that contaminates body and spirit, perfecting holiness [or sanctification] out of reverence for God" (2 Cor. 7:1).

"It is God's will that you should be sanctified..." (1Thes. 4:3).

Here the apostle Paul is urging believers to strive to be holy and sanctified -- something that is evidently not yet the case. By contrast, we "are justified freely by his grace..." (Rom. 3:24). Noted theologian J.C. Ryle notes:

"In justification our own works have no place at all, and simple faith in Christ is the one thing needful. In sanctification our own works are of vast importance and God bids us fight, and watch, and pray, and strive, and take pains, and labour. Justification is a finished and complete work, and a man is perfectly justified the moment he believes. Sanctification is an imperfect work, comparatively, and will never be perfected until we reach heaven. Justification admits of no growth or increase: a man is as much justified the hour he first comes to Christ by faith as he will be to all eternity. Sanctification is eminently a progressive work, and admits of continual growth and enlargement so long as a man lives." [16]

As to 1 Cor. 6:11, used by some to show that justification and sanctification are the same thing, Protestants note that the definition of sanctification there refers to the setting apart of a believer for God, and does not mean that all believers are perfectly sanctified or holy. Clearly we are not.

Also, reading the verse in context, the apostle Paul is trying to convince the Corinthians that they are holy enough to resolve legal matters themselves without going to court. He thus reminds them that they are already cleansed, set apart (sanctified, Gk. hagiasmos) and justified before God. Here he evidently has in mind the sense of sanctification as setting apart, not in the sense of striving to attain holiness. The word sanctification is defined as holiness, but also as "consecration" in Strong's Greek Dictionary, or setting apart for God All Christians, in this sense, are already consecrated and set apart for God's service. Thus 1 Cor. 6:11 is not mixing sanctification and justification, it is instead noting that all believers are set apart for Christ.

5) Special factors affecting salvation

THE CATHOLIC/ORTHODOX VIEW: *Many Catholic and Orthodox leaders say that a person must be a member in either the Catholic or Orthodox church to be saved.*

In an official papal ruling, the Catholic Church states that "there is one holy, catholic, and apostolic Church. And we firmly believe and profess that outside of her there is no salvation nor remission of sins... In it there is one Lord, one faith, one baptism." (Pope Boniface VIII, "Unum Sanctam,"). The Catholic Catechism says, "The sole Church of Christ is that which our Savior... entrusted to Peter's ... care... This Church subsists in the Catholic Church. For it is through Christ's Catholic Church alone....that the fullness of salvation can be obtained."

"The Church, a pilgrim now on earth, is necessary for salvation... Hence they could not be saved who, knowing that the catholic Church was founded as necessary by God through Christ, would refuse either to enter it, or to remain in it." [11] (This, however, seems to contradict the following statement in the Catechism (818) stating that non-Catholics can be saved: "All who have been justified by faith in Baptism are incorporated into Christ; They therefore have a right to be called Christians, and...are accepted as brothers in the Lord by the children of the Catholic Church.")

Orthodox Bishop Ware does not agree that the Catholic church is the true church, and writes instead that, "The Orthodox Church in all humility believes itself to be the 'one, holy, Catholic (universal) and Apostolic' church, of which the Creed speaks.... Many people may be members of the Church who are not visibly so; invisible bonds may exist despite an outward separation..... But there also exists in the Orthodox Church a more rigorous group, who hold that since Orthodoxy is the Church, anyone who is not Orthodox cannot be a member of the Church." [9] Orthodox Archimandrite Amvrosi agrees: "The Lord did not found many churches. He founded only one Church, only one faith. And these 22,000 sects were not founded by God, but by people, specifically human wanderers. These are not churches, but associations of people. There is no salvation there, no fullness of grace, only the grace of the call to repentance, which exists everywhere... We must keep the faith of Orthodoxy. In her only is there salvation, because the Church is the pillar and foundation of the truth." [10]

THE PROTESTANT VIEW: *Membership in a human church organization is not a condition of salvation with God.*

Membership in the body of Christ is determined by God, and not by any organization on the earth. Disagreements about minor doctrines do not divide Christians in God's eyes.

Rom. 14:1 says: "Accept him whose faith is weak, without passing judgment on disputable matters."

This shows that there are indeed "disputable matters" that divide Christians doctrinally, and yet we should still accept each other. There were divisions in the early church over circumcision (Acts 11:2, 15:5, Gal. 2:12), and over different leaders (1 Cor. 3:34). And yet they were still all called believers. (See the chapter, "THE CHURCH: Can it be divided?")

———

THE CATHOLIC/ORTHODOX VIEW: *A person can be saved through the prayers or money given for them by others.*

Catholic and Orthodox leaders accept the apocrypha as scripture, which teaches that money or prayers for the dead can save them:

"For alms doth deliver from death, and shall purge away all sin. Those that exercise alms and righteousness shall be filled with life..." (Tobit 12:9. See also Tobit 4: 8-11, 14:10-11)

"Water will quench a flaming fire, and alms maketh atonement for sin." (Ecclesiasticus/Sirach 3:30)

The Orthodox churches, like the Catholic, believe that prayers and good deeds done for the dead, even if they are in hell or purgatory, can result in their salvation: "The usefulness of prayers, public and private (at home), for souls — even if they are in hell — is written about in the lives of the saints and the ascetics, and by the holy Fathers."[12]

The Catholic Catechism (1479) says similarly regarding the dead, "one way we can help them is to obtain indulgences for them, so that the temporal punishments due for their sins may be remitted."

The Catholic church defines Indulgences as the forgiving of punishment for sins in purgatory ("temporal punishments," — see the chapter on purgatory).

They can be obtained from the Catholic church by "works of devotion, penance and charity," such as praying for them, or asking that they be mentioned in the liturgy or mass by the priest. *(Catechism, 1478. See the chapter on prayer for the dead.)*

THE PROTESTANT VIEW: *Prayers or money cannot save people in hell.*

There is no scripture showing prayer for the dead or giving money for the dead. (Protestants do not believe in purgatory, and do not accept the apocrypha as scripture.) The Bible condemns those who thought they could buy spiritual blessings. (See the chapter on praying for the dead and the chapter on purgatory.)

THE CATHOLIC/ORTHODOX VIEW: *A person can have their sins forgiven by the priest.*

This is related to the sacrament of penance, but includes the belief that priests have a special power to forgive sins that others don't. Some go so far as to say that it is impossible to be saved without a priest.

THE PROTESTANT VIEW: *No person on earth can forgive the sins of another.*

The Bible says only God can forgive sins. The Lord says in Isa. 43:25: "I, even I, am he who blots out your transgressions, for my own sake, and remembers your sins no more." *(See the chapter on the priesthood.)*

THE CATHOLIC/ORTHODOX VIEW: *A person must honor or venerate icons or statues in order to be saved.*

This statement may shock some Orthodox or Catholics, who may have never heard it. In all fairness, this is rarely or never spoken, but is nonetheless part of official Catholic and Orthodox teaching. It comes from the seventh ecumenical council (787 A.D.) which is held to be infallible. (See the chapter on the ecumenical councils.) That council stated, "...We salute the venerable images (icons and statues). We place under anathema those who do not do this."[13] (Anathema means a person is cut off from God and will go to hell unless they repent.)

THE PROTESTANT VIEW: *A person does not have to honor or venerate icons in order to be saved.*

It is interesting to note that even though icon veneration is required for salvation by the seventh ecumenical council (which is accepted as infallible by Catholic and Orthodox leaders), this is almost never repeated in Orthodox/Catholic publications. This shows that either (1) icon veneration is not essential to salvation, or (2) that church councils can make mistakes, or both.

If the world's salvation depends upon use of icons, one would expect it to be clearly taught to all. The fact that it is not, seems to imply that Catholic/Orthodox leaders in practice doubt this teaching, even though officially they must accept it as it comes from what they say is an infallible council. (See the chapters on icons and the seven ecumenical councils.)

THE CATHOLIC VIEW: *A person must submit to the pope to be saved.*

The Catholic church, in an official (infallible) papal ruling, states: "...that every human creature is subject to the Roman pontiff,—this we declare, say, define, and pronounce to be altogether necessary to salvation" (Unum Sanctam, 1302, Boniface VIII).

THE PROTESTANT/ORTHODOX VIEW: *There is no scripture that says salvation is limited to those who submit to the Pope.*

In fact, there is no scripture establishing a pope in the Bible. This doctrine (of submission to the Pope in order to be saved) was officially proclaimed 1,300 years after Christ and so could not have been taught by the early churches or the apostles. It is a late addition to Catholic theology.

Christ is the head of the church, not any man: "God placed all things under his feet and appointed him to be head over everything for the church." (Eph. 1:22-23). If Christ is the head of "all things" for the church, then the Pope cannot be. As Peter himself wrote, Christ, and therefore not the pope, is the chief shepherd and overseer of our souls (1 Peter 2:24, 5:4).

(See the chapter "Other differences" for more information on the Pope.)

———

In sum, the Protestant position on salvation can be answered by the response of the apostle Peter when asked this question (Acts 2:37-38): "Repent and be baptized in the name of Jesus Christ for the forgiveness of your sins." In Mark 16:16 the Lord Jesus said, "He who believes and is baptized will be saved; but he who does not believe will be condemned."

The apostle Paul wrote in Eph. 2:8-9: "For by grace you have been saved through faith, and that not of yourselves; it is the gift of God, not of works, lest anyone should boast."

Our works cannot save us. Is. 64:6 says, "All of us have become like one who is unclean, and all our righteous acts are like filthy rags."

Salvation is a gift of God that we cannot earn by doing good deeds. It is based on repentance (or turning away) from our sins and faith in the sacrificial death of Christ. The purpose of baptism is to show God, the world and even ourselves that our faith is sincere — that we have truly repented.

----

1) Ware, Timothy, *How are we saved?*, p. 49

2) Another distinctive of Orthodoxy is an emphasis on salvation as a restoration of a relationship ruined by sin. "Sin...is to be viewed not primarily in juridicial terms, as the transgression of a moral code... It is above all else a loss of relationship," (Ware, How are we saved?" p. 10) Sin in Orthodoxy is not seen as much as offending God as simply falling short of God's glory. "To sin is first and foremost to miss the mark." (ibid, p. 8) Catholic and Protestant doctrine puts more emphasis on sin as an offense to God, and salvation as atoning for those offenses through Christ's death. Protestants agree that salvation is a restoration of a lost relationship with God, but also believe the Bible stresses juridicial salvation. Col. 2:14 says: "... having cancelled the written code, with its regulations, that was against us and that stood opposed to us; he took it away, nailing it to the cross. 1 John 4:10 says: "...He loved us and sent his Son as an atoning sacrifice for our sins." 1 Peter 3:18 illustrates both the reconciliation and atonement: "For Christ died for sins once for all, the righteous for the unrighteous, to bring you to God."

3) Session 6, "Decree on Justification," canon 12.

4) Ware, *How are we saved?*, p. 79

5) Meyendorff, *Byzantine Theology*, p. 19, as cited in Biola report.

6) Ibid, 192-193

7) Ware, *How are we saved?* p. 6, 7, 14

8) Ibid, p. 66

9) Ware, *The Orthodox Church,* p. 315-317

10) *O vere i spacenii* (About Faith and Salvation), Book II, p. 41-42

11) Second Vatican Council, "Dogmatic Constitution on the Church", no. 14

12) *U Boga vse zhivi* (With God all are alive), Akafist, p. 17

13) Decree of the Seventh Ecumenical Council, Nicene/Post Nicene Fathers, p. 1326-1327

14) *The Gospel According to Rome*, p. 50

15) Ecclesiastical History of Theodoret, Book 1, chap. 30, Nicene & Post-Nicene Fathers

16) Ryle, J.C.,"Justification and Sanctification: How do they Differ?":
from http://www.monergism.com/thethreshold/articles/onsite/sanct_just_ryle.html

12. THEOSIS:
Becoming like God?

The Orthodox doctrine of theosis (or deification) is one of the doctrines unique to Orthodoxy. Neither Catholics[1] nor Protestants have a doctrine quite like it.

Simply put, theosis means becoming God or like God. In actuality, the Orthodox theosis doctrine combines the Bible's teachings on justification and sanctification as one thing.

The main scripture Orthodox use to support this doctrine is 2 Peter 1:4: "[God] has given us his very great and precious promises, so that through them you may participate in the divine nature...."

This participating in God's nature is called deification or theosis.

Author Daniel Clendenin says, "It is fascinating to observe the total absence of the doctrine of justification by faith in large segments of Orthodox history and theology. Instead, the idea of theosis or 'deification' takes center stage.[2] The startling aphorism—attributed to many early church fathers, including the champion of trinitarianism, Athanasius—summed it up well: 'God became man so that men might become gods.'" [3]

Such a statement sounds heretical. However, in Orthodox practice it means simply becoming more like God in our character — becoming holy and sanctified.

Theosis also reveals another distinction of Orthodoxy — its disinterest in judicial justification in favor of restoration of fellowship with God. In theosis, "the legal framework for understanding the work of Christ is played down and our mystical union with God is emphasized," Clendenin notes.[4]

Since theosis combines sanctification and justification, it is sometimes hard to understand if Orthodox writers are referring to one or the other.

Most of the time, it refers to sanctification, as Orthodox do not generally accept the Protestant teaching of salvation and justification occurring at repentance. Instead, they believe that salvation is not certain until death.

Biola's report on Orthodoxy says as much: "... justification holds little place in Orthodox theology. Rather Orthodox theology refers more to 'salvation' or 'deification' (being transformed into the likeness of God through union with Christ) and 'sanctification.' ...These terms, which overlap and are not clearly differentiated in Orthodox teaching, refer to a person's relationship with God. This means being right with him and enjoying fellowship with him and his life, as opposed to being alienated from him and without divine life... justification is included in the process of theosis or deification." [5]

Orthodox Bishop Timothy Ware's comments on deification (theosis) seem more suited to sanctification than justification: "...there is nothing ... extraordinary about the methods which we must follow in order to be deified. If someone asks 'How can I become god?' The answer is very simple: go to church, receive the sacraments regularly, pray to God 'in spirit and in truth', read the Gospels, follow the commandments." [6]

The problem with such statements is that they imply that salvation is attained by doing good works.

For instance, Orthodox theologian Christoforos Stavroupoulos writes: "Theosis... How is it possible for us to make this a reality? ... The Christian life comes into being with the sacraments and with holy works, those virtuous works which are done with a pure and holy motive in the name of Christ." [7]

According to Orthodox teaching, we attain deification or theosis by observing the church sacraments and keeping the commandments:

"Fastings, vigils, prayers, alms, and other good works which are done in the name of Christ are means which help us reach that goal which always remains the same: the reception of the Holy Spirit and the making him our own, that is, theosis. Good works are able to grant us the fruits of the Holy Spirit only when they are done in the name of Jesus Christ." [8]

The Protestant view of theosis

First, the Orthodox teaching on theosis usually corresponds to the Protestant doctrine of sanctification — becoming holy and one with God. As such it is a profitable doctrine. However, since the word theosis also sometimes is used to mean justification, it can cause problems, in that it implies we can earn forgiveness. (See below.)

Second, Protestants also note that the word theosis is not found in the Bible. It is a hybrid doctrine that neither Jesus nor the apostles taught.

Third, a careful reading of the principal scripture that is used to support the theosis doctrine (2 Peter 1:4) shows that sanctification was Peter's theme, not justification. "[God] has given us his very great and precious promises, so that through them you may participate in the divine nature...." God wants us to have the same holy character that he has.

This is similar to other passages in the Bible that refer to the process of sanctification (and not justification): "...Let us purify ourselves from everything that contaminates body and spirit, perfecting holiness out of reverence for God" (2 Cor. 7:1). "...We ... are being transformed into his likeness with ever-increasing glory..." (2 Cor. 3:18).

Fourth, adding justification to sanctification may seem minor, but it quickly leads to the belief that we must strive to attain justification just as we strive to attain sanctification. It destroys our peace with God because it is impossible through good deeds to justify ourselves to God. The prophet Isaiah noted: "... all our righteous acts are like filthy rags..." (Is. 64:6).

The "holy works" needed for theosis are helpful when it comes to sanctification, but are useless in obtaining justification for our sins, as Isaiah noted. Instead of justification by faith, the theosis doctrine inadvertently tries to attain justification by works. The role of faith is absent, as noted in Biola's report: "The Orthodox teaching on being born again as involving the necessity of the sacraments and the hierarchy of the church denies that the new birth is effected solely by faith through the instrumentality of the Word of God." [9]

Christians who do not understand that justification is a gift of God not obtained by works, can become discouraged.

Trying to reach God by good works, they soon discover that it is not possible. They have no peace with God. They also lack joy and thankfulness for their salvation, since they believe that it depends on their works, which they realize are insufficient. Confronted by their repeated failures, they may give up and fall back into sin. This can be the result of confusing these two doctrines. In its worst form, the doctrine of theosis is a dangerous mix of two doctrines that scripture treats separately for good reason. Christians are justified instantaneously by faith in Christ. But sanctification is a process that is ongoing until our death. (See the chapter on salvation.)

---

1) NOTE: Catholicism uses the term to refer to an advanced form of ascetical prayer.

2) "What the Orthodox believe,", *Christian History*, Issue 54, p. 35

3) Athanasius, "On the Incarnation," Nicene and Post-Nicene Fathers, s. 2, vol. 4, p. 65

4) "What the Orthodox believe,", *Christian History,* Issue 54, p. 35

5) *Eastern Orthodox Teachings in Comparison with The Doctrinal Position of Biola University,* p. 4

6) Ware, *The Orthodox Church,* p. 236

7) "Partakers of Divine Nature," p. 189, as cited in *Eastern Orthodox Teachings in Comparison with The Doctrinal Position of Biola University*, p. 4

8) Ibid, p. 190, as cited in *Eastern Orthodox Teachings in Comparison with The Doctrinal Position of Biola University*, p. 4

9) *Eastern Orthodox Teachings in Comparison with The Doctrinal Position of Biola University*, p. 11

13. CHRISMATION & CONFIRMATION:
Ritual or reality?

Another area of difference between Protestant, Catholic and Orthodox believers is over how Christians receive the Holy Spirit. Orthodox doctrine says it is by the ritual they call chrismation, and it occurs during infant baptism.

Catholic leaders and some Protestants say it is through the ritual they call confirmation, and occurs at about age 12.

Many evangelical Protestants say the Holy Spirit doesn't come through a ritual, or at any particular age, but comes by faith to believers when they are ready.

The Orthodox/Catholic viewpoint

In the Catholic church confirmation usually occurs at about age 12. The bishop or his delegate dips his right thumb in holy oil and makes the sign of the cross on the forehead of the child, saying, "Be sealed with the gift of the Holy Spirit." (Converts, of course, go through confirmation when they convert.)

The Orthodox churches don't wait until age 12, but anoint infants with holy oil immediately after their baptism. (Catholics also anoint children with holy oil at baptism, but this is not the same as confirmation.)

In the Orthodox ritual, the child's forehead, eyes, nostrils, mouth, ears, breast, hands and feet are anointed. Each time the priest says, "The seal of the gift of the Holy Spirit." This anointing makes the child " a full member of the people of God," Orthodox Bishop Ware says.[1]

Catholic and Orthodox doctrine says that the gifts of the Holy Spirit come through chrismation/confirmation. Orthodox theologian John Kamiris writes that, "Through chrismation baptized individuals receive the gifts of the Holy Spirit, together with a power which enables them to develop their new spiritual state, which they entered at baptism."[2]

The Catholic Catechism (1302) says, "The effect of ... confirmation is the full outpouring of the Holy Spirit as once granted to the apostles on the day of Pentecost."

Unlike the Catholic church, where confirmation is typically done by a bishop, Orthodox chrismation is usually done by a priest (but with oil that has been blessed by a bishop).

Orthodox leaders attach much importance to this ritual anointing of oil, according to Orthodox theologian Sergius Bulgakov. "It is only after Chrismation that they can partake of the other sacraments. Chrismation... corresponds to an individual Pentecost in the life of each Christian... He receives anew the glory inherent in the soul and body of the first Adam, lost after the fall..." [3]

Orthodox teaching on chrismation and water baptism is based on John 3:5, where Jesus said unless we are born of water (baptism) and the Spirit (chrismation) we cannot be saved. "The washing of regeneration, baptism, and renewing of the Holy Spirit, chrismation, form a unity in our salvation, which is clear throughout the New Testament. Jesus taught we are born from above through 'water and the Spirit' (John 3:5); Peter preached salvation in Christ through being 'baptized' and received 'the gift of the Holy Spirit' (Acts 2:38)." [4]

The Council of Trent, considered infallible by the Catholic Church, condemns to hell those who reject the sacrament of confirmation. [5]

The Protestant viewpoint

Evangelical Protestants believe that the Holy Spirit comes by faith, which depends on each person. Reaching a certain age does not qualify one for the Holy Spirit. In Gal. 3:2 the apostle Paul says: "I would like to learn just one thing from you: Did you receive the Spirit by observing the law, or by believing what you heard?" Faith, accordingly, is the key to receiving the Holy Spirit, not good deeds, or turning 12. The apostle Peter referred to the "gift of the Holy Spirit" in Acts 2:38. If it is a gift, we can't work for it.

Second, Protestants find no place in the Bible where the ritual of chrismation or confirmation occurs.

Third, in Luke 11:10,13, Jesus said the gift of the Holy Spirit comes in the process of seeking and asking. In the chrismation ritual, especially for infants, there is no seeking or asking possible, of course, as they can't speak and don't understand the ritual: "For everyone who asks receives; he who seeks finds; and to him who knocks, the door will be opened... how much more will your Father in heaven give the Holy Spirit to those who ask him!"

The apostles received the gift of the Holy Spirit after 10 days of seeking in the upper room (Acts 1-2).

Fourth, chrismation is called a "personal Pentecost" by Orthodox theologian Alexander Schmeeman[6] and by the Catholic Catechism (1288, 1232). Many Protestants, however, believe it has little resemblance to the day of Pentecost or how the early Christians received (Acts 2:1-5, 10:45-46, 19:1-7).

Fifth, Protestants note that the gift of the Holy Spirit follows repentance

in scripture. This is not the case in the chrismation ritual, as the infant is unaware of what is happening. Similarly for Catholics going through confirmation in groups, it is often the case that many are not sincerely repentant, but
are going through a ritual to please their parents.

The apostle Peter stated the conditions for receiving the gift of the Holy
Spirit (Acts 2:38): "Peter replied, 'Repent and be baptized, every one of you,
in the name of Jesus Christ for the forgiveness of your sins. And you will
receive the gift of the Holy Spirit.'"

Sixth, Protestants believe John 3:5 (born of the Spirit) does not refer to
the gift of the Holy Spirit or the baptism of the Holy Spirit, but to spiritual
birth as contrasted to physical birth. (See the chapters on water baptism for an
in-depth review of John 3:5.)

1) Ware, Timothy, *The Orthodox Church*, 278-79
2) Karmiris, John, p. 25, "Concerning the Sacraments." Chapter in *Eastern Orthodox Theology: A Contemporary Reader*, edited by Daniel B. Clendenin. Grand Rapids: Baker, 1995.
3) Bulgakov, Sergius, *The Orthodox Church*, p. 113, as cited in *Eastern Orthodox Teachings in Comparison with The Doctrinal Position of Biola University*
4) *Orthodox Study Bible* commentary on Titus 3:5.
5) "If any one saith, that the confirmation of those who have been baptized is an idle ceremony, and not rather a true and proper sacrament; or that of old it was nothing more than a kind of catechism, whereby they who were near adolescence gave an account of their faith in the face of the Church; let him be anathema." (On Confirmation, Canon I, Seventh Session)
6) *Eastern Orthodoxy through Western Eyes,* p. 87, Fairbairn

14. HESYCHASM:
Introspection or way to God?

Hesychasm, like theosis, is one of the unique doctrines of Eastern Orthodoxy. Protestants and Catholics don't have anything quite like it.

Basically, hesychasm is a form of meditation and prayer used primarily by monks, during which they hope to see an internal light and reach God through their hearts rather than through their minds. Hesychia is a Greek word meaning inner silence.

History of hesychasm

This movement began in the waning days of the Byzantine empire, based in part on the teachings of St. Symeon the New Theologian, who encouraged believers to experience God by seeing the "Light that transforms into light those whom it illumines, the Light that is uncreated and unseen, without beginning and without matter, but is the quality of grace by which God makes himself known."

St. Climacus, of the Mt. Sinai Orthodox monastery, followed up on this by instructing believers on how to see the light through breathing exercises, meditation and the help of a spiritual master.

This was further refined by a Mount Athos monk, who taught that a seeker "should sit down in a corner of his cell and bend forward until his forehead almost touched his navel, in search of his heart from whence his prayers should flow, rather than from his mind. This means of knowing and participating in God by seeing the same light that Christ's apostles saw at Christ's Transfiguration on Mount Tabor near Jerusalem, became the hallmark of hesychasm. The Prayer of the Heart, or the Jesus Prayer, the constant repetition of the words, 'Lord, Son of God, have mercy upon us' in time to regular breathing and so internalized, was another identifying mark of the true hesychast."[1]

The Catholic Encyclopedia says the hesychast must hold his body "immovable for a long time, the chin pressed against the breast, the breath held, the eyes turned in, and so on. Then in due time the monk began to see the wonderful light."

Despite criticisms by some Orthodox of the excesses of these "navel-gazers," the hesychast movement spread over Orthodox lands and is today experiencing a new revival.

A collection of writings important to hesychasts was made by a monk in 1782, and is known as the Philokalia. It is still used by hesychasts.

The hesychast movement came under fire in the 14th century by fellow

Orthodox who said the system was superstitious, absurd and blasphemous in that it said men could see the uncreated light of God.

The dispute lasted 20 years; it took six church synods from 1341 to 1351 to resolve it. The first two ruled in favor of hesychasm, the third against, the fourth for, the fifth against, and the sixth for.

The monk who had championed heyschasm during these disputes, Gregory Palamas, has been made a saint by the Orthodox church. His feast is celebrated twice a year.

The Protestant view of hesychasm

Very little has been written by Protestants about hesychasm, which is relatively unknown. Concerns can be raised in the following areas:

First, hesychasm lacks a biblical basis — there is no Bible verse telling Christians to seek the light of God or use hesychast exercises.

Second, hesychasm's contention that seeing this uncreated light is the supreme goal of every man contradicts the Bible. Jesus said the greatest commandment for a man is to love God and the second is to love his neighbor as himself (Luke 10:27).

Third, hesychasm is a relatively new teaching, having been accepted by Orthodox leaders 1,300 years after the apostles, and having never been accepted by Catholics or Protestants. Two Orthodox synods have called hesychasm an error.

Fourth, the many hours spent in self-centered hesychastic exercises drain energy from the church for activities that could help others. Hesychasm, like monasticism, calls for separation from the world, while the example of Jesus and the apostles show that we should be in the world as witnesses to the truth, serving God and man.

Fifth, the constant repetition of the eight-word hesychastic prayer contradicts Jesus' instructions in Matt. 6:7 against repetitive prayer: "And when you pray, do not keep on babbling like pagans, for they think they will be heard because of their many words."

Sixth, striving to reach God through breathing exercises and self-denial, while admirable, contradicts the free access we have to God through the blood of Jesus, as noted in Heb. 4:15-16: "Since we have a high priest who is sympathetic to our weaknesses, let us draw near with boldness to the throne of grace..."

---

1) Clark, Victoria, Why Angels Fall, p. 36, New York: St. Martin's Press, 2000

15. COMMUNION:
Key to eternal life?

One of the most contentious and significant differences between Protestant, Catholic and Orthodox doctrine is communion (the Eucharist).

Orthodox and Catholic leaders say that taking communion grants forgiveness and eternal life to the believer, at least in part.[1]

Orthodox theologian John Kamiris writes: "The flesh of the Lord, received by the believers... transmits to them ... divine life. This union of Christ with his faithful results in the remission of the sins of the latter. This remission of sins results in immortality and eternal life." [2]

The Catholic Catechism likewise says communion cleanses and forgives us from sin (1393). It is "the seed of eternal life" (1524) and keeps us from future mortal sins (1395). They say communion is necessary for salvation. [3]

Communion chalice from Notre-Dame cathedral in Paris.

Protestants say communion does not grant eternal life or forgiveness, and is not necessary for salvation.

Orthodox and Catholics say that communion is the actual body and blood of Christ. Catholics offer worship to the bread and wine accordingly.[4] "The Catholic Church has always offered and still offers to the sacrament of the Eucharist the cult of adoration, not only during Mass, but also outside of it, reserving the consecrated hosts with the utmost care, exposing them to the solemn veneration of the faithful, and carrying them in procession." Protestants say the bread and wine are symbolic and should not be worshiped.

Lastly, all three groups practice different ways of taking communion,[5] and often refuse communion to each other.

This is a sad state of affairs. During the Protestant Reformation 500 years ago, Protestants were burned alive because they did not believe that the communion was the actual body and blood of Christ. They were obviously convinced of what they believed — and that it was something for which they would be willing to die. Today that is not the case for many Protestants.

In fact, many Protestants have great difficulty answering Catholic and

Orthodox arguments about communion, which seem to be based on a literal interpretation of scripture, which is usually something Protestants support.

Look for instance at these scriptures used by Orthodox and Catholics:

"This is my body...." (Matt. 26:26). "Whoever eats my flesh and drinks my blood has eternal life..." (John 6:54). "...Unless you eat the flesh of the Son of Man and drink his blood, you have no life in you." (John 6:53).

These verses seem to support the Catholic/Orthodox position that communion is the actual blood and body of Christ,[6] and also that communion grants eternal life. This takes on even more importance when you add to it the Catholic/Orthodox argument that communion can only be offered by their priests — which means, if true, that Protestants are cut off from forgiveness and eternal life. Further, the Catholic Council of Trent says that those who do not accept their opinion on this issue are "anathema" or condemned to hell.[3] When the anathema ceremony is used in the Catholic church it reads: "we judge him condemned to eternal fire with Satan and his angels and all the reprobate, so long as he will not ... do penance and satisfy the Church." [7]

The belief that communion grants forgiveness of sins is part of the main liturgy used in the Orthodox church, that of John Chrysostom. The liturgy is considered part of Holy Tradition, and is therefore on a par with scripture in Orthodoxy. In several places it shows the Orthodox belief that taking communion results in forgiveness of sins:

"Then, wiping his lips and the edge of the chalice with the cloth that he holds in his hand, he says: This hath touched my lips and shall take away my transgressions and cleanse my sins." [1]

Belief that the communion elements have power in themselves is shown in a recent incident recounted by author Victoria Clark , in which Serb Orthodox Archbishop Amfilohije anointed bones of the dead with communion wine in the hope that it would help them to attain heaven.[8]

Since Orthodox doctrine teaches that communion grants eternal life, at least in part, it makes sense that communion would be offered to infants, and it is (but not by the Catholic church): "In the Eastern Church,... Immediately after receiving baptism and confirmation, the child is admitted to Eucharistic communion." [9]

In keeping with the conception of salvation as a process, both Orthodox and Catholic doctrine says that communion contributes to the obtaining of eternal life: "Communion...preserves, increases and renews the life of grace received at baptism" (Catechism, 1392).

The Protestant viewpoint

So why don't Protestants believe that communion grants forgiveness and eternal life?

First, because this belief contradicts other scriptures that show that salvation is by faith and repentance:

"Repent and be baptized...for the forgiveness of your sins" (Acts 2:38).

"He who believes and is baptized shall be saved" (Mark 16:16).

"If you confess with your mouth and believe in your heart, you will be saved...." (Rom. 10:9-10).

"For by grace you have been saved, by faith...." (Eph. 2:8-9).

Even the same chapter of John that is used to show that communion gives eternal life shows that salvation is by faith. In John 6:40 Jesus says "...everyone who looks to the son and believes in him shall have eternal life, and I will raise him up at the last day." In verse 47 he says again: "He who believes has everlasting life."

The basis of our salvation is faith, not communion, Protestants believe. The crowd arguing with Jesus in John 6 had no faith, as Jesus said in verse 36: "...You have seen me and still you do not believe."

They did not believe, and therefore misunderstood his words, and left. The apostles, no less mystified by his words, nonetheless believed in him and stayed.

Secondly, Protestants do not believe communion grants eternal life is because the context shows that Jesus was speaking spiritually in symbols, testing the crowd. Jesus said so in verse 63: "The words I have spoken to you are spirit and they are life."

Jesus often spoke symbolically even when he knew that his listeners would misunderstand. He apparently did it as a test to his listeners and to get their attention. To Nicodemus he said, "You must be born again" (John 3:7). Nicodemus clearly thought Jesus meant being born again physically, but Jesus was speaking spiritually.

To the woman at the well, Jesus offered living water that would end her thirst (John 4:10). She clearly thought he meant real water and asked for it, but Jesus was speaking spiritually. So now, two chapters later (John 6), Jesus tells the Jews that they must eat his body and drink his blood. He was again speaking symbolically and spiritually. Why did Jesus do this?

Because these people that followed him across the lake were not sincere disciples. Here is what he said to them in verse 26: "I tell you the truth, you are looking for me, not because you saw miraculous signs but because you ate the loaves and had your fill."

They just wanted Jesus to feed them as he had done the day before. They were not interested in becoming Christians. Not only that, they were going to force Jesus to become a king, as noted in verse 15: "Jesus, knowing that they intended to come and make him king by force, withdrew again to a mountain by himself." They were not Christians, and Jesus used symbolic language to test their allegiance. Most failed the test and left.

Thirdly, communion cannot be a condition of salvation, since the thief on the cross died without communion, and yet Jesus said, "Today you will be with me in paradise" (Luke 23:43).

Lastly, the belief that communion gives eternal life creates a false dependence upon a ceremony to save us, instead of faith in Christ.

The ceremony symbolizes our participation in the sacrifice of Christ on the cross. The ceremony has no power, but our faith in Christ does.

The ritual of communion looks back to the sacrificial death of Christ, as 1 Cor. 10:16-18 says: "Is not the cup of thanksgiving for which we give thanks a participation in the blood of Christ? And is not the bread that we break a participation in the body of Christ?... Consider the people of Israel: Do not those who eat the sacrifices participate in the altar?"

So communion is a memorial participation of the death of Christ on the cross. It is a renewal of our covenant with God, as Jesus said: "This cup is the new covenant in my blood" (1 Cor. 11:25). When Jesus said, "Whoever eats my flesh and drinks my blood has eternal life" he was saying when we enter into covenant with him by faith, we become partakers in the sacrificial altar of the cross, where his blood washes away our sins and his broken body opens the way to God. Communion is not therefore a separate way to God, but symbolizes the only way to God – through faith in the death and resurrection of Christ on the cross. When we take communion we participate in the sacrifice of Christ symbolically.

Is it really flesh and blood?

Another question dividing Christians about communion is whether or not the bread and the wine become the actual body and blood of Jesus during communion (transubstantiation).

Although there are different understandings of communion, no Protestant church (except Anglican/Episcopalian) believes that the communion elements are the actual body and blood of Jesus. The belief that the bread and wine are symbolic is distinctive of Protestant churches. (NOTE: Lutheran churches believe in consubstantiation — meaning that the blood and body of Christ are with the elements, but are not the elements themselves.)

Protestants don't believe in transubstantiation for several reasons:

First, because scripture shows that Jesus offered up his body once for all time — not every day during communion. Note the many times "once" or "one" are used in the following scriptures. Heb. 9:25-28 says, " Nor did he enter heaven to offer himself again and again... Then Christ would have had to suffer many times since the creation of the world. But now he has appeared once for all at the end of the ages to do away with sin by the sacrifice of himself. Christ was sacrificed once to take away the sins of many people..." Heb. 10:10-14 says: "...We have been made holy through the sacrifice of the body of Jesus Christ once for all. Day after day every priest stands and performs his religious duties; again and again he offers the same sacrifices, which can never take away sins. But when this priest had offered for all time one sacrifice for sins, he sat down at the right hand of God...by one sacrifice he has made perfect for ever those who are being made holy." *(See also 1 Pet. 3:18.)*

Second, once again Jesus was speaking symbolically when he said: "This is my body" and "This is my blood." He also said "I am the vine" and "I am the door." Christ is not, of course, a vine or a door. He was speaking symbolically then, just like when he referred to the bread and wine as his body and blood.

Church fathers said communion symbolic

Third, early church fathers (but not all) wrote that communion was symbolic: St. Clement of Alexandria in 195 A.D. wrote: "Elsewhere the Lord, in the gospel according to John, brought this out by symbols when he said, 'Eat my flesh and drink my blood,' describing distinctly by metaphor the drinkable properties of faith." [10] Notice that Clement said Jesus was using symbols and a metaphor. Tertullian (c. 210 A.D.) also accepted the teaching of communion as symbolic of the body and blood of Christ:[11] "They thought his discourse was harsh and intolerable, for they thought that he had really and literally directed them to eat his flesh....He also goes on to explain what he would have us to understand by spirit: 'The words that I speak unto you, they are spirit, and they are life.'"

Fourth, Jesus himself, after he had called the wine "blood" in Matt. 26:28, immediately called it wine again.

If Jesus had changed the wine into blood at the precise moment when he said, "Drink from it, all of you, for this is my blood..." it would still have been blood a second later. But Jesus said, "I will not drink of this fruit of the vine from now on until I drink it new with you in my Father's kingdom."

Therefore, Protestants believe he was speaking symbolically when he referred to it as blood. As has been noted by writer Muriel Welch, Jesus himself explains this symbolism in John 6:35: "Then Jesus declared, 'I am the bread of life. He who **comes** to me *[in repentance]* will never go **hungry**, and he who **believes** in me will never be thirsty." Here we see that our spiritual hunger is not satisfied by communion wafers, but by coming to Christ in repentance, and that our spiritual thirst is not satisfied by drinking the wine, but by believing.When Jesus referred to drinking wine again in his Father's kingdom, he was apparently speaking of the wedding supper of the Lamb mentioned in Rev. 19:9: "Then the angel said to me, "Write: 'Blessed are those who are invited to the wedding supper of the Lamb!'" It is hard to imagine that the guests would be given blood to drink at the wedding! It seems more likely that it will be wine, just as it was at the Last Supper.

Fifth, Jesus referred to communion as a memorial, saying "do this in remembrance of me" (1 Cor. 11:24)— recalling an event, not recreating it. Communion therefore is not an offering of the body of Christ all over again, but a memorial of that event.

Protestants believe communion is similar to a birthday. When a person has a birthday, they don't return to the hospital with his mother and the doctor and recreate the birth! It can't be done. It is simply a remembrance of that event. In the same way, communion is a remembrance of Christ's sacrifice, not a repetition of it. There can be no repetition of the death of Christ.

Sixth, taking the position that communion is the actual body and blood of Christ can lead people into worship of the bread and wine, which they believe have been changed into Christ.

Lastly, transubstantiation joins with other doctrines to exalt the priest into a position as someone who controls our eternal destiny. Under this view, we must confess our sins to them, and they can forgive our sins, or deny us the communion we need for eternal life. Such a role is not what the Bible teaches, and creates a dependency upon man rather than upon God. *(See the chapter on priests).*

Another, minor difference between Catholic, Orthodox and Protestant communion is how it is served. There are many differences here.

First, the Orthodox Church uses leavened bread, while Catholics and Protestants use unleavened bread. Which is right?

In the three gospel accounts and the passage in 1 Cor. 11:26 that mention the bread, all use the Greek word *artos* which is translated as bread, loaf or shewbread. *Artos* is defined by *Thayer's Greek-English Lexicon* as:

1) food composed of flour mixed with water and baked.

2) food of any kind.

It is interesting that the Greek word *azumos* was not used. This refers exclusively to unleavened bread. However, since *artos* can refer to food of any kind as noted, it can also mean unleavened bread.

Some Protestant theologians say it had to be unleavened bread as the Jews were obligated to remove all yeast even from their houses at this time of year, as noted in the following scriptures:

"For seven days you are to eat bread made without yeast. On the first day remove the yeast from your houses, for whoever eats anything with yeast in it from the first day until the seventh must be cut off from Israel" (Ex 12:15). "For seven days no yeast is to be found in your houses" (Ex. 12:19) "... nor shall any yeast be seen anywhere within your borders" (Ex. 13:7).

Why was this word used?

If this is the case, it seems certain that Jesus was using unleavened bread. If so, why doesn't the Bible use the word for unleavened bread, since clearly there was nothing but that in the house? It could be because the Lord did not want this to be a stumbling block — what is important in communion is not the condition of the bread, but the condition of our hearts.

For instance, in some parts of the world, wheat is not eaten at all, for it does not grow well there. By using the word artos, the Lord frees Christians worldwide from legalism when it comes to how they are to have communion — we do not need to worry whether the bread is leavened or unleavened.

Secondly, as to methods of communion, they are many and varied.

Orthodox communion (in Russia) involves a ritual of taking pieces of five loaves of leavened bread, mixing them with wine and water in a cup to form a mush. The priest then serves this to the congregation on a spoon.

Catholic communion usually offers the communicants a wafer that has been dipped in wine. The communicant does not touch the wafer but it is usually placed in their mouth by the priest. The wafers are unleavened. The cup of wine in which the wafer is dipped is then drunk by the priest in its entirety.[5]

Protestant communion varies. Some churches follow a more Catholic practice. Most evangelical churches offer communion, however, as unleavened flat loaves and nonalcoholic grape juice in separate tiny cups.

Thirdly, the three churches also differ in preparation for communion. Catholic and Orthodox doctrine calls for believers to fast before taking communion, and follow certain rules. To take communion in the Catholic church, for instance, one must be a baptized Catholic and "fully accept all of the Church's teachings." Communion is forbidden to those in "a separated sect that rejects some or all of the teachings" (i.e., Protestants) and to those "failing to observe the laws about marriage" (divorced and remarried without a church annulment of the first marriage), those who have not fasted, and those living a scandalous life. [12]

Most Protestants do not require fasting, because it is not required in the Bible. Many practice open communion, leaving it to the individual believer to determine their own worthiness to take communion.

1) The most used liturgy in the Orthodox church makes a strong statement that we receive forgiveness through taking communion. The importance of this distinction is that by denying communion (excommunication) they are in effect sending the person to hell. (The Orthodox Church takes doctrine from several sources, one of which is the liturgy — see the chapter on the liturgy). The main liturgy used in the Orthodox Church is that of John Chrysostom. It links forgiveness with communion several times. Some of these are quoted below: "Then, wiping his lips and the edge of the chalice with the cloth that he holds in his hand, he says: This hath touched my lips and shall take away my transgressions and cleanse my sins." "Impart unto me, Master, the precious and holy Blood of our Lord and God and Savior Jesus Christ, unto forgiveness of my sins and unto life eternal. "Unto thee, the servant of God, the deacon (Name), is imparted the precious and holy Blood of our Lord and God and Savior Jesus Christ, unto forgiveness of thy sins and unto life eternal."

2) Karmiris, John, p. 26.

3) The Council of Trent reminded Catholics that "If anyone shall say that the sacraments of the New Law are not necessary for salvation, but are superfluous, and that, although all are not necessary individually, without them or without the desire of them through faith alone men obtain from God the grace of justification: let him be anathema." (Geisler, N. L., & MacKenzie, R. E. 1995. *Roman Catholics and Evangelicals : Agreements and differences* . Baker Books: Grand Rapids, Mich)

4) Regarding worship of the bread and wine, the Roman Catholic Council of Trent ruled, "There is, therefore, no room left for doubt that all the faithful of Christ ... offer in veneration (can. 6) the worship of latreia [the act of adoration] which is due to the true God, to this most Holy Sacrament....If anyone says that in the holy sacrament of the Eucharist the only-begotten Son of God is not to be adored even outwardly with the worship of latreia (the act of adoration) . . . and is not to be set before the people publicly to be adored, and that the adorers are idolaters: let him be anathema. (Geisler, N. L., & MacKenzie, R. E. 1995., p. 257, *Roman Catholics and Evangelicals : Agreements and differences* . Baker Books: Grand Rapids, Mich.)

5) "About the middle of the 12th century the (Catholic) custom of withholding the wine, in communion, from the "laity" or private members, was begun, on the grounds that either element contained the whole of Christ's body, and that the wine, if handed around to so many, might be spilled, and that it was sufficient for the priest to receive both elements. The communion of children was discontinued during this century in the Roman, but not in the Greek Catholic Church." (Hassell, *History of the Church of God*, ch. 16)

6) "The Eastern Orthodox view dates back to the earliest times in Christendom, and interprets communion in much the same way as do Roman Catholics — with one important difference. Orthodox believers agree that when the priest consecrates the elements (the bread and wine), they become the very body and blood of Christ. However, while Orthodoxy has always insisted on the reality of the change, it has never attempted to explain the manner of the change." (Geisler, N. L., & MacKenzie, R. E. 1995. *Roman Catholics and Evangelicals : Agreements and differences.* Baker Books: Grand Rapids, Mich., p. 255)

7) *The Catholic Encyclopedia* — http://www.newadvent.org/cathen/01455e.htm

8) Clark, Victoria, *Why Angels Fall*, p. 97-98

9) Meyendorff, *Byzantine Theology*, p. 192

10) *The Instructor (Paedagogus)*, chap. 6, Ante-Nicene Fathers, vol. 1, p. 219

11) *On the Resurrection of the Flesh*, chap. 37, Part Second, Ante-Nicene Fathers

12) *Why do Catholics do that?*, 1994, p. 67-68, Kevin Orlin Johnson, Ballantine Books, New York. Imprimatur and nihil obstat.

16. ICONS AND STATUES:
Help or hindrance?

Should a Christian pray to paintings and statues, bow to them and kiss them? This is a controversial question, and it gets different answers among Catholics, Protestants and Orthodox.

In general, Catholic and Orthodox doctrine says officially that Christians not only may, but must pray to, bow to, kiss and venerate images.

Protestants do not use icons for several different reasons, listed below.

The Catholic/Orthodox viewpoint

The main source for Catholic and Orthodox veneration of images is found in the seventh ecumenical council, held in 787 A.D. in Nicea (modern day Turkey). Both Orthodox and Catholics hold that these ecumenical councils (including this one) were infallible — without error — and on a par with the Bible.

At the seventh council, more than 300 bishops, ordered to meet by the emperor, overturned a previous ecumenical council ruling outlawing icons in order to issue one requiring Christians to use them.

The bishops decreed that,

"the venerable and holy images...should be set forth in the holy churches of God...and on hangings and in pictures both in houses and by the wayside, to wit, the figure of our Lord God and Savior Jesus Christ, of our spotless Lady, the Mother of God, of the honorable Angels, of all Saints and of all pious people....to these should be given due salutation and honorable reverence (Gk. "proskuneo") not indeed that true worship of faith (Gk. "latreia") which pertains alone to the divine nature; but to these.... incense and lights may be offered according to ancient pious custom. For the honor which is paid to the image passes on to that which the image represents..." [1]

The council was very firm with those who do not venerate images.

Those who don't are to be deposed from church office, excommunicated and cursed to hell. ("Anathema", according to the Catholic Dictionary means that the persons cursed are "excluded from her communion and that they must, if they continue obstinate, perish eternally.")

The bishops decreed that "those, therefore who dare to think or teach otherwise, or as wicked heretics to spurn the traditions of the Church and to invent some novelty, or else to reject some of those things which the Church hath received (e.g., the Book of the Gospels, or the image of the cross, or the pictorial icons, or the holy relics of a martyr), or evilly and sharply to devise anything subversive of the lawful traditions of the Catholic Church or to turn to common uses the sacred vessels or the venerable monasteries, if they be Bishops or Clerics, we command that they be deposed; if religious or laics, that they be cut off from communion."

"...We salute the venerable images. We place under anathema those who do not do this. Anathema to them who presume to apply to the venerable images the things said in Holy Scripture about idols. Anathema to those who do not salute the holy and venerable images. Anathema to those who call the sacred images idols. Anathema to those who say that Christians resort to the sacred images as to gods."

Catholic and Orthodox doctrine (*Catechism*, 1159) also states that icons should be used because Jesus was an image of God (in Greek, "ikon"), as stated in Col. 1:15: "Who is the image of the invisible God, the firstborn of every creature:" Similarly in Heb. 1:3: "The Son is the radiance of God's glory and the exact representation of his being..." and 2 Cor. 4:4: "...Christ, who is the image of God."

Since God came and took on human flesh, thus deifying matter, it is also possible, Orthodox and Catholic doctrine argues, that the Holy Spirit can sanctify wood and paint as a source of God's grace. To deny that icons can be used of God, they say, is to deny that God could sanctify matter, and to deny the incarnation of Christ in a human body (Catechism, 2131).

Orthodox theologian Anthony Ugolnik thus calls icons "the image of the incarnation."[2] The Orthodox argue that if Jesus was, therefore, an icon, then it should be okay to honor other icons.

Catholics, while maintaining their tradition of holy images, do not go so far as to say that icons or paintings have power in themselves, at least as far as is stated in the Catechism (1159-1162).

The Catholic church has affirmed, however, that these images should be venerated or honored: "From the very earliest days of the Church there has been a tradition whereby images of our Lord, his holy Mother, and of saints are displayed in churches for the veneration of the faithful." [3] "...Whoever venerates an image venerates the person portrayed in it" (2132).

It also, like the Orthodox Church, accepts the seventh ecumenical council ruling requiring the use of icons and images (Catechism, 891, 2131), but rarely or never repeats the council's statement that those who don't venerate them are condemned to hell.

The Protestant viewpoint

Protestants, however, do not accept the Catholic/Orthodox conclusions about icons for several reasons, each explained in detail below. They believe that:

1) The Bible forbids icons.

2) Veneration of images began hundreds of years after the apostles.

3) The apostles and the angels rejected attempts to venerate them in the Bible, and would therefore reject the veneration of their images as well.

4) There is no example in the Bible of worship or veneration of icons.

5) Venerating of images may tempt Christians to sin.

6) The seventh ecumenical council approving the use of icons was invalid.

7) Reported miracles don't prove that God wants us to venerate and pray to icons.

8) Use of the incarnation as a basis for praying to paintings distorts the meaning of the incarnation.

1) They believe the Bible forbids it.

Protestants believe that the 10 commandments (specifically Ex. 20:4-6) forbid prayer to or giving of special honor to images:

"You shall not make for yourself an idol in the form of anything in heaven above or on the earth beneath or in the waters below. You shall not bow down to them or worship them; for I, the LORD your God, am a jealous God, punishing the children for the sin of the fathers to the third and fourth generation of those who hate me, but showing love to a thousand generations of those who love me and keep my commandments."

Protestants note two things in particular about this passage. First, the wide ban on images of anything — "any likeness of anything", and, second, the reason for the ban: "I, the LORD your God, am a jealous God."

Protestants believe that the wording and the detail in this warning means we are to be particularly careful in this area so as not to make God angry. Isaiah 42:8 says, "I am the LORD; that is my name! I will not give my glory to another or my praise to idols."

Lev. 26:1 says: "Do not make idols or set up an image or a sacred stone for yourselves, and do not place a carved stone in your land to bow down before it. I am the Lord your God."

Deut. 4:15-16 reinforces this. The Lord says: "You saw no form of any kind the day the Lord spoke to you at Horeb out of the fire. Therefore watch yourselves very carefully, so that you do not become corrupt and make for yourselves an idol, an image of any shape..."

Protestants note that the wording in this passage is particularly broad — the word "image" refers to "form, image, likeness, representation, semblance" (Hebrew: "temunah"). The warning to "watch yourselves very carefully" reiterates the concern expressed by the Lord in Ex. 20 regarding the use of images. The fact that the Lord did not allow himself to be seen shows that images — even of God — are not to be venerated or worshiped. Is. 40:18

says no image can represent God: "To whom, then, will you compare God? What image will you compare him to?"

Some argue, however, that the 10 commandments only forbid worship to graven images, so it must be okay to worship icons, which are flat. However, Lev. 26:1 has a broad prohibition against images in general used for worship — flat or three-dimensional: "Do not make idols or set up an image or a sacred stone for yourselves, and do not place a carved stone in your land to bow down before it. I am the Lord your God."

Some also say the biblical prohibition against images was temporary, superseded by the incarnation of Christ as a human image.

However, Protestants note that the prohibition against images is part of the 10 commandments, which are not temporary. If the 10 commandments were temporary, then we would now be permitted to worship other Gods, to commit adultery, steal and lie. Since these are still forbidden, we should also not make images and bow down to them, Protestants say.

Two versions of the 10 commandments

There are two versions of the 10 commandments — the Catholic version and the Protestant/ Orthodox version.*

In the Catholic version, the commandment against other gods is combined with the commandment against idols to make one commandment. (The Protestant/Orthodox version makes these separate commandments.)

To keep the list at 10, the Catholic version makes two commandments of the last one: one prohibiting coveting another man's wife, and one prohibiting coveting another man's possessions.

Why is this important?

Protestants believe it is important because making the commandment against images part of the commandment against other gods implies that it only prohibits images of other gods, therefore allowing images of God himself or saints or angels.

Keeping these two separate implies that the first commandment prohibits other gods and the second prohibits veneration of images, whether they be of other gods, other people, saints, angels or God himself.

So which version is correct? Protestants point to the apostle Paul's version of the 10 commandments for support: In Rom. 13:9 he listed the last five commandments, and did not split the 10th into two different kinds of coveting, but just referred to coveting: "You shall not covet."

In Rom. 7:7 he again refers to coveting as one commandment and not two: "For I would not have known covetousness unless the law had said, 'You shall not covet.'"

Besides the 10 commandments, a New Testament scripture also prohibits images (1 John 5:21): "Little children, keep yourself from idols."

John's word for idol is defined by *Strong's Greek Lexicon* as first "an image (i.e. for worship)." This would also forbid icons or statues.

---

* *The Lutheran Church and Judaism both use versions of the 10 commandments that are similar to the Catholic church.*

Lastly, true worship does not require the use of material paintings or statues, but a heart that is in tune with the Spirit of God. In John 4:23-24 Jesus told the Samaritan woman that it was not important where one worshiped, but that true worship is spiritual. "

A time is coming and has now come when the true worshipers will worship the Father in spirit and truth, for they are the kind of worshipers the Father seeks. God is spirit, and his worshipers must worship in spirit and in truth."

2) They believe veneration of images is a relatively new event that began hundreds of years after the apostles.

In A History of the Iconoclastic Controversy,[4] Dr. Martin notes of icons that, "No record of any of them can be traced earlier than the fourth century, and the sixth century is the period in which they really became significant. The attempt to establish an apostolic tradition by such a list of pictures definitely breaks down. The earliest authentic examples of distinct Christian pictures are those described by 4th-century writers like Gregory of Nyssa and St. John Chrysostom. Pictures of Christ are very rare among them. By far the majority still represented stories of the saints and symbolical Old Testament scenes like the sacrifice of Isaac. The appeal to authority does not help the Orthodox case much, while the appeal to tradition only carries it to the fourth century."

Similarly, in The Early Church,[5] author Glenn Hinson notes that "the earliest Christian vault and wall mosaics discovered thus far are located in a small mausoleum under St. Peter's in Rome ...The mosaics probably date from the middle of the third century and after. A mosaic in the center of the vault depicts Christ as the unconquered sun driving his chariot across the sky, with the nimbus around his head shooting out like the arms of the cross and bearing in his left hand an orb. The pagan sun god has been transformed into the risen Christ, triumphant over death and Lord of the universe. Church art in this period did not achieve the splendor it attained in the next two centuries, but at Constantine's urging it improved rapidly."

A contemporary account of a church persecution in 303 A.D. also shows that the churches at that time did not have images in them:

"When the prefect and his men entered the large and beautiful church at Nicomedia,...they were amazed to find no image of the deity. They burned the holy scriptures, pillaged what they wanted, and razed the building to the ground." [6]

Encyclopedia Britannica has this to say about the late arrival of icons:

"In the early church, the making and veneration of portraits of Christ and the saints were consistently opposed. The use of icons, nevertheless, steadily gained in popularity, especially in the eastern provinces of the Roman empire. Toward the end of the 6th century and in the 7th, icons became the object of an officially encouraged cult, often implying a superstitious belief in their animation. Opposition to such practices became particularly strong in Asia Minor."[7]

The earliest writings of the church fathers show consistent opposition to the use of images. Writing in the second century, Clement of Alexandria said: "It is with a different kind of spell that art deludes you...It leads you to pay religious honor and worship to images and pictures." [8]

Origen, writing in the third century, said: "Neither painter nor image-maker existed in the nation of Israel, for the law expelled all such persons from it. In that way, there was no pretext for the construction of images. For image-making is an art that attracts the attention of foolish men. It drags the eyes of the soul down from God to earth. Accordingly, there was among them a law to the following effect: 'Do not transgress the law and make to your-selves a carved image, or any likeness of male or female.'" [9]

In response to some who say that icons have an early origin, claiming that Christ was painted by Luke (the assistant to the Apostle Paul) Protestants note that there is no evidence that Luke ever painted Christ. Luke was a Greek, and ministry to the Greeks did not start until after Christ had ascended.[10]

Luke was evidently saved through the ministry of Paul many years after Christ had ascended to heaven and before Peter and Paul had begun ministry to the Greeks. It is very unlikely that he ever saw the Lord.

The fact that many of the past paintings of Jesus are similar is also not an evidence that they show what Christ looked like, Protestants believe. This is because these paintings are all of a handsome Christ, but the Bible says in Is. 53:2 that: "He had no beauty or majesty to attract us to him, nothing in his appearance that we should desire him."

3) They believe that the apostles and the angels rejected attempts to venerate them in the Bible, and would therefore reject the veneration of their images as well.

The bishops at the seventh ecumenical council argued that veneration shown to images transfers to the persons pictured in them.

However, Protestants note that these same persons — apostles and angels — rejected personal veneration as sinful when it was given to them in the Bible. It stands to reason they would also reject such veneration of a paint-ing or statue representing them. This is shown in Acts 10:25-26: "As Peter entered the house, Cornelius met him and fell at his feet in reverence. But Peter made him get up. 'Stand up,' he said, 'I am only a man myself.'"

Protestants note that, in the original Greek, the word "reverence" shown above is proskuneo and not latreia. The distinction is significant in that the bishops at the seventh council said it is permissible to offer proskuneo (wor-ship) to images but not latreia (service). [11]

Therefore, the Apostle Peter would seem to disagree with the decision of the seventh council — bowing down in worship before a man is forbidden from his point of view. It therefore stands to reason that worship before the same man's image (icon) is also forbidden, for the seventh council itself said that worship given to an image is the same as worshiping (or venerating) the individual.

Similarly, the Apostle John, overcome by awe at the presence of an angel, fell down twice to worship (proskuneo), but was forbidden each time: "At this I fell at his feet to worship him. But he said to me, "Do not do it! I am a fellow servant with you and with your brothers who hold to the testimony of Jesus. Worship (proskuneo) God!" (Rev. 19:1 as well as 22:9).

Note that the angel said that John should worship God, and for that purpose he used the word proskuneo and not latreia. Protestants accordingly believe that the distinction between proskuneo and latreia is an artificial one and is not useful. Protestants note that the attributes of worship — bowing, kissing, trusting in and praying — are all offered to images in the same way one would offer them to God. The boundary line between "veneration" and "worship" is not a clear one, Protestants argue, and it is therefore dangerous to do something that could easily become idolatry.

4) They believe there is no example in the Bible of worship or veneration of icons.

There is no scripture encouraging use of icons or images. Instead there are warnings to be careful to avoid such things: "Dear children, keep yourselves from idols" (1 John 5:21).

The Greek word used by the apostle John here is eidolon, from eidos, meaning an "image, likeness, whatever represents the form of an object," according to Strong's Greek Lexicon.

The importance of this distinction is that the Apostle John is not just warning us about strange foreign gods whose idols we may be tempted to worship — but about any image that we might worship — even Christian images. This is shown in two scriptures. Num. 21 shows the Lord told Moses to make an image of a snake and put it on a pole, resulting in the healing of the people from snake bites. But in coming years, they began to worship the image, and it was destroyed by King Hezekiah with God's approval (2 Kings 18:3-4): "He did what was right in the eyes of the Lord... He broke into pieces the bronze snake Moses has made for up to that time the Israelites had been burning incense to it."

It's therefore clear that the dividing line between this symbol of Christ and idolatry was when the people began praying to it and lighting incense to it. Accordingly, Protestants believe this passage teaches that we should not pray to or light incense before icons. (The snake on the pole represents Christ lifted up on the cross, as he said: "As Moses lifted up the snake in the wilderness, even so shall the Son of Man be lifted up."— John 3:14. The snake bite, of course, is a symbol of sin and death, which came through the snake in the garden.) In addition to the example of the snake image, the Bible includes God's instructions for statues of angels on the ark, and woven in the curtain surrounding the Holy of Holies. At the very least these images prove that religious art is not sinful.

However, this is not to say that we should pray to these pieces of art, kiss them, or bow to them. Here are five reasons why:

First, if we are to take these as a literal example of how we should worship, we should make statues and tapestries of angels or snakes.

Second, if we are to take these as literal examples of how to worship, then they should be largely invisible, as it was not possible for people to see most of these images — they were in the Holy of Holies behind the curtain, where only the high priest could go once a year. God ordered these images to be hidden behind the curtain to be rarely, if ever, seen. They were intended to show what the tabernacle in heaven was like, not to be objects of worship. Num. 4: 20 says that even the Levites working at the temple were forbidden from looking at the images: "But the Kohathites must not go in to look at the holy things, even for a moment, or they will die."

Third, these images were the only ones specifically allowed in regard to worship — there was no command to make images for every home and in every church or synagogue, as the seventh ecumenical council required.

Fourth, these Old Testament passages and form of worship are not to be seen in the New Testament. There are no instructions for, examples of or encouragement to use images in the New Testament.

Fifth, the history of the defeat of Israel in 1 Sam. 4 illustrates that no material object — not even the ark of the covenant — can guarantee victory. The Israelite army brought the ark into the battle, feeling that God would be with them and they would win. The Lord, however, not only let them be defeated but allowed the ark to be captured by the enemy. This is interpreted by some to be mean that no object (relic, icon, statue) should be relied upon. The Lord allowed this defeat and included it in his word to teach us that only dependence on him guarantees victory, not any image.

5) They believe that venerating of images may tempt some to sin.

Rom. 14:13 says "not to put a stumbling block or a cause to fall in our brother's way." Protestants believe that praying to icons, bowing to them, kissing them, trusting in them and venerating them may lead weaker Christians into the sin of idolatry, perhaps without realizing fully what they are doing. Therefore, for the sake of weaker brothers, we should not do it.

Orthodox and Catholic churches teach that icons and statues should not be worshiped, but some may worship them anyway.

Orthodox and Catholic leaders strongly reject the assertion that their images are idols. However, most Protestants believe if we treat anything with the respect and honor due to God, it is an idol, no matter what it is. This includes money, sex, power, houses, cars, and, of course, icons and statues. This is not to say, as noted, that all those who use icons are worshiping them. But the temptation to do so may be why God forbids them.

Deut. 4:15-16, already mentioned, shows this most clearly: "You saw no form of any kind the day the Lord spoke to you at Horeb out of the fire. Therefore watch yourselves very carefully, so that you do not become corrupt and make for yourselves an idol, an image of any shape..."

This verse shows that God did not show himself to us in order to prevent us from making images of him and worshiping them. He is saying, in effect, that we would be tempted to use an image of him and worship that instead of him. That seems to be why we also have no idea of what Jesus looked like.

The Bible does not describe his face, and no accurate statue or painting of him has come down to us. Research, mentioned above, shows that images of Christ did not appear until 300 years after his death at the earliest. It is clear from this that no one really knows what Christ looked like.

This is not to say that buying or keeping paintings of Christ are necessarily sinful, but they may cause us trouble, Protestants believe, especially if we pray to them or see the painting itself as something special.

For example, the story is told of a man testing drivers to see which he would hire; they had to drive on a very narrow road by the cliff's edge. The first man drove to within 8 inches of the edge to show how skilled he was.

The second drove within 4 inches of the edge to show he was better. The last drove so far from the edge and so close to the wall that he scraped paint off the car against the mountain. The others laughed at him. The owner, however, hired him because he wanted safety.

The point here is that in using icons we are perilously close to the edge of something dangerous — idolatry. We may never intend to cross that line, but well-intentioned people sometimes do. Since that is the case, should we use icons, since by so doing we may lead some into sin by our example? Rom. 14 says to do nothing that might tempt our brother to sin.

The tendency of the human heart toward idolatry is clearly shown in the Old Testament and the New. But some say the worship they offer icons transfers to God, who makes Himself present through the icon. Orthodox sometimes call icons, "windows to heaven."

Protestants see many problems with this argument. First is the fact that veneration is not just offered to God, but to saints, angels and Mary. This can easily lead to a dependence upon them instead of God.

Some argue, however, that it is possible to make a distinction between worship offered to God and that offered to icons. However, worshiping an image of God while trying to remember that it is not God is dangerously close to idolatry, despite what Orthodox theologian Sergius Bulgakov says, "The Orthodox prays before the icon of Christ as before Christ Himself; but the icon, the abiding place of that presence, remains only a thing and never becomes an idol or a fetish." [12]

It is an easy thing to say, but hard to do. The very words of Bulgakov make it difficult to believe, since he says the icon is "the abiding place of that presence." Trying to make a mental distinction between veneration of an icon and worship is not possible. Those who say such a distinction is possible often quote Jesus' statement in Matt. 4:10: "Worship (Greek: (proskuneo) the Lord your God, and serve (Greek: latreia) him only.'"

They argue that latreia (service or worship) is only for God but proskuneo (worship or honor) can be offered to icons also. To determine if icon veneration is worship (proskuneo) is therefore the question.

The word proskuneo is used of worship of God in many places. Ironically, when Satan asked Jesus to worship him, he used the word proskuneo, not latreia (v. 9). And Jesus refused. Clearly we should be careful about worshiping (proskuneo) anyone but God.

Interestingly, the word proskuneo literally means to come forward and kiss the hand in reverence. Icons are kissed routinely in Orthodox worship services. Ex. 20:4-6 says, "You shall not bow down" to images. Bowing is regularly done before icons. By both of these measures, icon veneration is worship of an image and therefore is prohibited.

6) They believe that the seventh ecumenical council approving the use of icons was invalid.

Protestants take issue with the seventh ecumenical council for several reasons. (See the chapter on the ecumenical councils.) Briefly, the seventh council is not accepted because it contradicts scripture, and because the emperor manipulated the bishops to get them to overturn the previous council's ban against icons. In addition, two church councils after the seventh banned icons. In 794, the Council of Frankfort rejected icon use.[13] In 815, another council under the reign of Byzantine Emperor Leo V outlawed icon use.[14]

7) They believe that reported miracles don't prove that God wants us to venerate and pray to icons.

Protestants often are faced with the argument that icons have done miracles for those who have prayed to them — healings especially. This is viewed as justification for their use by some. While not denying or accepting that some miracles may have occurred, Protestants note the Bible does not accept miracles alone as proof that God is at work. For instance, Deut. 13:1-5 says: "If a prophet, or one who foretells by dreams, appears among you and announces to you a miraculous sign or wonder, and if the sign or wonder of which he has spoken takes place, and he says, 'Let us follow other gods' (gods you have not known) 'and let us worship them,' you must not listen to the words of that prophet or dreamer. The LORD your God is testing you to find out whether you love him with all your heart and with all your soul. It is the LORD your God you must follow, and him you must revere. Keep his commands and obey him; serve him and hold fast to him. That prophet or dreamer must be put to death, because he preached rebellion against the LORD your God."

Similarly, Jesus in Matt. 24:24 said, "For false Christs and false prophets will appear and perform great signs and miracles to deceive even the elect—if that were possible.."

2 Thes. 2:9 says, "The coming of the lawless one will be in accordance with the work of Satan displayed in all kinds of counterfeit miracles, signs and wonders, and in every sort of evil that deceives those who are perishing." Rev. 13:13-14, speaking of the Antichrist, says, "And he performed great and miraculous signs, even causing fire to come down from heaven to earth in full view of men. Because of the signs he was given power to do on behalf of the first beast, he deceived the inhabitants of the earth. He ordered them to set up an image in honor of the beast who was wounded by the sword and yet lived."

It is more than interesting to note that the verse that follows this one refers specifically to a false miracle done by an image (Rev. 13:15): "He was given power to give breath to the image of the first beast, so that it could speak and cause all who refused to worship the image to be killed."

Given that it is possible to have false miracles, the question remains whether it is possible that a real miracle from God could occur in the course of a person's praying before an icon.

Protestants believe if a person is healed, it is in response to their faith, not an icon, because Jesus said, "Your faith has healed you." (Matt. 9:22). He never said, "your icon has healed you." Whether or not miracles have occurred in relation to an icon is not really the question, Protestants believe, because real miracles occur through faith in God. He does the miracle, and not the icon. Our faith should be in Christ, and not in an image.

In John 5 this situation is illustrated very graphically. Jesus came to the pool of Bethesda, which was surrounded by dozens of people waiting for the pool's waters to be disturbed, which they felt would allow them to be healed. While they were intently watching the water, they ignored Jesus, the true healer, walking right among them. Similarly, Protestants believe that it is a mistake to concentrate on an icon or statue as if it had the power to heal, despite reports of certain ones having healing power. The real healer is God, Protestants believe. No icon, relic or saint can heal us — only God. (For more on miracles in relation to icons or relics, see the chapter on relics.)

8) Use of the incarnation as a basis for honoring images distorts the meaning of the incarnation.

Protestants believe in the incarnation, but do not believe that it is a rationale for worshiping icons or venerating them.

Using the incarnation as a basis for icons or statues puts it into conflict with the many scriptural prohibitions against images (see above). Simply put, the Bible makes it clear that we are to worship Christ.

Similarly, worshiping images is forbidden.

It would seem that no matter which arguments are used to try to make a link between the two, it is proven false simply by the result obtained.

Protestants believe that once a person begins to see a painting or statue as supernatural, as something that can do miracles, as something to be respected and honored and even worshiped, the doctrine of the incarnation is inadequate justification.

But what about ...

Understanding the verses used by Orthodox leaders about Christ as an icon is important, nonetheless, if we are to arrive at the truth. One of those scriptures is Heb. 1:3 — "The Son is the radiance of God's glory and the exact representation of his being" This is taken as support for the use of icons or images, since some believe Christ himself was an image.

In support of that, the original Greek word used in Heb. 1:3 for "exact representation" of God the Father is "kharakter." It refers to "the instrument used for engraving or carving" and "the mark stamped upon that instrument or wrought out on it." It is "the exact expression" of any person or thing.

It's true that Jesus is that image of God, but he is not an image of how God physically appears. This is shown in John 5:37 where Jesus says of the Father, "You have never heard his voice nor seen his form."

The word "form" here is the Greek eidos which Thayer's Greek-English Lexicon defines as "the external or outward appearance."

Similarly in John 1:18 it says, "No one has ever seen God, but God the One and Only, who is at the Father's side, has made him known." So no one has seen God's external appearance. What, then, did Jesus mean when he told Thomas, "If you have seen me, you have seen the Father" (John 14:9)?

So what is going on here? Did Jesus look like the Father or not? Did they see God or not? The answer may be that Jesus didn't look like God the Father's external form, but he showed God's internal character.

This is clear when we realize that externally Jesus was ordinary looking. "He had no beauty or majesty to attract us to him, nothing in his appearance that we should desire him." (Is. 53:2).

God the Father's external appearance, however, is quite glorious (Dan. 7:9-10): "As I looked, "thrones were set in place, and the Ancient of Days took his seat. His clothing was as white as snow; the hair of his head was white like wool. His throne was flaming with fire, and its wheels were all ablaze. A river of fire was flowing, coming out from before him. Thousands upon thousands attended him; ten thousand times ten thousand stood before him." But internally, Jesus was exactly like his Father. Rom. 1:20 speaks of God's internal character, not visible externally: "For since the creation of the world God's invisible qualities—his eternal power and divine nature—have been clearly seen, being understood from what has been made..."

God the Father's invisible qualities were shown not by Jesus' external appearance, but in Jesus' internal qualities demonstrated in the many things he did for mankind. The incarnation shows his love because he was willing to come and live among us in this evil world, in order to save us.

1) Decree of the Seventh Ecumenical Council, Nicene/Post Nicene Fathers, p. 1326-1327

2) Fairbairn, Donald, Eastern Orthodoxy through Western Eyes, p. 106

3) Vatican II, Sacred Liturgy, A General Instruction on the Roman Missal, 278

4) Martin, Edward James, D.D, 1930, reprint 1978, Macmillan

5) Hinson, E. Glenn, Abingdon Press, 1996, p. 244

6) Renwick, A.M., The Story of the Church, p. 50.

7) p. 237, vol. 6, Micropedia (1987)

8) Exhortation to the Heathen, chap. 4, 195 A.D., vol. 2, p. 188 (382) Ante-Nicene Fathers

9) Origen Against Celsus, Book 4, chap. 31, p. 1048 (CD), 248 A.D,. Ante-Nicene Fathers

10) The arrival of the Greeks seeking to meet Jesus in John 12:20 signified to him that he had completed his work to reach the Jews because it had gone beyond the borders of Israel. Jesus was not sent to the Greeks or Gentiles, but to the Jews (Matt. 15:24). See John 12:20-23. The Four-Fold Gospel Commentary notes: "And the occasion forcibly suggested that the gospel invitation, which had hitherto been confined to the lost sheep of the house of Israel, should be extended to the vast throng of waiting Gentiles. But, according to the counsel of God, this extension was not to take place until Jesus had been glorified by his death, resurrection, and enthronement. "

11) Decree of the Seventh Ecumenical Council, Nicene/Post Nicene Fathers, p. 1326 (CD)

12) Bulgakov, Sergius. The Orthodox Church., p. 140

13) The Story of the Church, p.. 83

14) Encyclopedia Britannica, vol. 6, Micropedia (1987), p. 237

17. RELICS:
Do they have supernatural power?

Relics are body parts of dead Christians (saints), or objects used by them. Many believe these have special power. In fact, official Orthodox and Catholic doctrine says that no church building can be used unless it has a relic in it (see below).

Accordingly all Orthodox and Catholic churches have within them a body part of a saint. This is usually located under the table where the communion is prepared (Orthodox), or embedded in a cavity in it (Catholic). Relics may also be woven into the altar cloth, and may also be displayed in special places for prayer, usually encapsulated in a heavily ornamented gold or silver reliquary, since it is believed they have miraculous powers for healing and blessing.

Protestants as a rule do not believe

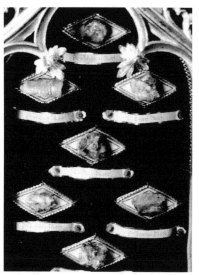

Seven relics (body parts) of deceased Christians at Notre-Dame Cathedral in Paris.

there is special power in the dead bodies of Christians, or in objects used by them, and they have no relics in their churches.

The Catholic/Orthodox viewpoint

Orthodox and Catholic doctrine says that relics have special power for several reasons.

1) There are verses in the Bible that seem to support that.

2) Church tradition has for centuries valued relics.

3) People sometimes report miracles caused by relics.

4) The seventh ecumenical council (787 A.D.) requires churches to have saints' relics in them and to honor them.

The most well-known verse supporting the use of relics is in 2 Kings 13:21: "Once while some Israelites were burying a man, suddenly they saw a band of raiders; so they threw the man's body into Elisha's tomb. When the body touched Elisha's bones, the man came to life and stood up on his feet."

Another verse used to support the doctrine of relics is Acts 19:11-12: "God did extraordinary miracles through Paul, so that even handkerchiefs and aprons that had touched him were taken to the sick, and their illnesses were cured and the evil spirits left them." In 787 A.D., the seventh ecumenical council required all churches to have relics: [1]

"That to churches consecrated without any deposit of the relics of the saints, the defect should be made good... We decree therefore that relics shall be placed with the accustomed service in as many of the sacred temples as have been consecrated without the relics of the martyrs. And if any bishop from this time forward is found consecrating a temple without holy relics, he shall be deposed, as a transgressor of the ecclesiastical traditions."

The veneration of relics was upheld at the Catholic Council of Trent in 1563 in which they commanded bishops and others to "instruct the faithful diligently touching... the honor paid to relics....Also, that the holy bodies of holy martyrs...are to be venerated by the faithful, through which [bodies] many benefits are bestowed by God on men..." [2]

Relics today are referred to in the Catholic church as one of the "sacramentals," which are defined as objects or rituals that bring a blessing (1667-1670). According to church law (Canon 1237), "the ancient tradition of keeping the relics of martyrs and other saints under a fixed altar is to be preserved according to the norms given in the liturgical books."

Orthodox Bishop Timothy Ware says (p. 234, *The Orthodox Church*): "Because Orthodox are convinced that the body is sanctified and transfigured together with the soul, they have an immense reverence for the relics of the saints. Like Roman Catholics, they believe that the grace of God present in the saint's bodies during life remains active in their relics when they have died, and that God uses these relics as a channel of divine power and an instrument of healing...."

The Protestant view of relics

At first glance, the scriptures on relics would seem to be sufficient evidence that there is power in the dead bones or clothes of a Christian of note (e.g., saint). How, then to explain this, if the doctrine of relics is not correct?

Protestants note that in 2 Kings 13, the miracle involved the bones of Elisha, who was Elijah's assistant, and who had asked for a double portion of the anointing on Elijah: "...Elijah said to Elisha, 'Tell me, what can I do for you before I am taken from you?' 'Let me inherit a double portion of your spirit,' Elisha replied" (2 Kings 2:9). He was promised that (v. 10). While alive, Elisha did almost twice the number of miracles that Elijah did, but was one short of double (19) when he died (Elijah has 10 miracles recorded in the Bible). So did God fail in keeping his promise because he gave Elisha "almost" double? Not at all. God gave him the rest of the double portion after he had died — making exactly 20 miracles. These miracles are cited below.

The 10 miracles of Elijah

1) 1 Kings 17:1 Prophecy of no rain
2) 17:5 Fed by ravens
3) 17:16 Miracle of unending supply of food at widow's house

4) 17:22 Boy raised from dead
5) 18:36-38 Called down fire from heaven
6) 18:41-45 Miraculous rainfall
7) 18:46 Ran faster than horses
8) 21:17-19 Prophecy about Ahab
9) 2 Kings 2:8 Parted Jordan river
10) 2 Kings 2:11 Taken to heaven supernaturally

The 20 miracles of Elisha
1) 2 Kings 2:14 Jordan river parted
2) 2:22 Undrinkable water restored
3) 2:24 Bear attack
4) 3:17 Water in the desert
5) 4:1-7 Unending supply of oil
6) 4:16 Child born to barren woman
7) 4:35 Boy raised from dead
8) 4:41 Poisoned food restored
9) 4:42-44 Hundred fed
10) 5:15 Naaman healed of leprosy
11) 5:27 Word of knowledge about Gehazi
12) 6:6 Ax head floats
13) 6:9 Word of knowledge about Aramean army
14) 6:18 Struck Aramean army with blindness
15) 7:1 Prophecy about end of siege in Samaria
16) 8:1 Prophecy about new seven-year famine
17) 8:13 Prophecy about Hazael and Benhadad
18) 9:1-6 Prophecy about Jehu and Ahab's destruction
19) 13: 17 Prophecy about defeat of Aram
20) 13:20-21 After his death, raised dead man who touched his bones

Hebrews 11:13 seems to refer to Elisha's posthumous miracle:: "They did not receive the things promised; they only saw them and welcomed them from a distance..."

Protestants therefore believe God gave us the scriptures about Elisha's dead body to teach us to trust him to keep his promises even after we die.

Protestant theologians also contend that Deut. 34:5-6 implies that veneration of relics is wrong. In this passage we see that the time had come for Moses to die. He was highly venerated by the people, and he had done many miracles of spectacular proportions. It is only reasonable that the people would have venerated his grave and the relics of his body.

That is why what happened next is very unusual:

"And Moses the servant of the LORD died there in Moab, as the LORD had said. He buried him in Moab, in the valley opposite Beth Peor, but to this day no-one knows where his grave is."

Note that God himself buried Moses, and hid the location of his grave. Why did he do this? And why would God include this little detail in the

Bible? What is he trying to tell us in this passage? Evidently the Lord put this in the Bible to prevent veneration of dead bodies, as they likely would have done with Moses' body if they had found it. Theologian Matthew Poole, in his commentary on this verse, notes the following: "No man knoweth of his sepulchre ... which God hid from the Israelites, to prevent their superstition and idolatry, to which he knew their great proneness. And for this very reason the devil endeavoured to have it known, and contended with Michael about it, Jude 1:9. And seeing God would not endure the worship of the relics or tomb of so eminent a person as Moses was, it is ridiculous to think God would permit this honour to be given to any of the succeeding saints, who were so far inferior to him." (*English Annotations on the Holy Bible*, Matthew Poole)

But what about the New Testament relics?

But if relics are powerless, what about the passage where Paul's handkerchiefs healed people? Doesn't that prove that there is healing power in the relics of saints? We should also note that, apparently, Peter's shadow healed people, Jesus' spit healed people, Jesus' robe healed people, oil healed people, and mud made from street dirt and Jesus' spit healed people (Acts 5:12,15, Matt. 14:36, Mat. 9:21, James 5:14, John 9:6).

These all refer to objects that seemed to do miracles.

All of these are interesting, but the most interesting is Peter's shadow. For what is a shadow? It is nothing. It is simply the absence of direct light — that's all. It really doesn't exist. It could not have healed anyone. So what then healed these people? Their faith.

That is what Jesus said. "Your faith has made you well" (Matt. 9:22). Just so with all the other healings. Faith is the key to understanding healings of icons or relics, most Protestants believe.

Note that Jesus never said, "my spit has made you well." Nor did he say "my robe has made you well." Nor did Paul ever say that a sweaty handkerchief healed anyone, nor did Peter say his shadow healed anyone. James did not say the oil healed anyone, but "the prayer offered in faith will make the sick person well" (James 5:15). Faith in God heals the sick.

But why, then, were spit, a robe, handkerchiefs, oil and shadows needed? Jesus said, "According to your faith will it be done to you." (Matt. 9:29) Some have faith that they must do something to be healed, like touch Jesus' robe. That was her faith, and that was her confession: "She said to herself, 'If I only touch his cloak, I will be healed.'" (Mat. 9:21) Did she really have to touch Jesus' robe to be healed? No. This is shown by the centurion, who believed that Jesus could just say a word and his servant would be healed (Luke 7:6-7): "Lord, don't trouble yourself, for I do not deserve to have you come under my roof... But say the word, and my servant will be healed."

And he was. But this woman didn't believe she could be healed without touching Jesus' robe. She somehow felt that this would be a condition of her healing. So that was the way it was, because "according to your faith will it be done to you." In the same way, sometimes relics or icons may be involved with someone's healing. Is there really power in the relic or icon?

Protestants believe there is not. But the person may believe that this is a condition of their healing. And so it will be, because "according to your faith will it be done to you." Note that immediately after the woman touched Jesus' robe, he said, "Take heart, daughter, your faith has healed you" (Matt. 9:22). Shouldn't he have said, "The holy relic of my robe has healed you"? She had touched the robe, and she had been healed. But no, Jesus said, "your faith has healed you."

Regarding the apostle Paul's miraculous handkerchiefs (Acts 19:12), theologian A. T. Robertson notes,[3] "If one wonders how God could honor such superstitious faith, he should remember that there is no power in superstition or in magic, but in God. ...God condescends to meet us in our ignorance and weakness where he can reach us." Albert Barnes in his commentary[4] on this passage wrote: "...The fact that the miracles were wrought... by garments which had touched his body, was a mere sign....to the persons concerned, that it was done by the instrumentality of Paul, as the fact that the Saviour put his fingers into the ears of a deaf man, and spit and touched his tongue, ...was an evidence to those who saw it, that the power of healing came from him."

Another passage that sheds light on this is Gen. 30:37-40, where Jacob made striped branches as a means of making his herds have striped offspring, because his employer promised all such animals would be his property: "Jacob, however, took fresh-cut branches ...and made white stripes on them by peeling the bark and exposing the white inner wood of the branches. Then he placed the peeled branches in all the watering troughs... When the flocks were in heat and came to drink, they mated in front of the branches. And they bore young that were streaked or speckled or spotted."

Do striped branches actually make sheep and goats have spotted or striped offspring? Of course not. It just doesn't work. It was Jacob's faith in God's blessing that made the change. God provided spotted and striped livestock in order to fulfill his promise to bless Jacob. It seems he tolerated the superstitious use of the striped poles, as that was how Jacob believed. Just so, many Protestants believe, God tolerates superstitious reliance upon relics, at times, and does miracles based upon the person's conditional faith.

Origin of veneration of relics

It is interesting to speculate how the practice of venerating dead body parts began, since it contradicts several Old Testament scriptures that say that those who touch the dead become unclean.

Num. 19:13 says, "Whoever touches the dead body of anyone and fails to purify himself defiles the LORD's tabernacle. That person must be cut off from Israel. Because the water of cleansing has not been sprinkled on him, he is unclean; his uncleanness remains on him." (See also Num. 5:2, 6:6, 6:11, 9:6-7, 9:10, 19:11, and Hag. 2:13.) Early church fathers indicate the practice arose out of respect for early Christian martyrs, such as Polycarp: "We afterwards took up Polycarp's bones — as being more precious than the most exquisite jewels, and more purified than gold. We deposited them in a fitting place."[5] Christians would go to their graves to pray, and apparently soon began believing there was power in their dead bodies.

The *Catholic Encyclopedia* reports relics were well established as objects of veneration by the fourth century.

"Neither is it quite easy to determine the period at which the practice of venerating minute fragments of bone or cloth, small parcels of dust, etc., first became common. We can only say that it was widespread early in the fourth century, and that dated inscriptions upon blocks of stone, which were probably altar slabs, afford evidence upon the point which is quite conclusive."

Steven Sora, in his book on relics, says the origin of relic veneration is "impossible to date" but that it became truly popular in the fourth century: "In the early fourth century the mother of the Roman emperor Constantine mounted an expedition to the Holy Lands. After Helena brought home her treasures, the collecting of relics began to reach a fever pitch..." St. Ambrose followed her example, and "the two created the cult of relics, and for the next 800 years it grew."[6]

Problems with relic veneration

The public fascination with relics has led to fraud in some cases.

For instance, Sora notes that there are currently three alleged heads of John the Baptist, each one venerated as a holy relic: in Amiens, France, in Damascus, Syria, and a new one from Wadi Kharrar in Jordan.[7] Even the *Catholic Encyclopedia* notes that "many of the more ancient relics ... must now be pronounced to be either certainly spurious or open to grave suspicion."[8] As early as the fourth century, St. Augustine warned of "hypocrites under the garb of monks" who were selling "limbs of martyrs, if indeed of martyrs."[9] In conclusion, Protestants believe the doctrine of relics is based on a misunderstanding of 2 Kings 13 and Acts 19. Power for healing does not reside in dead objects, but in God. Excessive devotion to relics can lead to a dependence on them instead of on God.

---

1) Canon 7, p. 1350

2) Conc. Trid., Sess. 25 December 3d and 4th, 1563. [Buckley's Trans.]

3) *Robertson, A.T., Word Pictures in the New Testament* (1930), The Online Bible Published by Larry Pierce, 11 Holmwood St., Winterborough, Ontario, Canada N0B 2VO.

4) *Barnes Notes on the New Testament*, (1872) New York, The Online Bibe, Published by Larry Pierce, 11 Holmwood St., Winterborough, Ontario, Canada N0B 2VO.

5) *Martyrdom of Polycarp*, chap. 18, p. 94 (CD), Ante-Nicene Fathers

6) p. 4-5, *Treasures from Heaven: Relics from Noah's Ark to the Shroud of Turin*, ISBN 0-471-46232-2, John Wiley and Sons, Hoboken, NJ, USA

7) Ibid, p. 89

8) *Relics*, III, The Catholic Encyclopedia, 1917, New York (http://www.newadvent.org/cathen/)

9) *The Works of Monks*, 36, Moral Treatises, p. 956 (CD).

18. THE APOCRYPHA:
Should it be part of the Bible?

The apocrypha (deuterocanon) is a collection of several small books and parts of books that are accepted by the Catholic and Ortho-dox churches as part of the Bible, but are not accepted by Protestants or Jews.

The Catholic and Orthodox viewpoint

Catholic and Orthodox leaders support the use of the apocrypha because it is a tradition (Catholic *Catechism* 120), and Catholics especially because of its Council of Trent. The council ruled in 1546 that those who reject these books won't be allowed in heaven: "If anyone, however, should not ac-cept the said books as sacred and canonical, entire with all their parts . . . and if both knowingly and deliberately he should condemn the aforesaid tradition, let him be anathema."

The Catholic church today, however, while accepting the council's ruling as infallible (*Catechism*, 891), rarely mentions the council's condemnation of those who reject the apocrypha.

The Orthodox church doesn't have an official position on the apocrypha, but it includes the books in its Bibles and cites them like scripture. It has all of the books of the Catholic apocrypha,[1] but adds more books to that, depend-ing upon the Orthodox church that publishes the Bible (Greek, Russian, Cop-tic and others — see the chart on the following pages). The additional books variously added are: 1 Esdras, 2 Esdras, 3 Esdras, 4 Esdras, 3 Maccabees, 4 Maccabees, the Prayer of Manasseh, Psalm 151, and sometimes Enoch and Jubilees. (NOTE: 1 and 2 Esdras are often called 2 and 3 Esdras in Orthodox Bibles.) Orthodox Bibles often mark the apocryphal/deuterocanonical books with an asterisk noting that they are non-canonical. Orthodox Bishop Timothy Ware says these books are of secondary value.[2] Nonetheless, they are cited to support doctrine, such as in the following example of an Orthodox book supporting prayer for the dead: "In the Book of Baruch (3:4) there is a prayer for the forgiveness of the sins of the dead...In 2 Maccabees Judah Maccabee speaks about the sinful warriors, who died due to their sins, that the 'sin committed might wholly be put out of remembrance...' (2 Macc. 12:42)..." [3]

Probably the strongest argument for the apocrypha is the fact that it was included in the Greek translation of the Jewish Old Testament, called the Septuagint. This very old translation was done in Alexandria, Egypt, for the Greek-speaking Jews, and was completed in the first century before Christ.

Orthodox writers also note that when the New Testament quotes an Old Testament scripture, it usually uses the Septuagint version. This, they say, shows that the Septuagint, including the apocrypha, is from God.

The apocryphal books were all written before the birth of Christ, starting from about 300 B.C. Most of them do not exist in Hebrew, but were written in Greek (except 4 Esdras, written originally in Latin).

The Protestant viewpoint

Protestants[4] don't accept the apocrypha as inspired by God for several reasons. **First** of all, Jesus never referred to any book of the apocrypha, and they are not quoted anywhere else in the Bible.[5] This is in contrast to the Old Testament scriptures, almost all of which were cited by Jesus and the New Testament writers, and referred to as scripture. (The five Old Testament books that aren't quoted in the New Testament are Ezra, Nehemiah, Esther, Ecclesiastes, and Song of Solomon. Some say, however, that since these books were normally included in the same scrolls as other Jewish Old Testament books that were quoted, they are therefore approved by association. This is not the case with the apocryphal books, which have never been officially included in the scrolls of Jewish scriptures. See below.)

Second, the Bible says that Jews were given the responsibility of preserving the Hebrew scriptures, as says Rom. 3:2, "Chiefly because to them were committed the oracles of God." Rom. 9:4 says God gave to the people of Israel "the covenants, the receiving of the law." Psalm 147:19-20 says: "He has revealed his word to Jacob, his laws and decrees to Israel. He has done this for no other nation." Therefore, since the Jewish people have this God-given authority over the Old Testament scriptures, it important to note that they have never accepted the apocryphal books as part of the Bible. A council of Jewish religious leaders in Jamnia in 90 A.D. rejected them, and that remains the case today.

Third, church fathers and early writers cast doubt upon the reliability of the apocrypha. Jerome (lived 340-420 A.D.), for instance, in his preface to the books of Solomon, wrote: "As the Church reads the books of Judith and Tobit and Maccabees but does not receive them among the canonical scriptures, so also it reads Wisdom and Ecclesiasticus for the edification of the people, not for the authoritative confirmation of doctrine."

Jewish historian Josephus, who wrote his history of the Jews in the first century, listed the Old Testament books used by the Jews. The list did not

include the apocryphal books. "For we do not have many books among us, ...
only 22....which are justly believed to be divine;....no one has been so bold as
either to add anything to them, or to make any change in them." [6]

(Note: The Jewish system of counting the books combined several that
today are treated separately, hence their traditional total of 22.)

Writing in 170 A.D., Melito, the bishop of Sardis, didn't include the
apocrypha in his list of Old Testament books.[7]

Fourth, the Bible forbids us to add to God's words. Proverbs 30:6 says,
"Do not add to his words, or he will rebuke you and prove you a liar." In
Deut. 4:2 and 12:32, God says not to "add to what I command you nor
subtract from it." 1 Cor. 4:6 tells us "not to go beyond what is written."
Rev. 22:18-19, although speaking about Revelation, stresses the principle of
leaving God's words alone: "if anyone adds to them, God will add to him the
plagues described in this book, and if anyone takes away from the words in
this prophetic book, God will take away his share in the tree of life."

Fifth, the Orthodox and Catholic churches don't agree on which books
should be in the apocrypha. *(See the charts.)* There are at least four versions.
This shows doubt about the authenticity of these books, Protestants believe.

Sixth, the apocrypha itself does not claim to be scripture. The writer
of Maccabees states that his book is simply a short history of the events of
the time: "...all such things as have been comprised in five books by Jason
of Cyrene, we have attempted to abridge in one book..." (2 Macc. 2: 24-32).
He also says he may have made mistakes: "...If I have done well, and as it
becometh the history, it is what I desired; but if not so perfectly, it must be
pardoned me. ..." (2 Macc. 15:38-39).

Seventh, the apocrypha wasn't officially recognized as scripture by the
Roman Catholic Church until the Council of Trent in 1546 A.D. This very
late affirmation was done apparently to address the controversies raised by the
Protestant Reformation, which was consuming Europe at that time. (Some of
the controversies were due to doctrines based on the apocrypha.)

Eighth, the fact that the apocrypha was included in the Septuagint does
not make it scripture, Protestants believe. (The Septuagint is an old Greek
translation of the Hebrew Old Testament.)

A) The three most ancient copies of the Septuagint dating from the fourth
century have different versions of the apocrypha, which shows there was
doubt about these books from the beginning. Codex Vaticanus does not have
the books of Maccabees. Codex Sinaiticus lacks 2 and 3 Maccabees, while
Codex Alexandrinus has all four. In addition, two of these — the Codex
Sinaiticus and the Codex Alexandrinus — include four books as part of the
New Testament that all churches reject today. (1 and 2 Clement, Epistle of
Barnabas, Shepherd of Hermas). Accordingly, if these old Bibles made errors
in the books of the New Testament, it's possible that they made errors in the
Old Testament, too.

B) The apostles apparently did not accept the Septuagint as without error,
as they sometimes preferred to use versions that differ with it.

Theologian F.F Bruce notes, "in Matthew 12:18-21 the announcement of

Different versions of the apocrypha [10]

Usual name	Catholic	Gk. Orth.	Russ. Orth.[†]	Eth. Coptic**
Ezra	Ezra[†]	Ezra	1Esdras[†]	Ezra
1Esdras	--	1Esdras	2Esdras[†]	1Esdras
2Esdras	--	--	3Esdras[†]	**
4Esdras	--	--	--	Ezra Apoc.**
Psalm 151	--	Ps. 151	Ps. 151	Ps. 151
3Maccabees	--	3Mac.	3Mac.	**
4Maccabees	--	4Mac.*	--	**
Prayer/Manasseh	--	Pr./Man.	--[†]	Pr./Man.
Enoch	--	--	--	Enoch
Jubilees	--	--	--	Jubilees
Pseudo-Josephus	--	--	--	Pseudo-Josephus

The four versions of the apocrypha have nine books in common (see footnote one) but disagree about the books listed above.

* Put in a separate appendix, and not with the other books of the Bible.

** The Ethiopian Coptic canon of scripture is not well-defined even today. There are differing lists, and some of the books have different information (e.g. Maccabees is completely different than that in other apocryphal collections.)[11] The Egyptian Coptic canon is like the Catholic Church, but adds Ps. 151.[12]

[†] Some Slavonic Bibles include Prayer of Manasseh. The Russian Orthodox Bible calls Ezra— 1 Esdras, and 1 Esdras — 2 Esdras, and 2 Esdras — 3 Esdras. Some older Catholic bibles call Ezra — 1 Esdras, and Nehemiah 2 Esdras.

the Servant of the Lord [Isaiah 42:1-4] is quoted in what appears to be a non-Septuagintal version. The statement, 'Vengeance is mine, I will repay' (from Deut. 32:35) is quoted in Rom. 12:19 and Heb. 10:30 in a form corresponding neither to the Hebrew text nor to the Septuagint, but to the Aramaic targums on the Pentateuch." Other places where the New Testament differs from the Septuagint are Mark 4:12 (see Is. 6:10) and Eph. 4:8 (see Ps. 68:18 — LXX 67:19).

The fact that the apostles felt free to modify the Septuagint translation shows that it was not regarded as infallible.

C) Jesus apparently endorsed the original Hebrew canon as opposed to its Greek translation (the Septuagint). This is shown by his references to the Old Testament as "the Law and the Prophets" (Mt. 5:17; 7:12; 11:13; 22:40; Rom 3:21), and the "Law, Prophets and Psalms" (Luke 24:44). This reflects the Hebrew canon and not the Septuagint, which has a different organization (Law, History, Poetry, Prophets). This is also shown in Mt. 23:35, where Jesus refers to "all the righteous blood shed on earth" and defines that as being "from the blood of righteous Abel to the blood of Zechariah, the son of Berechiah." Listing Zechariah last makes no sense chronologically, as he was not the last prophet killed in the Bible — Uriah was (Jer. 26:23) . However, Berechiah is the last prophet listed as killed in the Hebrew version of the Bible (2 Chr. 24:21). Accordingly, we can see that Jesus preferred the original Hebrew version, which has never included the apocrypha. Most New Testament citations, nonetheless, did follow the Septuagint, but Protestants believe this was because the New Testament was written in Greek, and the Septuagint was the only Greek Old Testament then available. Greek-speaking readers were familiar with it.

Different numbers of Old Testament books

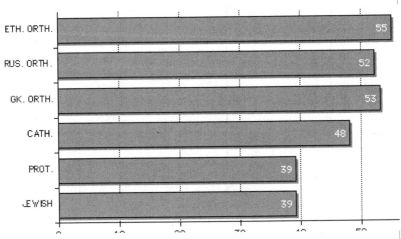

The differences in the Old Testaments of the different churches is due to the apocrypha. There are four versions of the apocrypha. Protestants and Jews do not accept any of the apocrypha books as scripture.

However, the New Testament never cites any part of the apocrypha in the Septuagint.

Ninth, the apocrypha contradicts the Bible in several places. For instance, the apocrypha says you can buy eternal life by giving money to the church. This contradicts Bible passages that say eternal life is a gift of God that cannot be purchased with money. The apocryphal passages are below, followed by the Bible passages:

a) Tobit 4: 7-11: " Give alms from your possessions...and the face of God will not be turned away from you.....So you will be laying up a good treasure for yourself against the day of necessity. For charity delivers from death and keeps you from entering the darkness; and for all who practice it charity is an excellent offering in the presence of the Most High."

b) Tobit 12:9: "For almsgiving delivers from death, and it will purge away every sin..."

c) Ecclesiasticus (Sirach) 3:30: "Water extinguishes a blazing fire: so almsgiving atones for sin."

These citations from the apocrypha contradict the following passages from the Bible (italic emphasis by the author):

"*Freely* you have received, freely give." (Matt. 10:8)

"For the wages of sin is death; but the *gift* of God is eternal life through Jesus Christ our Lord." (Rom. 6:23)

"Peter answered: "May your money perish with you, because you thought you could buy the *gift* of God with money!" (Acts 8:20)

"Whoever *believes* in the Son has eternal life..." (John 3:36)

"I tell you the truth, whoever hears my word and *believes* him who sent me has eternal life and will not be condemned; he has crossed over from death to life." (John 5:24)

" I *give* them eternal life...." (John 10:28)

"God has *given* us eternal life..." (1 John 5:11)

Notice especially the verses which refer to eternal life as a gift (Rom. 6:23, 1 John 5:11, John 10:28). Rom. 6:23 especially contrasts our wages (death) with the gift of God (eternal life).

Eternal life is not something we can buy, as the apocrypha says, but it is a gift of God given when we repent of our sins, as Acts 2:38 says: "Repent and be baptized, every one of you, in the name of Jesus Christ for the forgiveness of your sins."

That said, there are two Bible texts regarding the giving of money for atonement. Exodus 30:16 says : "Receive the atonement money from the Israelites... It will be a memorial for the Israelites before the LORD, making atonement for your lives." (See also Num. 31: 49-54.)

Here at first glance it seems that the giving of money is buying atonement (forgiveness). Can that be?

No. These actions and the sacrifice of animals look forward symbolically to Christ. He is the only way to heaven. There is no second way by giving money or sacrificing animals.

Note that the atonement money of Exodus 30:16 was melted to form the silver sockets which were the foundation of the tabernacle. These were therefore a symbol of Christ who is the foundation of our salvation. "For no-one can lay any foundation other than the one already laid, which is Jesus Christ." *(1 Cor. 3:11)*

The silver in the tabernacle is also a symbol of the 30 pieces of silver paid for Christ. "(Judas) asked, "What are you willing to give me if I hand him over to you?" So they counted out for him thirty silver coins." *(Mat. 26:15. See also Gen. 37:28, Ex. 21:32, Zech. 11:12-13)*

This money did not redeem anyone, as only the blood of Christ can atone for our sins, as the apostle Peter said: "Ye were not redeemed with corruptible things as silver and gold ...but with the precious blood of Christ." *(1 Peter 1:18-19)*

The half-shekel each one had to pay illustrates that each person must individually come to God. As M.R. DeHaan noted in his book, *The Tabernacle,* "Every man had to bring his own half shekel. The rich and the poor alike, without difference, must bring their bit of silver. It was an individual responsibility. And salvation, beloved, is also a personal, individual matter, and can never be obtained by proxy ...You cannot be saved by the religion of your parents."

The half shekel of silver amounts to about $5 in today's money.

If indeed it is possible to pay enough money to buy heaven, then the rich could be guaranteed eternal life. But in Luke 18:25 Jesus said, "Indeed, it is easier for a camel to go through the eye of a needle than for a rich man to enter the kingdom of God."

What Jesus meant was that no one, by his money or good deeds, can earn heaven. We must trust in God's mercy for our salvation, as the Bible says in Eph. 2:8-9: "For it is by grace you have been saved, through faith— and this not from yourselves, it is the gift of God— not by works, so that no one can boast." The prophet Zephaniah (1:18) said "Neither their silver nor their gold will be able to save them on the day of the LORD's wrath." Heb. 10:8-11 also says this old system of payment can't help us: "Sacrifices and offerings, burnt offerings and sin offerings you did not desire, nor were you pleased with them." Verse 11 says these sacrifices "can never take away sins." Verse 9 says God "sets aside the first to establish the second," meaning the new covenant of Christ. Verse 10 sums it up: "And by that will, we have been made holy through the sacrifice of the body of Jesus Christ once for all."

A fishy scripture

Another apocryphal passage that finds no support in the Bible is the teaching that you can cast out a demon by burning the inner parts of a fish:

Tobit 6:16-17 says: "When you enter the bridal chamber, you shall take live ashes of incense and lay upon them some of the heart and liver of the fish so as to make a smoke. Then the demon will smell it and flee away, and will never again return..."

The Bible shows no instance of anyone casting out demons by burning the parts of a fish. Instead, demons are cast out in the name of Jesus:

"...In my name they will drive out demons...." (Mark 16:17).

"...Lord, even the demons submit to us in your name" (Luke 10:17).

"...Paul became so troubled that he turned around and said to the spirit, 'In the name of Jesus Christ I command you to come out of her!' At that moment the spirit left her" (Acts 16:18).

This is not to say that Catholic or Orthodox teachers say that demons can be cast out by a fish — but the fact that it is in the apocrypha casts additional doubt on the reliability of these writings.

Another passage in the apocrypha shows a person praying to God to help them to lie (Judith 9:10,13): "By the deceit of my lips strike down the slave with the prince and the prince with his servant; ...Make my deceitful words to be their wound and stripe."

The Bible shows no case of someone asking God to help them to lie. The Bible says that lying is a sin (Rev. 21:8): "But ... all liars—their place will be in the fiery lake of burning sulfur. This is the second death." *(See also Ex. 20: 16, Lev. 19:11, Ps. 101:7.)*

The apocrypha also refers to praying for the dead:

2 Macc. 12:43-45 says: "He also took up a collection, ... and sent it to Jerusalem to provide for a sin offering.... to pray for the dead.... Therefore he made atonement for the dead, that they might be delivered from their sin."

There is no example in the Bible of anyone praying for the dead. In fact, in 2 Sam. 12:23, David, in referring to his infant son who had just died, quit praying for him, saying: "But now he is dead, wherefore should I fast? Can I bring him back again? I shall go to him, but he shall not return to me."

The Bible refers to immediate resolution of the state of persons who die. There is no delay mentioned in the Bible (such as 40 days) as some have believed. For instance, in Luke 23:43, Jesus told the repentant thief who died with him, "I tell you the truth, today you will be with me in paradise." The man went immediately to heaven.

Paul also referred to this immediate judgment in Phil. 1:23: "I am torn between the two: I desire to depart and be with Christ, which is better by far." Heb. 9:27 says, "Just as man is destined to die once, and after that to face judgment." *(See the chapter on praying for the dead.)*

Errors in the apocrypha

Tenth, the apocrypha also includes some evident errors, such as the two deaths of Antiochus Ephiphanes:

In 2 Macc. 9:5, 28 it is written that he died of bowel disease: "But the... Lord...struck him an incurable and unseen blow..... he was seized with a pain in his bowels for which there was no relief and with sharp internal tortures... So the murderer and blasphemer, having endured the more intense suffering... came to the end of his life...."

But 1 Macc. 6:8-9,10,16 says he died of grief: "When the king heard this news, he was astounded and badly shaken. He took to his bed and became sick from grief, ...and he concluded that he was dying...Thus Antiochus the king died there in the one hundred and forty-ninth year."

The apocrypha also says that Abraham, Isaac and Jacob never sinned: "Abraham and Isaac and Jacob, who did not sin against thee..." (Prayer of Manasseh 1:8). But the Bible says "all have sinned" (Rom. 3:23).

The apocrypha says Nebuchadnezzer was king over the Assyrians in Nineveh but the Bible says he was king over the Babylonians in Babylon. *(Judith 1:1, Jer. 50:17).*

The apocrypha says Christ will die a second time, but the Bible says he lives forever. *(2 Esdras 7:28-30 (3 Esdras in the Russian Bible), Heb 7:24.)*

The apocrypha says those who honor their father atone for their sins, but the Bible says it is by faith *(Sirach 3:3, Eph. 2:8-9)*

The apocrypha forbids helping a sinner, but Christ tells us to do good to them *(Sirach 12:4-7, Luke 6:27-36).*

The apocrypha says we should trust in our hearts, but the Bible says the heart is deceptive *(Sirach 37:13, Proverbs 14:12, Jeremiah 17:9).*

The apocrypha also includes several other strange passages:
Sirach (Ecclesiasticus) 25:19 says, "Any iniquity is insignificant compared to a wife's iniquity." This is an unusual criticism of wives. Are their sins really worse than other people's sins?

Sirach 22:3 says "the birth of a daughter is a loss." [8] Are girls really that bad? Sirach 26:29 says that businessmen are especially evil: "A merchant can hardly keep from wrongdoing, and a tradesman will not be declared innocent of sin."

Eleventh, parts of the apocrypha simply repeat other Bible verses. For instance, Baruch 2:6 says: "Righteousness belongs to the Lord our God, but

confusion of face to us and our fathers, as at this day." This repeats Daniel
9:7, "O Lord, righteousness belongeth unto thee, but unto us confusion of
faces, as at this day" (KJV).

Other repeated scriptures are in Baruch 2:6 (Daniel 9:7), Baruch 4:23
(Ps. 126:6), Baruch 2:17 (Is 38:18), Baruch 2:21 (Jer. 27:16-17), Baruch
2:23 (Jer. 7:34 (KJV), Baruch 5:7 (Is 40:4), Baruch 3:22-31 (Prov. 1:20-22),
Baruch 3:29 (Prov. 30:4), Baruch 2:2-3 (Lam. 2:20), Baruch 2:17 (Is. 38:18),
Baruch 2:21 (Jer. 27:16-17), Baruch 6:1 (Jer. 29:1), Baruch 6:3 (Jer. 29:10),
and Baruch 5:1 (Is. 52:1).

The Book of Sirach, while not copying other Bible passages, nonetheless
includes lengthy summaries of the lives of other Bible figures, starting with
44:1. Such summaries may be encouraging but are not necessarily scripture.

Conclusion

The apocryphal books consist of wisdom books (such as Sirach/Ecclesi-
asticus), religious romances (such as Tobit), and history (such as Maccabees),
or additional information, such as additions to Esther[9] and additions to Daniel[10].

While Protestants consider them useful for historical purposes in understanding the times in which they were written, they do not consider them to
be scripture for the reasons cited above. Insofar as the books promote false
doctrines, such as the possibility of praying for the dead or purchasing eternal
life, they may be harmful.

---

1) The apocryphal books accepted by both Catholic and Orthodox leaders are Tobit, Judith, additions to the Book of Esther, Wisdom of Solomon, Ecclesiasticus (or Sirach), Baruch, The Letter
of Jeremiah (or Baruch ch. 6), additions to the Book of Daniel (The Prayer of Azariah and Song
of the Three Hebrew Children, Susanna, Bel and the Dragon), 1 Maccabees, and 2 Maccabees.
Slavonic and Russian Orthodox bibles add to this 3 Maccabees, 1 and 2 Esdras (which they call
2 and 3 Esdras), the Prayer of Manasseh (sometimes) and Ps. 151. The Greek Orthodox Bible
is like the Russian/Slavonic Bible but it rejects 3 Esdras, and adds 4 Maccabees as an appendix.
Ethiopian Coptic adds Enoch and Jubilees and some others.
2) Ware, Timothy, *The Orthodox Church*, p. 208-209 (1963)
3) *Shto suzhdeno nam za chertoi zhizni*, ("What is destined for us behind the veil of life), p. 218,
Blago, Moscow, 2003, ISBN 5-94972-012-3
4) Among Protestants only the Anglican Church puts the apocrypha in its Bible, but it does so on
a literary basis and not as a source of doctrine.
5) Jude quotes Enoch, and the Ethiopian Coptic church has a Book of Enoch containing the
quote. But this book is not in the apocryphas of Catholics or other Orthodox.. The *Jamieson,
Fausset and Brown* commentary on Jude 14 and the Book of Enoch says: "There is no certain
proof that [the book of Enoch] existed so early as the time of Jude...Both Jude and the author of
that book may have quoted a common tradition of their time...There are reasons given by some
for thinking the Book of Enoch copied from Jude rather than vice versa."
6) Flavius Josephus, *Against Apion*, Book 1, Section 8.
7) Bruce, F.F. *The Canon of Scripture*, p. 71, InterVarsity Press, Downers Grove, IL 60515, 1988,
ISBN 0-8308-1258-X. Also in Eusebius *Hist. Eccl.*, 4.26.12-14.
8) The Russian translation adds by implication "ill bred" daughters, as do some other translations,
but the word is not in the original Greek. The Revised Standard apocrypha leaves it out.
9) Some parts of the apocryphal/deuterocanonical books are not listed separately, but are included
in other books of the Bible. Additions to Esther are found either at the end of the book (10:4 to
16:24) or interspersed throughout the book of Esther, after the following verses: 1:1, 3:13, 4:17,
8:12, 5:1, 5:2, 10:3. The Letter of Jeremiah is found either as a separate book or as the sixth

chapter of Baruch. Ps. 151 is found at the end of Psalms. *Additions to Daniel:* Song of Azariah, and Song of the Three Young Men (or Song of the Three Holy Children) are found after Daniel 3:23. Susanna is found as Daniel chap. 13. Bel and the Dragon is found as Daniel 14. Prayer of Manasseh is sometimes found as a separate book or in *Odes,* a collection of hymns or poems after Psalms. Sometimes the apocrypha is included in a separate section of the Bible, however.

10) Below is an excerpt from the *New Oxford Annotated Bible with the Apocrypha:* New Revised Standard Version. Ed. Michael D. Coogan. 3rd ed. New York: Oxford University Press, 2001. "The Eastern Orthodox Churches recognize several other books as authoritative. Editions of the Old Testament approved by the Holy Synod of the Greek Orthodox Church contain, besides the Roman Catholic Deuterocanonical books, 1 Esdras, Psalm 151, the Prayer of Manasseh, and 3 Maccabees, while 4 Maccabees appears in the Appendix. Slavonic Bibles approved by the Russian Orthodox Church contain besides the Deuterocanonical books, 1 and 2 Esdras (called 2 and 3 Esdras), Psalm 151, and 3 Maccabees." See also "The Old Testament in the Orthodox Church," by Fr. R. Stergio, *Voice in the wilderness,* v. 5(4-6), 1997, Greek Orthodox Church of St. George, South Brisbane, 1 Kidwelly St, CARINDALE Qld 4152 AUSTRALIA. See also http://orthodoxyinamerica.org/article.php?id=48, accessed Nov. 1, 2015.

11) See R. W. Cowley's research in Ostkirchliche Studien, 1974, Volume 23, pp. 318-323, or http://www.islamic-awareness.org/Bible/Text/Canon/ethiopican.html, accessed Nov. 1, 2015.

12) http://www.suscopts.org/evangelism/frames/know_your_bible.html, accessed Nov. 1, 2015.

19. PRAYER TO SAINTS:
Right or wrong?

Should we pray to the saints and Mary? The Orthodox church and the Catholic church both practice and encourage praying to saints, meaning notable men and women of God who have died. Protestants do not.

The Orthodox/Catholic viewpoint

The Catholic *Catechism* (2683) says regarding saints that, "We can and should ask them to intercede for us and for the whole world." Prayer to Mary is also encouraged (2683): "...The Church loves to pray in communion with the Virgin Mary,...and to entrust supplications and praises to her."

Many support prayer to saints and Mary because they feel that God is too awesome for us to approach. A fellow human, it is felt, can better understand us and will be more accepting of us, as Orthodox theologian Sergius Bulgakov noted: "It is naturally necessary to hide ourselves in awe before the Judge of all, and here we take our refuge beneath the protection of the Virgin and the Saints"[1] "Prayers addressed to the Virgin occupy a large place in the Orthodox service. Besides the feasts and the days specially consecrated to her, every office contains innumerable prayers addressed to her and her name is constantly spoken in the temple together with the name of our Lord Jesus"[2] Gal. 5:24 is said to be about saints: "Those who belong to Christ Jesus have crucified the sinful nature with its passions and desires."

Catholic and Orthodox leaders also say they are not praying to saints, but merely asking them to pray for us. They point out that the Holy Spirit also intercedes for us (Rom. 8:26-7), as do other believers. They argue that it is just as acceptable to ask a saint or Mary to pray for one's needs as it is to ask another Christian at church, as there is no separation between living and dead believers — they are part of the same family, united in Christ. This is called the "communion of saints." So why can't we ask a fellow Christian in heaven to pray for us? What's wrong with that?

The Protestant viewpoint

Most Protestants say there are eight things wrong with praying to saints:
1) There is no special category of believer called a saint.
2) There are no examples of praying to saints in the Bible.
3) Jesus taught us only to pray to the Father.
4) The Old Testament warns against prayers to others than God.
5) Early church fathers opposed prayer to departed Christians.
6) God has established a separation between living and dead Christians.
7) The Bible says there is only one mediator between us and God.
8) God is sympathetic to our needs — we don't need to pray to others.

First, Protestants do not believe there is a special category of believer who is called a saint. Protestants say the biblical word "saints" refers to all Christians, and not just to persons especially noted for their piety, as is made clear in Paul's letter to the Corinthians.

"By "saint" is not meant the morally perfect, but the one who belongs to Christ... Thus Paul can salute the disciples at Corinth as saints and a little later rebuke them as carnal and babes, as those among whom are jealousy and strife, who walk after the manner of men (1 Cor. 1:2; 3:1-3)." [3]

Similarly, in 2 Cor. 1:1, Eph. 1:1, and Phil. 1:1 Paul uses the word "saints" as a general term for all Christians.

Second, the Bible has no example of prayer to saints or anyone who had died. When Jesus spoke to Moses and Elijah (Luke 9:30-31) he was not praying to them. They were speaking a message sent to him by the Father: "Two men, Moses and Elijah, appeared in glorious splendor, talking with Jesus. They spoke about his departure, which he was about to bring to fulfillment at Jerusalem."

Third, when Jesus taught us to pray in Matt. 6:9, he said nothing about praying to saints, but only about prayer to God the Father: "This, then, is how you should pray: 'Our Father in heaven, hallowed be your name'" In his own prayers, Jesus is never recorded as praying to anyone but the Father.

Fourth, the Old Testament gives a strong symbolic warning against praying to anyone but God.

In Ex. 30:9, when the Lord is directing Moses about building the altar of incense, he warns him: "Do not offer on this altar any other incense...." Incense represents prayer, as is shown in Rev. 5:8: "...They were holding golden bowls full of incense, which are the prayers of the saints." (Also in Rev. 8:3-4). So the Lord was forbidding, in effect, prayers to anyone but him. The Lord struck dead two priests who offered unauthorized incense (prayers) in Lev. 10:1: "Aaron's sons Nadab and Abihu took their censers, put fire in them and added incense; and they offered unauthorized fire before the LORD, contrary to his command. So fire came out from the presence of the LORD and consumed them, and they died before the LORD."

Similarly Korah and his 250 followers were killed by the Lord while offering unauthorized incense before the Lord (Num. 16). Even the making of incense like that of the temple was forbidden: "Do not make any incense with this formula for yourselves; consider it holy to the LORD. Whoever makes any like it to enjoy its fragrance must be cut off from his people." (Exodus 30:37-38)

Protestants therefore believe that prayer, like this incense, is "holy to the Lord" — it is only for him, and not for any saint or Mary.

Even asking a departed Christian to pray for us is a form of prayer, Protestants believe. It is also unnecessary, as the Christians in heaven are already praying to God and see our situation: (Heb. 12:1: "...Since we are surrounded by such a great cloud of witnesses...")

Church fathers opposed prayer to saints

Fifth, the earliest church writings (immediately after the time of the apostles) show opposition to the idea of praying to the dead:

Tertullian wrote in approximately 197 A.D that it is not possible to contact the saints or the dead: "We speak of paradise, the place of divine bliss appointed to receive the spirits of the saints. There, the saints are cut off from the knowledge of this world by that fiery zone, as by a sort of enclosure." [4]

Lactantius, a century later, wrote that praying to the saints is actually dangerous: "...It is clear that those who...make prayers to the dead...do not act as becomes men, and that they will suffer punishment for their impiety and guilt, who, rebelling against God, the Father of the human race, have undertaken inexpiable rites, and violated every sacred law." [5]

Origen was also against it: "We judge it improper to pray to those beings who themselves offer up prayers. For even they themselves would prefer that we should send up our requests to...God." [6] "Celsus forgets that he is addressing Christians, who pray to God alone through Jesus." [7]

Sixth, Protestants believe God has established a separation between living and dead Christians. Deut. 18:11-12 says, "There shall not be found among you any...necromancer." The word necromancer literally means one who communicates with the dead (Hebrew, "darash" to consult, inquire of, seek, or pray and "muwth", the dead). God condemned Saul for contacting the prophet Samuel after he had died (1 Chron. 10:13-14).

This prohibition may be because the difference between asking a saint to pray and actually praying to that saint is a very narrow one. An emotional attachment to that "saint" can easily develop. We can become more comfortable in speaking to them about our needs than with God, feeling a fellow human will understand us better. This leads us to the sin of idolatry, in which a person takes the place of God. Further, Christians who think they are in contact with a saint may actually be in contact with a demon, as the Bible says "Satan himself masquerades as an angel of light" (2 Cor. 11:14).

Seventh, 1 Tim 2:5 forbids reliance upon others to mediate between us and God: "For there is one God and one mediator between God and men, the man Christ Jesus..." This is not a prohibition against asking others to pray for us, but it does prohibit reliance upon those others — living or dead — to reconcile us to God. Christ is the only one who can reconcile us to God by his death and resurrection. Clearly no one else will ever do that — Jesus is the only mediator between God and man.

The Greek word used here ("mesites") is defined by *Thayer's Greek-English Lexicon* as "one who intervenes between two, either in order to make or restore peace and friendship, or form a compact, or for ratifying a covenant." Christ has restored us to peace and friendship with God by his own blood.

Eighth, Protestants believe God is very sympathetic to our troubles. We don't need a saint or Mary to intercede for us, as if they would understand us better or would be more sympathetic than Jesus Christ. The Lord says his compassion is even greater than a mother's: "Can a mother forget the baby at her breast and have no compassion on the child she has borne? Though she may forget, I will not forget you! See, I have engraved you on the palms of my hands..." (Is. 49:15-16).

The scars in the hands of Jesus are eternal reminders of his love for us.

The Bible says the Lord came to earth and lived just as we do, and he understands us and cares for us. Heb. 7:25 says Christ is our high priest who, "always lives to intercede" for us. Heb.4:15-16 says the Lord is sympathetic: "We do not have a high priest who is unable to sympathize with our weaknesses, but we have one who has been tempted in every way, just as we are — yet was without sin. Let us then approach the throne of grace with confidence, so that we may receive mercy and find grace to help us in our time of need."

Heb. 2:18 says of Jesus, "Because he himself suffered when he was tempted, he is able to help those who are being tempted."

Ps 103:13 says, "As a father has compassion on his children, so the LORD has compassion on those who fear him."

God's love for us is clearly shown in Is. 54:10: "Though the mountains be shaken and the hills be removed, yet my unfailing love for you will not be shaken nor my covenant of peace be removed, says the LORD, who has compassion on you."

1) Bulgakov, *The Orthodox Church*, p. 122
2) Ibid, p. 118
3) *International Standard Bible Encyclopedia*, 1939, electronic edition, article under "sanctification"
4) Part First, *1- The Apology*, chap. 47, p. 101 (CD), Ante-Nicene Fathers
5) *The Divine Institutes*, Book 2, chap. 18, p. 140 (CD), Ante-Nicene Fathers
6) *Against Celsus*, Book 5, chap. 12, p. 1128 (CD), Ante-Nicene Fathers, c. 248 A.D.,
7) *Against Celsus*, Book 8, chap. 37, p. 1349 (CD), Ante-Nicene Fathers, c. 248 A.D

20. MARY:
Sinless intercessor?

Protestants, Catholics and Orthodox all agree that Mary, the mother of Jesus, was a great person worthy of our respect, a virgin before Christ's birth. However there are still big differences between the three about Mary.

In general, Catholic and Orthodox doctrine says Mary never sinned, is eternally a virgin, and is someone to whom Christians should pray and show special honor.

Most Protestants believe Mary was a sinner as we all are, had a normal marriage and should not be prayed to or shown special honor.

If official Catholic/Orthodox teaching is right, then Protestants are sinning by not praying to Mary and showing her honor. If Protestants are right, then those who pray to Mary and venerate her are sinning. So is devotion to Mary a path to God, or does it lead us away from God? This is the question facing us.

Shared Catholic/Orthodox beliefs

1) Catholicism and Orthodoxy both teach that Mary is the mother of all Christians and has special power to intercede for us. The Orthodox Study Bible notes: "In saying to ... John, Behold your mother..., Jesus symbolically establishes Mary's role as mother of all faithful disciples — of the entire Church."[1] The argument is also sometimes made that since Jesus did not refuse his mother's request to change the water into wine at the wedding in Cana (John 2), he will not refuse requests she brings to him now on behalf of believers who pray to her.

2) Both churches pray to and venerate Mary. The Catholic church teaches that devotion to Mary is an essential part of Christian worship (*Catechism* 971): "The Church rightly honors the Blessed Virgin for special devotion." Our prayers should include "supplications and praises...to the Mother of Jesus..." (2675). Orthodox theologian Bulgakov says: "The Church sees in her the Mother of God, who, without being a substitute for the One Mediator, intercedes before her Son for all humanity. We ceaselessly pray her to intercede

for us"[2] Both churches say that this veneration is not the same as the worship Christians offer to God. [3]

3) Both churches believe that Mary never sinned, and was a virgin her entire life. Regarding the brothers of Jesus, the *Orthodox Study Bible* comments: "In the Greek patristic tradition; these brothers are identified as stepbrothers of Jesus, sons of Joseph by a previous wife. In the Latin tradition, they are seen as relatives, such as cousins." [4]

Catholic and Orthodox leaders say the gate in Ezekiel's vision of the temple (Eze. 44:2) refers to Mary's eternal virginity: "This gate shall be shut, it shall not be opened, and no one shall enter by it, for the Lord God of Israel has entered by it; therefore it shall be shut."

It is also argued that Jesus would not have given charge of Mary to John at his death, if Mary had had other children. (See John 19:26-27.)

4) Both churches argue that Mary is shown in scripture in an exalted position. Orthodox Bishop Ware says Mary is "the most exalted of God's creatures." [5]

Some Catholic/Orthodox writers say that the ark of the covenant in the tabernacle, which carried the 10 commandments, represents Mary, who carried Jesus in her womb. The special reverence shown to the ark of God should also be shown to Mary today, they say.

It is often said that the woman clothed with the sun in Revelation 12:1-6 represents Mary: "A great and wondrous sign appeared in heaven: a woman clothed with the sun, with the moon under her feet and a crown of twelve stars on her head. She was pregnant and cried out in pain as she was about to give birth. ...She gave birth to a son, a male child, who will rule all the nations with an iron scepter. And her child was snatched up to God and to his throne. The woman fled into the desert to a place prepared for her by God, where she might be taken care of for 1,260 days."

5) Lastly, both churches support veneration of Mary based upon church tradition and the writings of the church fathers. They believe devotion to Mary is an ancient practice of the church, going back many centuries.

Unique Catholic beliefs about Mary

Catholicism has several beliefs and practices about Mary that set it apart from both Orthodoxy and Protestantism.

1) The most popular prayer in Catholicism is about Mary, the "Hail Mary." Most Protestants do not use the prayer, and it is rarely used in Orthodoxy. The "Hail Mary" is part of the rosary, said by millions daily: "Hail Mary, full of grace, the Lord is with thee. Blessed art thou among women, and blessed is the fruit of thy womb, Jesus. Holy Mary, Mother of God, pray for us sinners, now and at the hour of our death."

This prayer is repeated 150 times each time the rosary is prayed. The rosary is a common method of Catholic prayer that uses beads as a reminder.

2) Catholicism has several internal organizations devoted to Mary. Neither Orthodox nor Protestants [7] have such organizations. These include:
   • The Marian Movement of Priests, with worldwide membership of more

than 100,000 priests and bishops, and reportedly millions of Catholics, with the goal of being united to the immaculate heart of Mary.

• The Society of Mary (Marists), formed in 1816 and active in 36 nations.

• The Militia of the Immaculata (1917) with official membership of almost four million. It encourages total consecration to the Virgin Mary. Other groups include the Blue Army of our Lady of Fatima, the Medjugorje Star association, and the Marian Renewal Ministry.

3) Catholic leaders believe Mary has appeared in dozens of places over the centuries. The most famous were in Fatima, Spain, in 1917; in Lourdes, France, in 1858; in Guadalupe, Mexico, in 1531; and recently in Medjugorje, Bosnia-Herzegovina. Appearances of Mary and prophecies from her are common in Catholic literature, but are rare in Orthodox literature [6] and nonexistent in Protestant experience. There have been at least 22 apparitions of Mary that have been officially approved by the Catholic church since 1347 (http://www.apparitions.org/#references).

4) The Catholic church teaches that Mary helped Jesus redeem us from our sins, and is a mediator (mediatrix) between God and man (*Catechism*, 969). Protestants and most Orthodox believe Jesus alone redeemed us from our sins. The Catholic *Catechism* (963) speaks of the "union of the mother with the Son in the work of salvation..." Pope Pius XI said she "participated with Jesus Christ in the very painful act of redemption" *(Explorata Res)*.

5) Catholic popes have often promoted devotion to Mary. Pope John Paul II, for instance, took as his personal Latin motto, "totus tuus", a well-known phrase of devotion to Mary meaning, "I am all yours." [8] His coat of arms had an "M" for Mary, beside a cross. One of the last things he said before he died was, "totus tuus," which was also written on top of his coffin.

6) The Catholic church has officially approved new doctrine about Mary as late as 1950 (her ascension into heaven without dying) and in 1854 (her birth without original sin — the Immaculate Conception). Protestants disagree with both new doctrines. Orthodox leaders disagree with them in part. *(See below.)*

7) Catholic teaching also especially encourages reliance upon Mary when near death (*Catechism*, 2677): "By asking Mary to pray for us, we acknowledge ourselves to be poor sinners, and we address ourselves to the 'Mother of Mercy,' the All-Holy One. We give ourselves over to her now, in the Today of our lives. And our trust broadens further...to surround 'the hour of our death' wholly to her care. May she be there as she was at her son's death on the cross. May she welcome us as our mother at the hour of our passing to lead us to her son, Jesus, in paradise."

Unique Orthodox beliefs about Mary

Orthodox teaching about Mary, while not as pronounced, is still closer to the Catholic than the Protestant.

1) Orthodox use a rosary (a prayer rope with knots instead of beads), but instead of prayers to Mary, they usually pray the Jesus prayer: "Lord Jesus Christ, Son of God, have mercy on me, a sinner." This prayer is repeated

continuously as part of hesychasm. (*See the chapter on hesychasm.*)

2) All personal pronouns regarding Mary are capitalized in the Russian Orthodox Bible, something that is usually done only for God. This is not done in either Catholic or Protestant Bibles.

3) Orthodox doctrine agrees with the Catholic that Mary never committed any sin[9] but it doesn't accept the Catholic doctrine of the Immaculate Conception,[10] (that Mary was conceived in her mother's womb without the stain of original sin).

4) Unlike Catholicism, Orthodoxy believes that Mary died physically (Catholicism teaches that she ascended without dying). However, Orthodox believe Mary nonetheless ascended into heaven, after she was raised from the dead, as Bulgakov notes: "The Church believes that, dying a natural death, she [Mary] was not subject to corruption, but, raised up by her Son, she lives in her glorified body at the right hand of Christ in the heavens."[11]

5) Apparitions by Mary in the Orthodox church are extremely rare. One that is commonly accepted by the Orthodox (but not by the Catholic) allegedly occured in Constantinople in the 10th century. According to Orthodox tradition, Mary appeared in the church at Blachernae Palace, praying for the protection of Christians. Orthodox churches commemorate this with the Feast of the Protection (Pokrov) on Oct. 1. Mary's importance in the Orthodox church is shown in other feasts as well. Of their 12 major feasts, four are for Mary.

The Protestant viewpoint

Protestants find Mary to be a wonderful example of godly Christian character. Many of her statements are still models of Christian virtue today — examples we would do well to follow.

Living in a very strict Middle Eastern culture, the angel of God told her she would be the mother of the Messiah. She faced certain shame, loss of the love of her life, and possibly death as an unwed mother, but she nonetheless agreed: "I am the Lord's servant," Mary answered. "May it be to me as you have said" (Luke 1:38).

However, most Protestants do not venerate or pray to Mary for several reasons — reasons they feel Mary would agree with, from where she is in heaven today:

1) There are no prayers to Mary or veneration of her in the Bible.

2) Devotion to Mary can replace devotion to God.

3) Jesus did not support special honor for Mary.

4) Jesus did not always answer Mary's requests.

5) The ark of the covenant and the woman in Rev. 12 are not Mary.

6) Mary had a normal marriage and other children.

7) The Bible indicates that Mary sinned like all of us.

8) Mary is not the mother of all Christians, nor the queen of heaven.

9) Devotion to Mary arose after the apostles and grew over the centuries.

10) Only Jesus redeemed us from our sins.

First, there are no prayers to Mary or veneration of her in the Bible. There is no place in the Old or New Testament where Christians are found praying to Mary or where they venerate her. If this is an important part of the Christian life, Protestants believe it would be seen in the history of the church recorded in the New Testament.

The fact that it isn't, they believe, shows that it developed after the apostles. For instance, the Hail Mary prayer is not a biblical prayer, Protestants say. The parts of it that are from the Bible are not prayers, but greetings to Mary by her cousin and an angel: "And the angel came in unto her, and said, 'Hail, thou that art highly favored, the Lord is with thee: blessed art thou among women.' And when she saw him, she was troubled ... what manner of salutation this should be" (Luke 1:28-29 KJV).

"And it came to pass, that, when Elisabeth heard the salutation of Mary, the babe leaped in her womb; and Elisabeth was filled with the Holy Ghost: And she spake out with a loud voice, and said, 'Blessed art thou among women, and blessed is the fruit of thy womb'" (Luke 1:41-42, KJV). The only part of the prayer that is a prayer — "Holy Mary, Mother of God, pray for us, sinners, now and at the time of our death" is not in the Bible.

Second, Protestants believe devotion to Mary can create a dependency that takes the place of God, leading to the sin of idolatry. This is illustrated, some Protestants believe, in the Catholic rosary. Of its 165 prayers, 150 are to Mary and only 15 are to God.

Protestants further are concerned that the constant repetition of the Hail Mary prayer (150 times each time the rosary is prayed) falls under Jesus' warning in Matt. 6:7: "And when you pray, do not keep on babbling like pagans, for they think they will be heard because of their many words."

Protestants pray only to God, since Jesus said, "This, then, is how you should pray: 'Our Father in heaven, hallowed be your name...'" (Matt. 6:9. *See the chapter on prayer to saints*.)

This dependency on Mary instead of Christ is illustrated, for example, in the following citations from a book of prophecies reportedly made by Mary, printed by the Marian Movement for Priests (with an imprimatur): "...you must entrust yourselves to me with absolute confidence, you must believe in me and you must let yourself be led by me with docility and filial abandonment..." [12]

Trusting in another to that degree is prohibited by Jer. 17:5: "This is what the LORD says: 'Cursed is the one who trusts in man, who depends on flesh for his strength and whose heart turns away from the LORD.'"

Most Protestants also believe it is difficult to determine when veneration or honor of Mary crosses the line into worship of her (idolatry). To avoid this, Catholic and Orthodox writings use different Greek words to distinguish one from the other. Protestants feel this doesn't help, however, as those words are used interchangeably in the Bible — sometimes meaning worship, sometimes meaning veneration.

For instance, the word *proskunesis* and its verb *proskuneo* mean to bow down or worship. Catholic/Orthodox leaders say this word refers to veneration, and so can be used of Mary and the saints. Although the word is sometimes used of honoring people, in the New Testament the word is used only of worship to God. Rev. 14:7 says, "...Worship (*proskuneo*) him that made heaven, and earth..." The apostle John was rebuked twice by angels for offering them worship (*proskunesis*): "At this I fell at his feet to worship him. But he said to me, 'Do not do it! I am a fellow-servant with you and with your brothers who hold to the testimony of Jesus. Worship God!'" (Rev. 19:10, 22:9. *See also Acts 10:25.*)

Other words used by Catholic/Orthodox theologians to mean only veneration is *dulia* (honor), and the related *hyperdulia*. (great honor). Accordingly, it is taught that one can offer *dulia* to saints and *hyperdulia* to Mary. But this word is also used of God in the Bible (Acts 20:19: "I served the Lord;" Rom. 12:11: "serving the Lord;" Col. 3:24: "It is the Lord Christ you are serving" (*douleuo*).

Accordingly the use of these different words as a defense against idolatry is really no defense at all, many Protestants believe.

The Biola Task Force on Eastern Orthodoxy notes: "Orthodox theologians clearly make the above distinction between the veneration of Mary and the worship of God by the use of these different Greek words (as is done also by Roman Catholics). However, the strong exaltation and veneration of Mary in words and practices raises the question of whether this clear distinction is always made in the minds of the lay worshipers." [10]

Third, Jesus did not support special honor for his mother. This is shown in the one recorded instance of devotion to Mary in the New Testament, shown below: "As Jesus was saying these things, a woman in the crowd called out, 'Blessed is the mother who gave you birth and nursed you.' He replied, 'Blessed rather are those who hear the word of God and obey it'" (Luke 11:27-28). Here Jesus had an opportunity to affirm this woman's devotion to Mary. He could have shown us all that we should honor his earthly mother in a special way. Instead of doing so, he directs our attention to the word of God and away from his mother.

Fourth, Jesus is shown in scripture as publicly refusing to meet with his own mother. This would speak against the argument that Jesus, as an obedient son, would grant any request his mother makes of him (Mark 3:20-21, 3:31-35): "Then Jesus entered a house, and again a crowd gathered, so that he and his disciples were not even able to eat. When his family heard about this, they went to take charge of him, for they said, 'He is out of his mind.'... Then Jesus' mother and brothers arrived. Standing outside, they sent someone in to call him. A crowd was sitting around him, and they told him, 'Your mother and brothers are outside looking for you.' 'Who are my mother and my brothers?' he asked. Then he looked at those seated in a circle around him and said, 'Here are my mother and my brothers! Whoever does God's will is my brother and sister and mother.'"

Fifth, Protestants believe the ark of the covenant and the woman in Rev. 12 do not symbolize Mary. These symbols are often used to teach that Mary is the greatest of humankind, but Jesus said that John the Baptist, not Mary, was the greatest (Matt. 11:11): "I tell you the truth: Among those born of women there has not risen anyone greater than John the Baptist..."

The Bible does not say the ark of the covenant symbolizes Mary. To say that it does is simply a matter of opinion, many Protestants believe.

Further, the ark was lost, and the Bible says it will be forgotten. If the ark represents Mary, then the Bible is saying therefore that she will be forgotten, too, which is very unlikely: "'In those days...' declares the LORD, 'men will no longer say, 'The ark of the covenant of the LORD.' It will never enter their minds or be remembered; it will not be missed...'" (Jer. 3:16)

As to the woman clothed by the sun in Rev. 12, Protestants note that none of the church fathers support the Catholic position. They wrote that she does not represent Mary, but represents the church, those of humankind who are faithful to the Lord, persecuted by Satan. Hippolytus, for instance, writing about 220 A.D., wrote: "By the woman clothed with the sun" he meant most manifestly the Church....The Church, always bringing forth Christ, the perfect man-child of God..." (*Treatise on Christ and Anti-Christ*, 61, as cited by Larry Harper in "The Antichrist" p. 52).

Note also that the passage (see Rev. 12) says, "The woman fled into the desert to a place prepared for her by God, where she might be taken care of for 1,260 days." The "1,260 days" may be the key to understanding this passage. It refers to the three and a half years of the great tribulation of the church described in Daniel 9:27 and Revelation 11:3. (1,260 days is three and a half years, half of seven, or 42 months).

If this interpretation is correct, then this is not a case of Mary hiding three and a half years, of which the Bible says nothing, but it refers to the future of the church during the Great Tribulation.

Noted Bible commentator Albert Barnes writes: "The meaning of the passage before us is ... the true church would not in fact become extinct. It would be obscure and comparatively unknown, but it would still live."

Was Mary a virgin her entire life?

Sixth, most Protestants believe Mary had a normal marriage with several children. The question of Mary's perpetual virginity is not a vital question to many Protestants. However, since it contributes to a false picture of Mary as different from other humans, Protestants note Matt. 1:25, speaking of Mary's husband Joseph: "He had no union with her until she gave birth to a son."

Most Protestants believe that this verse shows that Mary and her husband Joseph had normal marital relations. Indeed, 1 Cor. 7 says that it is wrong to deny normal physical relations in a marriage. Since Joseph was with Mary when Jesus was at the temple as a young man, they had to have been married at least 12 years. The fact that they had a normal marriage is especially shown in the many verses about Jesus' brothers and sisters:

"Then Jesus' mother and brothers arrived..." (Mark 3:31).

"Even his own brothers did not believe in him" (John 7:3-5:).

"...his mother and brothers stood outside, wanting to speak to him..." (Matt. 12:46).

"Now Jesus' mother and brothers came to see him..." *(Luke 8:19. See also John 2:12, Acts 1:14, 1 Cor. 9:4-5, Gal. 1:19, Mark 6:3.)*

The context of these passages, especially those where Mary and Joseph are mentioned, can only be seen in the context of their children, and not someone else's children. Matthew 13:55-56 says: "Is not this the carpenter's son? Is not his mother called Mary, and his brothers, James and Joseph and Simon and Judas? Aren't all his sisters with us?..."

The context of this passage is of a nuclear family — father, mother, brothers and sisters, not cousins. This is further shown in the prophetic Messianic Psalm 69 which Jesus quotes twice in the New Testament as referring to himself (Psalm 69:4, quoted in John 15:25, and Psalm 69:9 in John 2:16-17). In verse 8, between these two citations, Jesus says, "I have become estranged from my brothers, And an alien to my mother's sons." Here Jesus says his mother, Mary, had sons, who were his brothers. Accordingly Mary must have had other children than Jesus.

As to Eze. 44:2, ("This gate shall be shut, it shall not be opened, and no one shall enter by it, for the Lord God of Israel has entered by it...") Protestants do not believe this refers to the eternal virginity of Mary, but it refers to the temple in heaven. Only Christ entered into the sanctuary in heaven to redeem us from our sins, and no one else will ever do so. There is only one savior. "...(Christ) entered the Most Holy Place once for all by his own blood, having obtained eternal redemption." (Heb. 9:12). Accordingly, this verse does not refer to Mary, but to the temple of God in heaven, and to Christ.

Was Mary a sinner?

Seventh, the Bible indicates that Mary sinned like all of us. Scripture shows that "all have sinned" (Rom. 3:23). Eccl. 7:20 says, "There is not a righteous man on earth who does what is right and never sins." Psalm 53:3 says, "there is no one who does good, not even one." 1 Kings 8:46 says, "there is no one who does not sin." This must include Mary or else the Bible is untrue. (Jesus, being God, is not included.)

If Mary never sinned, then she could go to heaven without the sacrifice of Christ for her sins. This would mean she would have attained heaven by obeying the law of the Bible — by keeping God's rules. But the Bible (Gal. 2:16) says, "by observing the law no one will be justified." Gal. 2:21 says, "...If righteousness could be gained through the law, Christ died for nothing!"

Christ is the only way to heaven. Christ himself said, "I am the way, the truth and the life, no one comes to the Father but by me" (John 14:6). If no one goes to heaven without Christ and his payment of our sins with his blood, then that would include Mary.

For instance, Mark 3:21 shows that Mary and Jesus' brothers did not fully believe in Jesus, and thought that "He is out of his mind." Mary accordingly came with Jesus' brothers to get him and forcibly take him home (v. 31). She did not believe in her own son.Rom. 14:23 says, "Whatever is not of faith, is sin." Accordingly, if she did not believe in him, she was sinning. Mary also called God her savior (Luke 1:47). Jesus is the savior of sinners.

As Matt. 1:21 says, "He shall save his people from their sins." If Mary was sinless, she would have needed no savior.

Protestants also note that the idea that Mary was born without a sinful human nature (immaculate conception) was a late addition to Christianity. It wasn't believed by the early church, according to Hassell: "The doctrine of the Immaculate (or Sinless) Conception of the Virgin Mary was broached, about 1140, by certain canons of Lyons, in France. It was opposed by Bernard and Thomas Aquinas and other leading Catholic theologians of the twelfth and thirteenth centuries, as being in conflict with the doctrine of Original Sin; but it was defended by Duns Scotus and adopted by the Franciscans in the fourteenth century, impliedly sanctioned by the Council of Trent in the sixteenth century, and finally affirmed by Pope Pius IX in 1854." [13]

Church fathers who apparently did not believe Mary was sinless include Tertullian, Origen, John Chrysostom and Basil. Origen stated it plainly: "Scripture clearly records that, at the time of the passion, all the apostles were scandalized (e.g., fell away, into sin. See Matt. 26:31). The Lord himself said, 'This night you will all be scandalized.' ... Why do we think that the mother of the Lord was immune from scandal when the apostles were scandalized? If she did not suffer scandal at the Lord's passion, then Jesus did not die for her sins. But, if 'all have sinned and lack God's glory,' but are justified by his grace and redeemed, then Mary too was scandalized at that time." [14]

Tertullian wrote that Mary and Jesus' brothers treated him badly (see Mark 3:20-35): "...While strangers intently listened to him, his very nearest relatives were absent. By and by they turn up, and stayed outside; they do not go in, because, it seems, they did not think much of what was going on inside; nor do they even wait... but they prefer to interrupt him, and wish to call him away from his great work... Now, I ask you, ...would you not have exclaimed, 'What are mother and brothers to me?'...When denying one's parents in indignation, one does not deny their existence, but censures their faults." [15]

Commenting on the same passage, Chrysostom also seemed to believe that Mary had sinned. He wrote that Mary had "superfluous vanity" (pride) when she expected Jesus to stop preaching and come out to see her ("She wanted to show the people that she had power and authority over her Son, not thinking as yet anything great about him..." [16]

St. Chrysostom also wrote the liturgy used in most Orthodox churches. The liturgy is one of the seven sources of Holy Tradition in Orthodoxy, as is the Bible. In it he calls Jesus "the only sinless One." If Christ is the only one who never sinned, then Mary must have been a sinner.

St. Basil, another great church father, believed Mary sinned. Writing in the fourth century, he said Mary was "reached by some doubt" when she saw Christ crucified, and was restored after the resurrection:

"Now every soul in the hour of the passion was subjected, as it were, to a kind of searching. According to the word of the Lord it is said, 'All ye shall be offended because of me.' Simeon therefore prophesies about Mary herself... 'Even thou thyself, who hast been taught from on high the things concerning the Lord, shalt be reached by some doubt....' He indicates that after the offense at the cross of Christ a certain swift healing shall come from the Lord to the disciples and to Mary herself, confirming their heart in faith in him." [17]

Eighth, Protestants don't believe Mary is the mother of all Christians, or the queen of heaven. The only time the phrase "queen of heaven" is used in the scripture is in reference to an idol (Jer. 44:25-27). None of the descriptions of heaven in the Bible show or speak of a queen. The crown of 12 stars on the woman in Rev. 12 likely refers to the crown of righteousness and glory that all believers will wear, since this woman represents the church, the bride of Christ, and not Mary. For insatnce, 2 Tim. 4:8 says: "Now there is in store for me the crown of righteousness, which the Lord, the righteous Judge, will award to me on that day — and not only to me, but also to all who have longed for his appearing." 1 Pet. 5:4 says: "And when the Chief Shepherd appears, you will receive the crown of glory that will never fade away." (See also James 1:12, and Rev. 2:10 and 3:11.)

The Bible also does not say that Mary is the mother of all Christians. When Jesus spoke to John at the cross, "behold your mother" and to Mary "behold your son" he was assigning responsibility for taking care of her to John. He was not saying she is the mother of all Christians. The context makes this clear — Jesus was on the cross, close to death. He was making arrangements for his departure. John 19:26-27 says: "When Jesus saw his mother there, and the disciple whom he loved standing near by, he said to his mother, 'Dear woman, here is your son,' and to the disciple, 'Here is your mother.' From that time on, this disciple took her into his home."

Ninth, Protestants believe devotion and prayer to Mary were not practices of the apostles or the early church. They believe devotion to Mary began later and grew over the centuries. This is evident, they say, by the lack of any devotion or prayer to Mary in the New Testament.

The earliest writings of the church (after the New Testament) also seem to show that devotion to Mary came later.

For instance, the comments of church father Irenaeus, writing in the second century, indicate that the doctrine of Mary's eternal virginity was not one he held. He says Christ was born of "Mary, who was as yet a virgin" (*Against Heresies*, 3:21:10). Similarly, Irenaeus notes in the same chapter that "before Joseph had come together with Mary, while she therefore remained in virginity, she was found with child of the Holy Ghost."

As mentioned above, Tertullian, writing close to the time of Irenaeus, believed Mary sinned. John Chrysostom, writing in the fourth century, felt the same way, as did Origen and Basil.

The development of doctrine about Mary is also shown, many Protestants believe, by the late date of the approval of some of these doctrines. For instance, Catholic leadership officially ruled that Mary was sinless from her conception (Immaculate Conception) in 1854, more than 1,800 years after she was born. The doctrine of the Ascension of Mary into heaven was not formally approved by the Catholic church until 1950.

Similarly, the Hail Mary prayer, received "official recognition ... in its complete form, ... in the Roman Breviary of 1568," according to the *Catholic Encyclopedia*. The earliest reference to a part of the Hail Mary (only the first part) was in 1030. The first official pronouncement of the church promoting the use of the phrase was in 1196, when the bishop of Paris encouraged the clergy to teach the "Salutation of the Blessed Virgin" to their congregations.

Accordingly, Protestants believe that the Hail Mary prayer is not something the apostles prayed or taught, and like many other doctrines on Mary, arose hundreds of years after Christ.

NOTE: It is sometimes mistakenly said that the Hail Mary prayer was composed by the church at the Council of Ephesus in 431 A.D. However, a careful reading of the council shows no reference to the prayer or even part of it, except the three words "Mother of God," which the council ruled could be used to refer to Mary.

Tenth, Protestants believe that only Jesus saved us from our sins, and he is the only mediator between God and man. Although Mary suffered as any mother would when losing a son, her suffering did not help save us. The Bible says we have only one Savior and mediator, not two: "But I am the LORD your God... You shall acknowledge no God but me, no savior except me" (Hos. 13:4). "I, even I, am the LORD, and apart from me there is no savior" (Is. 43:11). " For there is one God and one mediator between God and men, the man Christ Jesus" (1 Tim. 2:5).

In every case where our redemption is shown in the Bible, only God is credited, never Mary. For example:

a) "He himself will redeem Israel from all their sins" (Ps. 130:8).

b) "...who gave himself for us to redeem us from all wickedness" (Titus 2:14).

1) *Orthodox Study Bible* commentary on John 19:25-27

2) Bulgakov, *The Orthodox Church*, p. 116

3) Ware, *The Orthodox Church*, p. 257

4) *Orthodox Study Bible* commentary on Mark 3:31

5) Ware, *The Orthodox Church*, p. 257

6) There is an Episcopalian Society of Mary, but it is not known if it is an approved Episcopalian/ Anglican group.

7) Mary is reported to have appeared in Constantinople at the Blachernae church, coming through the air. She prayed, and then took her veil and spread it over the people (a symbol of protection). In honor of this apparition, the Russian Orthodox Church celebrates the Feast of the Intercession of the Holy Virgin (Pokrov) Oct. 14.

8) It is part of a famous phrase by St. Louis de Montfort. The rest of the phrase is, "and all I have is yours. I welcome you into all my affairs and concerns. Show me your heart, O Mary."

9) Ware, *The Orthodox Church*, p. 259

10) *Eastern Orthodox Teachings in Comparison with the Doctrinal Position of Biola Univ.* (1998)

11) Bulgakov, *The Orthodox Church*, p. 118

12) Gobbi, Don Stefano, *To the Priests: Our Lady's Beloved Sons*, p. 256, 1990, Marian Movement of Priests, St. Francis, Maine 04774.

13) Hassell, C.B. and Sylvester, *History of the Church of God*, ch. 16

14) Origen: *Homilies on Luke; Fragments on Luke*. 17.6) Translated by Joseph T. Lienhard, S.J. The Catholic University of American Press, Washington, D.C. 1996. ISBN 0-8132-0094-6. "The Fathers of the Church: A New Translation", vol. 94

15) *On the Flesh of Christ*, 7

16) *Homilies on Matthew*, 44.

17) Basil the Great, letter 260 (or 259) "To Optimus." 329-379 A.D.

21. PURGATORY:
Does it exist?

As with many other questions in this book, Catholics, Orthodox and Protestant have three answers to the question of purgatory.

Catholic leaders teach that there is a definite place called purgatory, between heaven and hell. Orthodox leaders officially deny belief in purgatory, but in practice they pray for the dead just as Catholics do.

Protestants do not believe that there is a purgatory, mainly because it is not mentioned in the Bible.

The Orthodox and Catholic viewpoint

(Note: for simplicity's sake in this article purgatory will be referred to as an Orthodox belief, as it is in practice if not in name.)

Catholic and Orthodox arguments in favor of purgatory include 1 Cor. 3:9-15, which they believe refers to purification of a believer through suffering in purgatory. The passage was written by the apostle Paul to the church in Corinth, as a defense of his work as an apostle. It reads as follows:

"...No one can lay any foundation other than the one already laid, which is Jesus Christ. If any man builds on this foundation using gold, silver, costly stones, wood, hay or straw, his work will be shown for what it is, because the Day will bring it to light. It will be revealed with fire, and the fire will test the quality of each man's work. If what he has built survives, he will receive his reward. If it is burned up, he will suffer loss; he himself will be saved, but only as one escaping through the flames."

Another verse used to support the doctrine of purgatory is 1 Peter 3:18-20: "For Christ...was put to death in the body but made alive by the Spirit, through whom also he went and preached to the spirits in prison who disobeyed long ago when God waited patiently in the days of Noah while the ark was being built..."

It is argued that this "prison" in which Christ preached is purgatory, and that these disobedient people had a second chance at salvation.

Other verses used to support purgatory include Matt. 5:26-26 (Luke 12:58-59): "Settle matters quickly with your adversary who is taking you to court. Do it while you are still with him on the way, or he may hand you over to the judge, and the judge may hand you over to the officer, and you may be thrown into prison.I tell you the truth, you will not get out until you have paid the last penny." It is argued that this implies that we can pay for our release from purgatory ("prison") by our suffering there.

Also Matt. 12:32: "...anyone who speaks against the Holy Spirit will not be forgiven, either in this age or in the age to come." The argument is that this verse implies that we can be forgiven in the next life, in purgatory.

And Luke 12:47-48: "That servant who knows his master's will and does not get ready or does not do what his master wants will be beaten with many blows. But the one who does not know and does things deserving punishment will be beaten with few blows." This verse is seen as supporting the belief that we will be punished in purgatory.

The Catholic *Catechism* teaches that Christ, Mary and the saints have stored up good deeds in a treasury in heaven that can be used to help persons in purgatory (1476-1478): "We also call these spiritual goods of the communion of saints the Church's treasury ... the infinite value ... which Christ's merits have before God... This treasury includes as well the prayers and good works of the Blessed Virgin Mary... In the treasury, too, are the prayers and good works of all the saints..."

Catholic and Orthodox leaders also look to the apocrypha as a basis for purgatory. 2 Maccabees 12:43-45 says:

"And when he had made a gathering throughout the company to the sum of two thousand drachmas of silver, he sent it to Jerusalem to offer a sin offering,... to pray for the dead. ...Whereupon he made a reconciliation for the dead, that they might be delivered from sin."

Catholics also point to writings of church fathers that support the concept of prayer for the dead or purgatory. In the fourth century Augustine wrote of "those who suffer temporary punishments after death... for to some... what is not remitted in this world is remitted in the next, that is, they are not punished with the eternal punishment of the world to come" (*City of God,* 21.13).

Catholic leaders officially confirmed their belief in purgatory more than a thousand years after the apostles, at the Council in Florence in 1439. This was reaffirmed at the Council of Trent in 1563, as well as at Vatican 1 (1870) and Vatican II (1965). They believe in a cleansing fire that is in proportion to the sins of the person — the more sins, the more suffering in purgatory.

Orthodox doctrine is "not entirely clear and has varied somewhat at different times," according to Orthodox Bishop Timothy Ware.[1] He notes that in the 17th century the Orthodox church position was similar to that of the Catholic church, but he believes the majority of Orthodox today are inclined to reject the idea of suffering in purgatory.

The Orthodox understanding of purgatory includes prayer for the dead while (officially at least) rejecting an atoning fire.

In addition, Catholic/Orthodox doctrine argues for the concept of purgatory because it is a tradition of the church.

The Protestant viewpoint
Protestants do not accept purgatory because the Bible does not mention it, and speaks against the concept of purgatory

Heb. 10:14 says "by one sacrifice he has made perfect for ever those who are being made holy.." Protestants take this to mean that Christians are perfected by Christ alone, not by suffering after death or by the prayers of others. Christ's sacrifice on the cross is sufficient. If suffering in purgatory or the sacrifices of others can help deliver a person from purgatory, then it would not be by "one sacrifice" but by many. Heb. 10:18 says that Christ's forgiveness of our sins eliminates the need for any subsequent payment or suffering: "Now where there is forgiveness of these things, there is no longer any offering for sin." In other words, no suffering in purgatory (or offering) is needed, if we've been forgiven.

The Catholic teaching that there is a treasury of merit in heaven, stored up by the saints to help people in purgatory, is not in the Bible, Protestants note. The parable of the 10 virgins shows that sharing of spiritual merit is not possible: "The foolish ones said to the wise, 'Give us some of your oil; our lamps are going out.' 'No,' they replied, 'there may not be enough for both us and you. Instead, go to those who sell oil and buy some for yourselves.'" (Matt 25:8-9).

The word "purgatory" literally means a place of cleansing. However, 1 John 1:9 (NAS) says, "If we confess our sins, he [God] is faithful... to forgive us our sins and cleanse us of all unrighteousness." Accordingly, if the Lord forgives us and cleanses us when we confess our sins, there is no need for a purgatory after death.

Protestants also believe the example of the thief on the cross contradicts the idea of purgatory (Luke 23:43). He reviled Christ until almost the last moment of his life, but when he repented, Jesus told him, "I tell you the truth, today you will be with me in paradise." Logically, if anyone would be in need of purgatory after death, it would have been this thief, yet he went straight to paradise after death.

Christ's parable of the laborers who worked only an hour (Matt. 20:8-16) additionally supports the idea of complete forgiveness. They received the same pay (symbolizing eternal life) as those who worked the entire day.

This is taken to refer to those who have lived in sin many years but repented late in life. There is no mention of them having to "make up" or compensate for their late repentance. Additionally, Christ's description of hell in Luke 16 refers only to paradise and hell. There is no mention of purgatory. The word purgatory is not in the Bible.

As to 1 Cor. 3:9-15, Protestants believe it refers to the judgment day ("the Day will bring it to light") and not a period of days or years, as would be the case if it was referring to purgatory. On that day the works of Christians will be tested. Note that the test is for the works of each Christian, not for the Christian himself ("the fire will test the quality of each man's work").

The purpose of this testing is to determine the believer's reward ("if what he has built survives, he will receive his reward"). It does not affect his salvation ("he himself will be saved"). There is no mention here of atoning for sins by suffering.

Protestants also don't believe Peter's comments refer to purgatory, when he wrote in 1 Pet. 3:18-20 and 4:6 that Christ preached to the dead. First note that Peter said Christ did not speak to all the dead but only to those "who disobeyed ... in the days of Noah." If he was referring to purgatory, then Christ would have spoken to people who died at other times also. Secondly, many believe Jesus spoke only to the righteous who had died — not the unrighteous in hell.   These people were in the upper half of Sheol or Hades until Christ's resurrection. (Note that the Greek word *Hades* corresponds to the Hebrew word *Sheol*, and simply means the place of the dead or the grave, not necessarily a place of punishment. Gehenna and the lake of fire refer to hell, but Hades simply means the place of the dead.) The people Christ preached to were in paradise, and yet not in heaven, just as is shown in Luke 16 regarding Abraham and Lazarus, comforted in paradise, and yet not seen with the Lord. Christ freed these captives and took them with him when he ascended to the father, as Eph. 4:8 says: "When he ascended on high, he led captives in his train..." This is also shown when Christ said to the thief on the cross, "I tell you the truth, today you will be with me in paradise" (Luke 23:43). And yet, three days later we see when Jesus spoke to Mary after his resurrection that he had not yet been to heaven: "Do not hold on to me, for I have not yet returned to the Father" (John 20:17).

Where had he been then, for those three days, if he was not with the Father? Many believe he was in this upper part of Hades with Abraham, Lazarus and the other righteous ones. It was to the righteous to whom he spoke, not to the unrighteous suffering punishment, because the Bible says no one can leave hell (Luke 16:26): "And besides all this, between us and you a great chasm has been fixed, so that those who want to go from here to you cannot, nor can anyone cross over from there to us."

Christ's preaching in Hades was not a second chance to repent for the wicked, but a proclaiming of the gospel to the righteous.

These righteous men apparently couldn't appear before the Father until the death and resurrection of Christ had occurred, as noted in Eph. 4:8 above.

As to Matt. 5:25-26, Protestants believe it shows we have a debt to God, but one that is impossible to pay back. For instance, there is no chance of earning money while in prison. McGarvey's commentary on this passage notes: "It is intended to teach that men cannot pay their debts to God, and therefore they had better obtain his forgiveness through faith during these days of grace."

Jesus shows how impossible this is in Matt. 18:23-25: "Therefore, the kingdom of heaven is like a king who wanted to settle accounts with his servants. As he began the settlement, a man who owed him ten thousand talents was brought to him. Since he was not able to pay, the master ordered that he and his wife and his children and all that he had be sold to repay the debt."

The man's debt of 10,000 talents is incredibly large. It amounts to at least $57 million in today's money — not the kind of money one could earn while locked up in prison.

Matt. 12:32 also does not support the purgatory doctrine, Protestants believe: ("...anyone who speaks against the Holy Spirit will not be forgiven, either in this age or in the age to come."). It simply says that there is no hope for forgiveness of blasphemy against the Holy Spirit, ever. Indeed, it can just as easily be used to show that there is no forgiveness in the next life.

As to Luke 12:47-48, (the punishment of wicked servants) note that the preceding verse says God's rebellious servants will be assigned "a place with the unbelievers." Unbelievers, of course, go to hell. This verse is therefore about the punishment of hell, not purgatory. Theologian John Gill said this verse "signifies that persons who have light and knowledge...and act not according to them, shall...endure the greatest degree of torments in hell..."

As to the verses in the apocrypha used to support purgatory, Protestants and Jews, of course, reject the apocrypha as not from God. *(See the chapter on the apocrypha.)* The passage mentioned, further, contradicts other passages in the Bible because it implies that forgiveness for sins can be bought.

At least four church fathers (leaders of the church who arose after the time of Christ and the apostles) opposed the idea of purgatory: Clement, Justin Martyr, Tertullian and Cyprian. *(See the chapter on praying for the dead for their statements).*

Misunderstanding

The idea for purgatory may have come from a misunderstanding about the "intermediate state" of people who have died and are awaiting the final judgment of God.

Christians go immediately to heaven (Phil. 1:23, Luke 23:43), and unbelievers go immediately into punishment (Luke 16:22-23, 2 Pet. 2:4,9, Jude 1:6), and yet their final reward or punishment will not be determined until the great white throne judgment of God (2 Cor. 5:10, Acts 17:31, 2 Pet. 3:7, Rev. 20:12).

Some may have mistakenly assumed that while waiting for the final judgment, Christians may atone for their sins or be purified. That is not the case, as we have seen.

The disagreement over purgatory may also have its roots in a misunderstanding of atonement (justification) and sanctification.

Atonement is the payment for our sins, which Christ alone has provided, and which occurs immediately upon repentance for every believer. Sanctification is the process of becoming more like Christ, which continues throughout the life of the believer, and is completed at death.

Christ, who is our high priest, has already atoned for our sins, as is shown in Heb. 10:10-12: "And by that will, we have been made holy through the sacrifice of the body of Jesus Christ once for all. Day after day every priest stands and performs his religious duties; again and again he offers the same sacrifices, which can never take away sins. But when this priest had offered for all time one sacrifice for sins, he sat down at the right hand of God."

In the eyes of God we "have been made holy" — meaning our sins are forgiven. But our minds still need to be renewed, as Paul said in Romans 12:2: "...Be transformed by the renewing of your mind." Note just prior to this passage (Rom. 12:1-2) Paul mentions giving our bodies as a living sacrifice, and our minds (souls) to be renewed, but does not mention our spirits.

This is because those who have repented have already received justification (forgiveness), and our spirits are right before God. Our souls (our minds), however, are still in the process of sanctification. Both atonement and sanctification are shown in Hebrews 10:14: "because by one sacrifice he has made perfect forever those who are being made holy."

The "one sacrifice" of Christ makes us perfect in God's eyes by atoning for our sins, while at the same time we "are being made holy" by the renewing of our minds in the process of sanctification. Notice the words "has made" (past tense) regarding atonement and "are being" (present continuous) regarding sanctification.

How sanctification may be completed

If then, this intermediate state does not involve purification or suffering for sin, how exactly, then, will the process of sanctification be completed?

It may be when we meet the Lord after death, as noted in 1 John 3:2: "Dear friends, now we are children of God, and what we will be has not yet been made known. But we know that when he appears, we shall be like him, for we shall see him as he is."

This transformation is echoed in other passages as well:

Rom. 8:29: "For those God foreknew he also predestined to be conformed to the likeness of his Son...."

1 Cor. 15:49: "And just as we have borne the likeness of the earthly man, so shall we bear the likeness of the man from heaven."

Phil. 3:21: "who, by the power that enables him to bring everything under his control, will transform our lowly bodies so that they will be like his glorious body." (See also 2 Cor. 3:18.)

Too late

Additionally, Protestants are concerned the doctrine of purgatory can mislead sinners into believing that they can atone for their own sins after death in purgatory, and therefore the incentive to repent in this life is removed — they assume they can do it later.

In fact, the scripture shows that only in this life can we repent. In such cases, the doctrine of purgatory gives a dangerously false hope about a place that does not exist.

Protestants note several cases in scripture where it is shown that there is a point when it is too late to repent after death. Among these are the parable of the unwise virgins in Matt. 25, and in the story of Esau in Heb. 12; and of the rich man in hell in Luke 16. *(See the chapter on praying for the dead.)*

---

1) Ware, Timothy, *The Orthodox Church*, p. 259

22. PRAYING FOR THE DEAD:
Does it do any good?

The idea of praying for the dead is another one that divides Christians.

Catholic/Orthodox teaching says such prayers help the dead get to heaven. Most Protestants (except for Anglicans/Episcopalians) believe that they don't help.

Praying for the dead is closely related to the idea of purgatory. *(See the preceding chapter on purgatory).*

The Catholic/Orthodox viewpoint

Orthodox and Catholic doctrine teaches praying for the dead. Muslims and Jews also practice praying for the dead.

The following Orthodox publication notes: "Hymns and prayers at home for the deceased, good deeds done in his memory (charity or gifts to the church) — are all useful for the dead. But especially useful for them is to remember them in the divine liturgy....There is nothing better and nothing greater that we can do for the deceased than to pray for them, remembering them in the liturgy. There have been many appearances of the dead and other events, confirming how useful such remembrances are. Those who have died in repentance, even if they did not show that when they were alive, are freed from suffering and receive peace." [1]

"Some souls, after 40 days, appear in the state of anticipation of eternal joy and blessings, and others tremble in expectation of eternal tortures, which will occur after the Judgment Day (the return of Jesus Christ, when he will judge the living and the dead). But before that it is quite possible to change the fate of souls, especially due to prayers for them by the Church and by good deeds done in memory of the deceased." [2]

The Catholic *Catechism* says prayers for the dead help them:

"Catholics still living can help a deceased loved one in purgatory by saying prayers, giving alms and performing good works (958, 1032, 1475). The Catholic then offers up these meritorious acts for the poor soul in purgatory. The most effective means of helping the dead, says the Church, is the sacrifice of the Mass (1055, 1689). Parishioners can ask a priest to say a Mass for the benefit of a person believed to be in purgatory. Normally a small amount of money accompanies the request." [3]

The Biola Task Force on Eastern Orthodoxy[4] reports: "Orthodoxy universally upholds some notion of prayers for the dead. This belief is logically connected with their view that the ultimate fate of the individual is not determined until the last day of Judgment. Thus, Orthodoxy often emphasizes the individual's ongoing journey of freedom toward or away from the love of God after death. That is, the person still has opportunity prior to final judgment to turn from his or her wickedness and toward God or from justification and away from God."

Asking priests to pray for the dead is usually something for which payment is expected. This payment, along with other means of income such as sales of candles and icons, support the churches in Russia, as they do not believe in tithing. (Some Orthodox churches in the US, however, practice tithing, the giving of 10 percent of one's income to God.) The cost in Moscow for prayer for the dead is usually about 150 rubles for a year ($7).

The importance of such prayers is shown in *Azy Pravoslavia* (Fundamentals of Orthodoxy): "After the death of the body, the soul receives either eternal blessing, or eternal torture. This depends on how he lived his earthly life. But it also depends in no little part on prayers for the deceased." [5]

The Orthodox tradition of praying for the dead involves observing special anniversaries three days, nine days, forty days and every year after his/her death. "On the ninth and fortieth days after death it is necessary to order a panicide — prayers for the forgiveness of the sins of the departed. The fortieth day is especially important, because it is on that day that God's judgment of the departed is completed, determining where he will spend his time until the return of Christ." [6] The origins of such dates are obscure, but they are mentioned as far back as 390 A.D. when the Apostolic Constitutions were compiled:[7]

"Let the third day of the departed be celebrated with psalms, lessons, and prayers — on account of him who arose with the space of three days. And let the ninth day be celebrated in remembrance of the living and of the departed. Do this also on the fortieth day, according to the ancient pattern. For the people lamented Moses in this manner. Also the anniversary day should be kept in memory of him. And let alms be given to the poor out of his goods, for a memorial to him. Now, we say these things concerning the godly. As for the ungodly person — if you gave the whole world to the poor, you would not benefit him at all. For to whom the Deity was an enemy while he was alive, it is certain it will be the same way when he is departed."

By the time of Augustine, prayer for the dead was established: "...In the prayers of the priest which are offered to the Lord God at his altar, the commendation of the dead hath also its place."[8]

Praying for the dead is linked to belief in the communion of the saints.

Orthodox theologian Meyendorff writes: "Prayer for the departed, as well as intercession by the departed saints for the living, express a single and indivisible 'communion of saints.'" Meyendorff says it is not too late for a person to repent even after death. "Man's freedom is not destroyed even by physical death; thus, there is the possibility of continuous change and mutual intercession."[9]

Nonetheless he writes that the Orthodox church does not accept "the notion of redemption through 'satisfaction,' of which the legalistic concept of 'purgatory pains' was an expression."[10]

However, some Orthodox say it is even possible to pray a person, not just out of purgatory (which they technically do not accept) but also out of hell, as Sergius Bulgakov writes: "This offers, consequently, the possibility of liberation from the pains of hell and of passing from an estate of reprobation to that of justification. In this sense it may be asked not if a purgatory exists, but even more if a 'definite hell' exists. In other words, is not hell a sort of purgatory? The Church at least knows no bounds to the efficacy of prayers for those who have quitted this world in union with the Church, and it believes in the effective action of these prayers."[11]

Bulgakov, notes, however, that for those who never were part of the Church, "the church passes no judgment but leaves them to the mercy of God."[11] Regardless of Bulgakov's statement, there is no unanimity among Orthodox about exactly what happens to the deceased after death, or how prayer helps them, according to Bishop Ware: "Orthodox are convinced that Christians here on earth have a duty to pray for the departed, and they are confident that the dead are helped by such prayers. But precisely in what way do our prayers help the dead? What exactly is the condition of souls in the period between death and the Resurrection of the Body at the Last Day? Here Orthodox teaching is not entirely clear, and has varied somewhat at different times."[12]

The Protestant viewpoint

Protestants do not pray for the dead primarily because there is no command or example to do so in the Bible. Jesus never prayed for the dead, nor did any of the apostles.

When Jesus spoke about hell in Luke 16:26 he said it is not possible to leave it, so prayer for people there won't help them: "And besides all this, between us and you a great chasm has been fixed, so that those who want to go from here to you cannot, nor can anyone cross over from there to us."

The Bible stresses that we must repent before death. After that it is too late. Eccl. 12:6-7 warns us to "Remember him— before the silver cord is severed, or the golden bowl is broken; before the pitcher is shattered at the spring, or the wheel broken at the well, and the dust returns to the ground it came from, and the spirit returns to God who gave it."

If there was an additional opportunity to repent beyond the grave, such a warning would be meaningless. The fact that it is in the Bible shows us that death is the closing chapter on a persons' life. Nothing else can be added to it before the judgment. This finality is also shown by Jesus in Luke 13:24-25 when he warned us:

"Make every effort to enter through the narrow door, because many, I tell you, will try to enter and will not be able to. Once the owner of the house gets up and closes the door, you will stand outside knocking and pleading, 'Sir, open the door for us.' But he will answer, 'I don't know you or where you come from.'"

Matt. 25:46 speaks of eternal punishment for the wicked: "Then they will go away to eternal punishment, but the righteous to eternal life."

If indeed it is possible to pray for a person in hell and see them delivered, then their punishment would not be eternal. Esau could not receive the blessing even though he asked for it with tears. It was too late. "Afterward, as you know, when he wanted to inherit this blessing, he was rejected. He could bring about no change of mind, though he sought the blessing with tears." (Heb. 12:17)

So it is with those who die without repentance.

There is a time when it is too late to repent. In Rev. 2:21 the Lord speaks of a false prophet: "I have given her time to repent of her immorality, but she is unwilling." God gives us time to repent. After that it may be too late, "because you did not recognize the time of God's coming to you." (Luke 19:44)

There is a time when God is favorable and a time when that door of favor will be closed. Luke 4:19 and Is. 61:2 both speak of the "year of the Lord's favor."

God sets a time for each of us in this life to repent: "God again set a certain day, calling it Today, when a long time later he spoke through David, as was said before: 'Today, if you hear his voice, do not harden your hearts'" (Heb. 4:7).

Psalms 32:6 says "let everyone who is godly pray to you while you may be found" Is. 55:6 says, "Seek the LORD while he may be found; call on him while he is near." In John 8:21 Jesus told the unbelieving Jews, "...you will look for me, and you will die in your sin. Where I go, you cannot come."

They would seek him in the future but it would be too late. They would die in their sins without repentance, because they had not accepted him at their appointed time.

This is because repentance is a gift of God that he can take back if we reject it. The following scriptures show repentance is a gift from God that we neglect at our peril.

2 Tim. 2:25 says, "Those who oppose him he must gently instruct, in the

hope that God will grant them repentance..."

Acts 11:18 says, "When they heard this, they had no further objections and praised God, saying, "So then, God has granted even the Gentiles repentance unto life."

Notice in both these scriptures repentance is something that is granted us from God. What we do with it is our responsibility. If we reject it, we may never have it again — even in purgatory, as Heb. 6:4-6 says: "It is impossible for those who have once been enlightened, who have tasted the heavenly gift, who have shared in the Holy Spirit, who have tasted the goodness of the word of God and the powers of the coming age, if they fall away, to be brought back to repentance..."

If there are people who can never repent again, it means that it is too late for them. And if it is too late, then there must not be a purgatory where they could repent, and praying for such people after death will not help.

All these scriptures show that there is a time when God cannot be found – a time when it is too late. By contrast, the doctrine of praying for the dead means that there is a chance to repent even after death, that it is never too late. The scriptures show that this is not true.

Another mysterious verse that seems to speak to this issue is Ecclesiastes 11:3b: "Whether a tree falls to the south or to the north, in the place where it falls, there will it lie."

Most theologians take the falling to refer to death, and the direction it falls to refer to where the person goes after death — heaven (north) or hell (south).

Theologian Adam Clarke, in his commentary on this passage, says it means that we should "acquire a heavenly disposition while here; for there will be no change after this life. If thou die in the love of God, and in the love of man, in that state wilt thou be found in the day of judgment. If a tree about to fall lean to the north, to the north it will fall; if to the south, it will fall to that quarter. In whatever disposition or state of soul thou diest, in that thou wilt be found in the eternal world."

Prayer for the dead an unnecessary burden

Protestants additionally feel the doctrines of purgatory and of praying for the dead are not a comfort to grieving relatives, but instead are a burden that God never intended for anyone to bear. For instance, after the death of a relative the surviving family members do not know if the deceased is in heaven, in hell, or in purgatory. If he is in heaven or hell, there is no need to pray for them, since nothing will change. And if they are in purgatory, it is not known when prayers have sufficed to deliver them from there.

Accordingly, Christians could spend many years praying for someone who is either already in heaven or who is eternally in hell. Further, in the case of purgatory, they would be praying, Protestants believe, for deliverance from a place that does not exist. Such Christians would be weighed down with guilt if they do not pray and give enough for the salvation of departed relatives, since few pray as much as they can. Protestants also contend that time spent praying for the dead detracts from prayers for real needs.

Church fathers opposed prayer for dead

Early church leaders (after the apostles) spoke out strongly against the practice of praying for the dead by noting that it is not possible for the dead to repent. Ignatius wrote less than 80 years after Christ: "While yet we have opportunity, [let us] exercise repentance towards God. For in Hades there is no one who can confess his sins." [13]

Justin Martyr said: "It is likely enough that they themselves are now lamenting in Hades and repenting with a repentance that is too late."[14]

Tertullian wrote: "There is not a soul that can at all procure salvation, unless it believes while it is still in the flesh. For it is an established truth that the flesh is the very condition on which salvation hinges."[15]

Cyprian likewise stated: "When once you have departed yonder, there is no longer any place for repentance. And there is no possibility of making satisfaction. Here life is either lost or saved. Here eternal safety is provided for the worship of God and the fruits of faith. Do not let anyone be restrained from coming to obtain salvation either by his sins or by his years. To him who still remains in this world, no repentance is too late."[16]

Note that Cyprian said, "there is no possibility of making satisfaction," meaning prayers or money given by the living cannot help the dead, nor can suffering in purgatory pay for their sins.

Does giving money for the dead help?

The Bible speaks against giving of money for the dead: "No man can redeem the life of another or give to God a ransom for him" (Ps. 49:7). Zeph. 1:18 says, "Neither their silver nor their gold will be able to save them on the day of the LORD's wrath."

The only ransom for a man's soul is the blood of Jesus. 1 Pet. 1:18-19 says: "For you know that it was not with perishable things such as silver or gold that you were redeemed ... but with the precious blood of Christ."

Hosea 13:14 says: "I will ransom them from the power of the grave; I will redeem them from death." Matt. 20:28 (Mark 10:45) says: "The Son of Man did not come to be served, but to serve, and to give his life as a ransom for many." 1 Tim. 2:6: "(Christ) gave himself as a ransom for all men..."

The idea of paying money for prayers for the dead is also not accepted by Protestants, since Jesus said in Matt. 10:8 that Christians should help others without charge: "Freely you have received, freely give."

Additionally Micah 3:11 speaks out against ministry for money: "Her priests instruct for a price, and her prophets divine for money."

Peter in Acts 8:20 followed a similar principle in rejecting money for a spiritual blessing: "May your money perish with you, because you thought you could buy the gift of God with money!"

Although the apocrypha refers to paying money for the dead, Protestants do not accept the apocrypha. *(See the chapter on the apocrypha.)*

1) *U Boga vse zhivi* (With God all are alive), Akafist, p. 19

2) Ibid, p. 17

3) McCarthy, James. G., *The Gospel According to Rome*, p. 95

4) *Eastern Orthodox Teachings in Comparison with The Doctrinal Position of Biola University*

5) *Azy Pravoslavia* (Fundamentals of Orthodoxy), p. 55

6) Ibid

7) *Certain Prayers and Laws,* Book 8, section 4.42, p. 1021 (CD), Ante-Nicene Fathers

8) *On care to be had for the dead*, 3. Moral Treatises, Nicene and Post-Nicene Fathers (p. 985)

9) *Byzantine Theology*, p. 222

10) Ibid, p. 96

11) Bulgakov, Sergius, *The Orthodox Church*, p., 183

12) Ware, Timothy, *The Orthodox Church*, p. 255

13) *Epistle of Ignatius to the Smyrnaeans*, chap. 19, Ante-Nicene Fathers, c. 107 A.D.

14) *Justin's Hortatory Address to the Greeks*, chap. 35, p. 597 (CD), Ante-Nicene Fathers, c. 160 A.D.,

15) *On the resurrection of flesh,* chap. 8, Ante-Nicene Fathers, c. 210 A.D.

16) *Treatises of Cyprian*, 5.25, c. 250 A.D., vol. 5, *Ante-Nicene Fathers.*

23. THE LITURGY:
Is this how we should worship?

Probably nothing is more familiar and more essential in many churches
than the liturgy (or mass as it is called in Catholic churches). Indeed, Orthodox Bishop Timothy Ware counts it as one of the seven sources of the
church's tradition.

A liturgy is a collection of written prayers and unwritten rituals used by
priests before, after and during communion. It is basically a written church
service. Orthodox, Catholic and even some Protestant churches use liturgies
(Episcopalian, Anglican, most Lutheran, etc.).

How the liturgy began

The liturgy used in most Orthodox churches was composed by John
Chrysostom more than 300 years after the time of the apostles.

The Catholic liturgy has evolved over the centuries, and was most
recently changed by Vatican II, which turned the altar around to face the
congregation, and recommended that the liturgy be done in the language of
the local population, and not in Latin. The liturgy is also not the same in each
place (*Catechism* 1203): "The liturgical traditions or rites presently in use...
are the Latin....and the Byzantine, Alexandrian or Coptic, Syrica, Armenian,
Maronite and Chaldean rites."

The trend toward a written liturgy was a gradual process. A major factor
in its development was the naming of Christianity as the state religion of the
Roman empire in the fourth century, as noted in *Eerdman's Handbook to the
History of Christianity* : [1]

"The toleration of Christianity under Constantine produced a few immediate changes...Sunday services became bigger occasions and worship
imported some practices from court ceremonial, such as the use of incense,
the carrying of candles as a mark of honor, and curtaining around the altar
used at the Eucharist. With Christian worship evolving into public ceremonial, there came a move towards fixed, written forms of service. During the
fourth century this change was fairly slow. The catecheses given at Jerusalem
by Bishop Cyril (348-86) and Bishop John (386-417) include fixed wording
but also opportunity for extempore prayer. ....Prominent churches such as
Rome used their power to try to enforce some kind of uniformity, but local
variations continued for a long time....In the East the ritual tended to become
uniform, leaving no room for variation."

This uniformity is surprising given the words of Bishop Ware: [2] "The
Holy Spirit is a Spirit of freedom....Life in the church does not mean the iron-

ing out of human variety, nor the imposition of a rigid and uniform pattern upon all alike, but the exact opposite."

Another possible reason for the development of the liturgy could have been the desire of church leaders to make sure services were properly run, even if the priest were himself an unlearned man. A written order of service obviously has advantages in such a case.

Some Catholic and Orthodox leaders argue that the Bible supports the use of liturgies, noting that a related word is used three times in the New Testament (*leitourgeo*).

The Protestant viewpoint

Some Protestant churches, as mentioned, use liturgies. Most do not, however, for the reasons cited below:

1) Many liturgies are in a language people don't understand. The Russian Orthodox Church uses Old Church Slavonic instead of Russian, the Greek Orthodox Church uses Ancient Greek, and some Catholic Churches use Latin, all of which are often not understood by the worshippers. The apostle Paul said, "in the church I would rather speak five intelligible words to instruct others than ten thousand words in a tongue" (1 Cor. 14:19). "Unless you speak intelligible words with your tongue, how will anyone know what you are saying? You will just be speaking into the air." (1 Cor. 14:9). Unless a person can understand the language of a service, they cannot be "transformed by the renewing of (their) mind" (Rom. 12:2).

2) Repetitious prayers are discouraged by Jesus in Matt. 6:8: ""And when you pray, do not keep on babbling like pagans, for they think they will be heard because of their many words."

Jesus did teach a written prayer in the following verse: "This, then, is how you should pray: 'Our Father in heaven, hallowed be your name...'"

The fact that the prayer does not have an ending in the Bible is seen by some to mean that it is to be used as a framework or model to start our prayers, rather than one we should repeat without modification.

Insincere repetition of words is also discouraged in Is. 29:13: "The Lord says, "These people come near to me with their mouth and honor me with their lips, but their hearts are far from me." From these scriptures, we can conclude that written prayers are not wrong, if they are sincere and from the heart.

3) An unwritten, spontaneous church service (e.g., without a liturgy) is shown in 1 Cor. 14:26, with no mention of written prayers (Amplified Version): "What then, brethren, is [the right course]? When you meet together, each one has a hymn, a teaching, a disclosure of special knowledge or information, an utterance in a strange tongue or an interpretation of it."

This scripture implies a small meeting in which everyone is encouraged to participate ("each one"). It seems very similar to a cell group or a house church. Such meetings, while spontaneous, are to be orderly, as Paul notes in the same chapter: "Let everything be done decently and in order." A spontaneous service is also shown in Acts 13:2, where the Holy Spirit told them to ordain Paul and Barnabas, something they apparently had not expected. In a written church service, this would not have been possible.

4) The Bible also indicates a central role to preaching in church services. For example, when preaching in Troas (Acts 20: 7-12), Paul preached until midnight to the point that one young person fell asleep and fell out the window! Paul raised him from the dead, then continued preaching until dawn. The importance of preaching is also shown in 2 Tim. 4:1-2: "In the presence of God and of Christ Jesus, ...I give you this charge: Preach the word, be prepared in season and out of season, correct, rebuke and encourage with great patience and careful instruction."

5) Christians who do not use liturgies note that liturgies are a relatively new arrival, not being found in the New Testament.[3]

6) The New Testament verb that is related to liturgy, *leitourgeo*, is defined by Strong's as "to perform religious or charitable functions (worship, obey, relieve)" and is generally translated as minister (serve). The context of the passages in which it is used do not support the use of a written church service. In fact, a liturgy could not have been used, especially in Acts 13:2, because the Holy Spirit spoke spontaneously to those gathered in prayer in the form of a personal prophecy to Paul and Barnabas. Such spontaneity is not possible in a written church service. The three times the verb is used in the King James it is always translated as minister (Acts 13:2, Rom. 15:27, Heb. 10:11). The NIV translates it respectively as "worshipping", "shares" and "offers."

In conclusion, then, many Protestants believe the New Testament pattern of the apostles for a church service is much more spontaneous than the ones we have today, with wider participation, use of the gifts of the Spirit, in the language of the people, and with an emphasis on preaching.

Reform of the liturgy

Several efforts have been made by Orthodox, Catholic and Protestant churches to renew or reform the liturgy.

Certainly one of the most well-known is the change in the liturgy in the Catholic church after Vatican II, as previously mentioned.

Protestant churches that have liturgies and have reformed or modernized them include the United Presbyterian church (1977), the Lutheran Church in the United States (1978) and the Episcopalian church (1979).

Orthodox Bishop Ware notes that a liturgical reform movement has also been active in Orthodox churches: "Certainly the Orthodox Church, as well as the west, stands in need of a Liturgical Movement; indeed, some such movement has already begin in a small way in several parts of the Orthodox world (revival of congregational singing; gates of the Holy Door left open in the Liturgy; more open forms of iconostases, and so on.)" [4]

Many Christians have alternatively organized their own prayer groups outside of the regular liturgy. This leaves the liturgy unchanged while allowing the spontaneity and Spirit-led worship that so many seek.

These meetings are often held at night in homes or rented halls. The

Catholic, Orthodox and Protestant renewal movement has for years provided Spirit-led meetings based on 1 Cor. 14:26, while encouraging prayer group members to remain in their churches and renew them from within.

To date, this movement has not had as much of an impact in Orthodox churches as it has in Catholic and Protestant churches, but movements are active, including the "Zoe" movement in Greece, the "Lord's Army" in Romania, and the "Orthodox Brotherhood of Saint Simeon the New Theologian" in the United States, led by Greek Orthodox Archimandrite Eusebius Stephanos, an evangelical charismatic priest.[5]

---

[1] p. 147-148

[2] Ware, *The Orthodox Church,* p. 246-247

[3] A word in Acts 13:2 is translated as "liturgy" in one Catholic translation but in all other translations as "ministered." . The word is translated as "minister" in Rom. 15:27, Heb. 10:11

[4] Ibid, p. 279

[5] Clendenin, Daniel, *Eastern Orthodox Christianity,* p. 12

24. THE SEVEN CHURCH COUNCILS:
Were they infallible?

The seven ecumenical church councils were a series of meetings of bishops of the church, held from 325 A.D. until 787 A.D. to resolve religious contro-versies.

Catholics, Orthodox and Protestants in general accept the rulings of the first six councils. There are major differences, however, on why they accept the rulings, explained below, and complete disagreement on the seventh council.

The first six councils dealt primarily with the nature of Christ, while the seventh required the use of icons and the relics (body parts) of dead saints.

The Orthodox/Catholic viewpoint

First, Orthodox and Catholic leaders say the Bible shows church councils were used by the early church (Acts 15). In this council the church resolved a controversy, and the council's pronouncement was accepted by the church as from God.

Accordingly, many believe that we must also accept the seven church councils, since the principle of a divinely inspired church council is laid down in the Bible.

Second, Orthodox/Catholic doctrine teaches that when a church council is properly convened, the result is always perfect, because God protects the council from error.

This, they say, is what Christ meant when he said, "I will build my church, and the gates of hell shall not prevail against it" and "for where two or three come together in my name, there am I with them." (Matt. 16:18, 18:20).

Orthodox leaders view the seven councils as equal to scripture, as if they were added to the Bible, according to Bishop Ware. "The doctrinal definitions of an Ecumenical Council are infallible. Thus in the eyes of the Orthodox Church, the statement of faith put out by the seven councils possess, along with the Bible, an abiding and irrevocable authority."[1]

Similarly the Catholic church writes: "The infallibility promised to the Church is also present in the body of bishops....above all in an Ecumenical Council" (*Catechism*, 891).

Third, Orthodox and Catholics say a church council established which books would be included in the New Testament. *(See the chapter, "The Bible: Who gave it to us?")* Since Protestants accept the results of this council, it is argued, then they must also accept the results of later councils, or they are being hypocritical.

Lastly, accepting the seven councils is not optional to the Orthodox or Catholic believer. It is required, because both churches accept them as infallible and divinely inspired. The seventh council report says any who reject its report are put under anathema (cursed to hell).

According to Orthodox theologian Sergius Bulgakov, denial of the seven ecumenical councils "would be truly in contradiction — direct or indirect — with the profession of faith which is the foundation stone of the Church: 'You are the Christ, the Son of the living God' "[2]

The Protestant view of ecumenical councils

The Protestant position is well put by the Biola report on Eastern Orthodoxy:[3] "While conservative Protestants do respect and even endorse the conclusions of at least certain of the ecumenical councils (particularly Nicea 325 and Chalcedon 451), they do not regard these as infallible or inspired. Protestants accept conciliar decisions only in so far as they reflect Scripture, which alone is infallible and inspired. Therefore, even where Protestants agree with a conciliar decision, they still do not regard such decisions as inspired, infallible, or inerrant any more than they would attribute such properties to their own confessions of faith."

Specific Protestant concerns with the doctrine of conciliar infallibility are listed below:

First, two identically convened councils (in 754 A.D. and 787 A.D.) contradicted each other. If God is obligated to protect the councils from error, then he failed since these two had opposite viewpoints on the question of icons. One forbid Christians to use icons, and the other required them. They cannot both be right.

Since the council outlawing use of icons was in effect for 34 years, the church was in error at least 34 years, or the Catholic/Orthodox churches are in error now. Either way it can be said with certainty that at least one of the councils was wrong. This, therefore, proves the doctrine of infallible councils false.

Similarly, there were six synods of the Orthodox church on the issue of hesychasm in the 14th century. *(See the chapter on hesychasm.)* Four ruled in favor of hesychasm and two were against it. If church councils are infallible, such contradictory rulings would not be possible.

People are sinful and make mistakes. In the same way their councils will make mistakes, since they are made up of people.

Second, the example in Acts 15 of a church council simply establishes that a church council can help resolve disputes; it does not go so far as to say that these councils will never err. To say that it does is to fall under the apostle Paul's admonition: "Do not go beyond what is written" (1 Cor. 4:6). Protestants note that there is no verse in scripture that guarantees that council decisions will always be correct.

Third, even though Christ is present when the church is gathered, it can still make mistakes. In Rev. 2:14-15 and 2:20 the Lord rebukes the churches for doctrinal errors. The Bible says, "we all make many mistakes" (James 3:2 RSV).

Fourth, the scripture that the "gates of hell will not prevail" against the church means the church will overcome the defenses of hell, but is no guarantee that the church will be without sin or error. *(See the chapter "THE CHURCH: Can it be wrong?")*

Fifth, Protestants accept some councils and reject others based on what the Bible says, not because of tradition. (It should be noted that Orthodox and Catholic leaders also reject some of the councils, such as the ecumenical council outlawing icons in 754 A.D. and the synods against hesychasm in the 14th century.)

The council approving the books of the New Testament is accepted by Protestants simply because it confirmed the de facto practice of Christians. *(See the chapter "THE BIBLE: Who gave it to us?")*

Similarly, some of the councils are accepted by Protestants because their decisions are in keeping with scripture and the witness of the Holy Spirit, not because the rulings came from a council. *(See the chapter, "THE BIBLE: Who has the right to interpret it?")*

Sixth, some actions of Catholic/Orthodox leaders imply that they also may not believe the councils are infallible. For instance, Canon 20 of the first ecumenical council forbids kneeling on Sundays in church. This rule is obviously not kept today. Canon 16 of the seventh council forbids clergy from wearing expensive clothes, but many patriarchs and bishops, for instance, wear robes with silver and gold woven into the fabric, and jewels. The Council of Trent (fourth session) also ruled that all persons who don't accept the apocrypha as part of the Bible will go to hell (anathema). The seventh ecumenical council ruled that those who don't venerate icons will go to hell (*Decree of the Ecumenical Synod*). If this was the case it would be expected that warnings would be issued to the millions who don't use the apocrypha or icons. The fact that these rulings are not put into practice seems to imply that the councils' rulings are not really believed to be infallible.

Lastly, Protestants don't accept the seven councils as infallible as that would make them equal to scripture, and would in effect be adding to God's words. Prov. 30:6 says, "Do not add to his words, or he will rebuke you and prove you a liar." Protestants believe the Bible alone is the "inspired, inerrant, infallible, and absolutely authoritative rule of faith and practice" as noted in the Biola Report on Eastern Orthodoxy.

Why Protestants reject the seventh council

Protestants don't believe that church councils are infallible, but they are especially concerned with the seventh council. Protestants don't accept this council, which required the use of icons in 787 A.D., for several reasons.

1) The council's ruling goes against biblical teaching on icons *(see the chapter on icons)* and on relics *(see the chapter on relics)*.

2) The council contradicted a previous council ruling made just 34 years earlier.

3) The council was not a free and open discussion, called and led by the church. Instead it was called and controlled by the emperor. The scriptural model for church councils in the book of Acts gives only the church the right to call a council. Protestants accordingly question whether a church council controlled by a secular ruler should be accepted as from God. *(See below.)*

4) The council wasn't ecumenical as not a single western bishop attended, and the churches in Charlemagne's empire in Western Europe rejected the council. (Two men attended as representatives of the pope — no others from Western Europe were there.)

5) The council ruled against the supremacy of scripture over tradition, going against Jesus' statement in Mark 7 that scripture is more important than tradition. The council cursed those who hold scripture above tradition: "Anathema to those ...taking as a pretext ... that unless we were evidently taught by the Old and New Testaments, we should not follow the teachings of the holy fathers and of the holy ecumenical synods, and the tradition of the catholic church."

6) The council called Mary "ever virgin" going against scriptures that show Mary had a normal married life and had other children: Matt. 12:46, Luke 8:19, John 2:12.

7) The Catholic and Orthodox churches in practice ignore the seventh council's ruling that all those who don't venerate icons will go to hell. This very serious pronouncement is rarely or never acknowledged today. This shows doubt about the reliability of the council's condemnation to hell (anathema) of those who do not venerate icons.

To understand how the council could have made so many errors it is necessary to look at how the council was called and run.

Fortunately, history provides detailed information on this controversial seventh council. Excerpts below are from the 1899 issue of "The Seven Ecumenical Councils of the Undivided Church," edited by Henry R. Percival, included in Nicene and Post-Nicene Fathers, series 2, vol. 14, p. 1276ff:

History of the seventh council

By the time of the council, the Roman empire had ended. In the west Rome was under the influence of Charlemagne's empire. In the east, Muslims had conquered most of the former Roman and Byzantine empires. The Greek-speaking Byzantine empire was a shadow of itself, clinging to part of what is now Turkey. The emperor of this little area was Constantine, who was only 10 years old. He ruled under the regency of his mother, Irene.

It had been 34 years since the council condemning the use of icons, but the issue was still a hot one. There was division in the empire, with the monasteries for icons and many government officials and the army against them. Queen Mother and Regent Irene ordered a council to be convened expressly for the purpose of overthrowing the decision of the ecumenical council condemning icons.

Because of fear of forces opposed to this change, she moved the location of the council from the original planned site of Constantinople to Nicea.

Her letters make it clear that it was not going to be an impartial review of the previous council's ruling, but that it would overturn it. She wrote the pope saying, "..... Your paternal blessedness knows what hath been done in times past in this our royal city against the venerable images, how those who reigned immediately before us destroyed them and subjected them to disgrace and injury: ...and how they seduced and brought over to their own opinion all the people who live in these parts — yea, even the whole of the East...."

Although Irene was later canonized for her actions (made a saint), history shows her to not have been very saintly. In coming years, after her son had formally taken the throne, she forcefully took the throne back, and ordered him to be blinded. (See *Encyclopedia Britannica*.)

In her letter to the pope, Irene continued by asking him to "make no delay, but come up hither to aid us in the confirmation and establishment of the ancient tradition of venerable images. It is, indeed, incumbent on your holiness to do this..."

Note her phrase: "confirmation and establishment of the ancient tradition of venerable images" (icons) and the phrase "it is incumbent" (required). The queen mother is making it clear that she expects the council and the pope to rule in favor of icons.

Percival notes that the pope was hoping to have certain lands in southern Italy that were under Irene's authority and the eastern church restored to him. He was hoping by cooperating in this case to get those lands back. In the end, he did not succeed.

In the statement read to the bishops at the opening of the council, Irene noted that she had "caused you, his most holy priests, to meet together ..."

The council then opened with three bishops confessing publicly that they were wrong to have opposed icons at the previous council, in a scene reminiscent of the Stalin show trials. The presentation of these bishops as the first order of business seems to have been intended to sway other bishops who were not yet convinced.Bishop Basil of Ancyra , the first of the three, started by issuing a curse on those opposed to icons: "Anathema to those who do not salute the holy and venerable images. And if at any time ...I shall be opposed to what I have now professed, may I be anathema from the Father, the Son and the Holy Ghost..."

Basically, Basil took an oath of self-condemnation, which is forbidden in the Bible. In James 5:12 the Bible says: "Above all, my brothers, do not swear—not by heaven or by earth or by anything else. Let your 'Yes' be yes, and your 'No', no, or you will be condemned."

Basil was followed by two other bishops who similarly turned publicly from the decision of the previous council and asked to be forgiven. Then a letter from Pope Hadrian to the emperor was read: "If the ancient orthodoxy be perfected and restored..., and the venerable icons be placed in their original state, ..., your most pious and heaven-protected name likewise will be set forth as that of another Constantine and another Helena...."

It is interesting to review what has happened so far: first, the bishops were commanded to attend, then heard a letter from the emperor clearly telling them to approve icons, then three bishops start off the program confessing their "sin" against icons and cursing those opposed to icons, and then the pope weighs in to support the emperor.

Everyone knew from the opening bell that this question was already settled. Debate would be useless....even perhaps dangerous, since the Empress Irene, the pope and some bishops were supporting the change.

The seventh council is evidence of how church councils are no guarantee of infallibility. If they are not called in accordance with scripture, and are unduly influenced, then the results will be wrong. This is particularly the case when they are called by the government (not the church) and controlled by the government, like the seventh council, with a conclusion that had been agreed upon before the bishops ever met.

---

1) Ware, Timothy, *The Orthodox Church*, p. 202

2) Bulgakov, *The Orthodox Church*, p. 29

3) *Eastern Orthodox Teachings in Comparison with The Doctrinal Position of Biola University*

25. THE CHURCH FATHERS:
Did they agree?

The early church fathers were prominent church leaders who lived in the first few centuries after the apostles. Since these men lived closer to the time of the apostles, their writings are seen by Catholic/Orthodox leaders as authoritative in determining what we should believe today. The writings of the fathers are often used to support Catholic and Orthodox teachings.

Protestants, while valuing their writings as helpful, do not consider them to be authoritative, and do not rely upon them as a source of doctrine. Instead they rely upon the Bible, and only accept writings of the church fathers that don't contradict the Bible.

The Orthodox church counts the church fathers' writings to be one of its authoritative sources of doctrine, alongside the Bible, the ecumenical councils, icons, the liturgy, and canon law, as Orthodox Bishop Ware has noted. The Catholic Council of Trent in 1546 also emphasized the church's reliance upon the church fathers. It ruled that all Catholics must "never accept nor interpret it [Holy Scripture] otherwise than in accordance with the unanimous consent of the Fathers." This decision was upheld by Vatican I in 1870.

Protestants do not accept the writings of the church fathers as authoritative for several reasons.

First, elevating these writings to be equal with scripture is like adding books to the Bible. The Lord forbids this. In Deut. 4:2 the Lord says not to "add to what I command you nor subtract from it." 1 Cor. 4:6 tells us "not to go beyond what is written." Prov. 30:6 says "Do not add to his words, or he will rebuke you and prove you a liar."

Second, Protestants consider the New Testament to a better source of doctrine than the church fathers. Most church fathers wrote several hundred years after the apostles, and so they may have drifted from the example set by them. Even church father Irenaeus criticized those who said the apostles "preached before they possessed 'perfect knowledge,' as some dare to say, boasting themselves as improvers of the apostles." [1]

Third, the church fathers cannot be relied upon because they often contradicted each other. Here are some examples:

BIBLE SUPERIOR TO TRADITION:
Gregory of Nyssa was for it: "...We make the Holy Scriptures the rule and the measure of every tenet; we...approve that alone which may be made to harmonize with the intention of those writings." [2]
Origen was against it: "...That alone is to be accepted as the truth which

differs in no respect from ecclesiastical and apostolic tradition."[3]

INFANT BAPTISM:

Tertullian was against it: "...The delay of baptism is preferable. This is particularly true in the case of little children....Let the children come when they are growing up."[4] Cyprian was for it: "Nobody is hindered from baptism...How much more should we shrink from hindering an infant."[5]

FATE OF UNBAPTIZED INFANTS:

Augustine said they are under God's wrath: "..surely [infants] who have lacked the sacrament [of baptism] ... shall not have life, but the wrath of God abideth on them."[6] Gregory of Nazianzus said they are not punished. "Others are not in a position to receive it [baptism], perhaps on account of infancy... [They] will be neither glorified nor punished by the righteous Judge..."[7]

COMMUNION SYMBOLIC:

Clement of Alexandria said it was symbolic: "...the Lord...brought this out by symbols when he said, 'Eat my flesh and drink my blood,' describing distinctly by metaphor the drinkable properties of faith."[8] Justin Martyr said it was not: "We do not receive these as common bread and common drink.... The food which has been blessed by the prayer of his word...is the flesh and blood of that Jesus who was made flesh."[9]

SALVATION BY FAITH ALONE:

Clement of Rome was for it: "We are not justified by our own works, but by faith."[10] Lactantius was against it: "The spirit must earn immortality by works of righteousness."[11]

PRAYER FOR DEAD:

Cyprian was against it: "When once you have departed yonder, there is no longer any place for repentance...no possibility of making satisfaction."[12] Augustine was for it: "...In the prayers of the priest which are offered to the Lord God at his altar, the commendation of the dead hath also its place."[13]

MARY SINLESS:

Origen was against it: " If she did not suffer scandal at the Lord's passion, then Jesus did not die for her sins. But, if 'all have sinned and lack God's glory,'..., then Mary too was scandalized."[14] Ambrose (possibly) was for it: "She was a virgin not only in body but also in mind,...stained... by no guile..."[15]

---

1) *Against the Heresies*, chap. 1.1

2) *On the Soul and the Resurrection*, Philosophical Treatises, p. 439 (CD — p. 859)

3) *Origen de Principiis*, preface (2). Ante-Nicene Fathers, c. 225 A.D.

4) *On Baptism*, chap. 18, Ante-Nicene Fathers, c. 198 A.D.

5) *Epistles of Cyprian*, 58.5, Ante-Nicene Fathers, c. 250 A.D.

6) *Merits and Forgiveness of Sins and On the Baptism of Infants*, chap. 28, p. 167, Anti-Pelagian Writings, Nicene & Post-Nicene Fathers

7) *Oration 40*, chap. 23, Ante-Nicene Fathers
8) *The Instructor (Paedagogus)*, chap. 6, Ante-Nicene Fathers
9) *Of the Eucharist*, First Apology of Justin, chap. 66. Ante-Nicene Fathers
10) *Epistle to the Corinthians*, chap. 32.
11) *The Divine Institutes*, book 4, chap. 25., and book 7, chap. 5.
12) *Treatises of Cyprian*, 5.25, c. 250 A.D., vol. 5, *Ante-Nicene Fathers*.
13) *On care to be had for the dead*, 3. Moral Treatises, Nicene &Post-Nicene Fathers (p. 985)
14) *Homilies on Luke*, 17.6
15) *Concerning Virgins*, 2.7

26. Concise Comparison of Catholic, Orthodox and Evangelical Protestant Beliefs

	CATHOLIC	ORTHODOX	EVAN. PROTESTANT
Water baptism	Infant	Infant	Believer
	Saves us	Saves us	Symbolic
Salvation	Faith + Works	Faith + Works	Faith
	Process	Process	Event + Process
Church government	Pope/Hierarchy	Patriarchs/Hierarchy	Various
Purgatory	Yes	Yes; undefined	No
Apocrypha	Yes	Yes (4 extra books)	No
Bible interpretation	Only church leaders	Only church leaders	Individual believer
Tradition	Superior to Bible	Superior to Bible	Inferior to Bible
Priesthood	Can forgive sins	Can forgive sins	Can't forgive sins
	Elite	Elite	All believers priests
	Mediator	Mediator	Christ only mediator
Communion	Literal blood/body	Literal blood/body	Symbolic
	Needed for salvation	Needed for salvation	Not needed for salvation
	Age 7	Baptized infants	Believers only
	Wafer in wine	Bread/wine mixed	Various
Confession	Priest only	Priest only	Any believer
Holy Spirit	At confirmation	At infant baptism	Believer only
Icons/Statues	Must venerate	Must venerate	Forbidden
Prayer to saints	Yes	Yes	No
Prayer for dead	Yes	Yes	No
Mary	Co-redemptrix	Special intercessor	No
	Sinless	Sinless	Sinner
	Eternal virgin	Eternal virgin	Had normal marriage
	Hail Mary	Jesus prayer	No Hail Mary prayer
	Immac. Conception	No Immac. Conc.	No Immac. Conc.
	Never died	Died	Died
	Many apparitions	Few apparitions	No apparitions
True Church	Catholic	Orthodox	All believers
Hesychasm	No	Yes	No
Filioque	Yes	No	Yes/unimportant
Theosis	Yes/No	Yes	No
Rapture	Post-Trib	Post-trib	Pre or Post-trib
Calvinism	Free-will	Free-will	Free-will or Calvinist
Homosexuality	Sinful	Sinful	Sinful

27. HOLY AND UNHOLY PLACES:
Where should we meet?

Can a Christian church meet in any place? Or must it be sanctified?

Often people ask how Protestant Christians can have church services in places that are not holy or sanctified, such as movie theaters.

Protestants point to Matt. 18:20, "For where two or three are gathered together in My name, there am I in the midst of them."

Protestants believe this means that what sanctifies a church service is not the place or the building it is held in, but the presence of Christ in the midst of the believers.

The Bible also says that Christians are the temple of God, and not buildings: "Don't you know that you yourselves are God's temple and that God's Spirit lives in you?" (1 Cor. 3:16. See also 1 Cor. 6:19 and 2 Cor. 6:16)

In John 4:20-24 Jesus had a discussion with a Samaritan woman, who was disputing with Jesus about whether it was more proper to worship God at a Samaritan mountain or in Jerusalem. Note that Jesus emphasized that true worship has nothing to do with the location of the worship, but with the spirit of the believer:

"...A time is coming when you will worship the Father neither on this mountain nor in Jerusalem....the true worshippers will worship the Father in spirit and truth, for they are the kind of worshippers the Father seeks. God is spirit, and his worshippers must worship in spirit and in truth.""

It is interesting to note that the temple of God built at Jerusalem was destroyed in 70 A.D., and has never been rebuilt.

Many Protestants think that this is because God wants to show us that we can worship him anywhere, as long as we are gathered in his name, and he will be with us, even if we are surrounded by evil, such as in a prison. For example, the Bible shows that an angel of God appeared twice to the apostles in prison. (Acts 5:19 says, "But during the night an angel of the Lord opened the doors of the jail and brought them out." See also Acts 12:7.)

It is a wonderful thing, of course, to have a building dedicated to the use of God, where believers may pray seven days a week. But often that may not be possible. That is why it is important to know that we do not have to have a special building in order to worship God or be in his presence.

The Bible shows that early Christians met in many places.

These include a school (Acts 19:9, "the lecture hall of Tyrannus"), Jewish synagogues (18:4, 26, 19:8), the Jewish temple (Acts 3:1), and (primarily) in private homes. (Acts 2:46, 5:42, 18:7, Philemon 1:2, Col. 4:15, Rom. 16:5, and 1 Cor. 16:19: "Aquila and Priscilla greet you warmly in the Lord, and so does the church that meets at their house.")

Evangelistic meetings recorded in the Bible were held outside by a river (Acts 16:13), to a crowd on the street (Acts 2:14), and in the public market (Acts 17:17). There is no record in the Bible of the early Christians ever meeting in a church building they constructed for that purpose. And yet the first century church was the strongest the church has ever been in terms of holiness, miracles and church growth.

28. APOSTOLIC SUCCESSION:
Is there such a thing?

Several Christian denominations — Catholic, Orthodox, Anglican and some Lutheran — hold to the theory of apostolic succession. The theory says that only those who can trace their ordination back to the apostles can serve as priests, bishops or ministers. Most Protestants don't accept the theory and say that the Bible doesn't require it to be a minister.

In its most strong form, apostolic succession teaches that those who don't have it can't baptize, serve communion or ordain others, and lack the anointing of the Holy Spirit.

The Catholic *Catechism* (77) reads: "In order that the full and living Gospel might always be preserved in the Church the apostles left bishops as their successors. They gave them their own position of teaching authority.... to be preserved in a continuous line of succession until the end of time." The *Catechism* (862) says "the bishops have ... taken the place of the apostles ... whoever listens to them is listening to Christ and whoever despises them despises Christ..." The Catholic church sometimes refers to apostolic succession as "apostolicity."

The Greek Orthodox Church defines apostolic succession as: "The direct, continuous, and unbroken line of succession transmitted to the bishops of the church by the apostles. ...The duties and powers given to the apostles ...are transmitted ...to the bishops and priests..." [1]

Without apostolic succession, a minister or priest cannot transmit the gifts of the Holy Spirit, according to Orthodox theologians. Bulgakov writes: "the abolition of the apostolic succession in Protestantism... has deprived the Protestant world of the gifts of Pentecost... Christ... has established ...recognized modes for the reception of the Holy Spirit... These modes are the sacraments of the Church administered by a priest of the apostolic succession".[2]

The Orthodox/Catholic viewpoint

Catholic and Orthodox church arguments for the theory of apostolic succession are:

1) Jesus gave authority to Peter and the apostles, who transferred that authority to their successors.

2) The church fathers consistently taught the theory.

The scripture most often cited is Matt. 16:18-19, where Jesus spoke to Peter saying: "And I tell you that you are Peter, and on this rock I will build my church, and the gates of Hades will not overcome it. I will give you the keys of the kingdom of heaven; whatever you bind on earth will be bound in heaven, and whatever you loose on earth will be loosed in heaven."

It is argued that Christ gave the keys to eternal life to Peter and built his church on him. Those who succeeded Peter are said to have these keys and his authority. Those who cannot prove their "link" with Peter therefore lack the grace he received from Christ.

The writings of the church fathers consistently support the theory of apostolic succession. In 180 A.D. Irenaeus wrote: "It is necessary to obey the presbyters who are in the church — those who, as I have shown, possess the succession from the apostles." [3]

The Protestant viewpoint

Most Protestants do not accept the theory of apostolic succession for at least nine reasons, listed below:

1) There is no verse showing a transferrable apostolic anointing in scripture. Jesus' statement in Matt. 16:19 giving Peter the keys does not say that Peter could or would pass this authority on to others. The verse uses a singular Greek pronoun (you). In other words, these keys were only for Peter. Peter used them to open the gospel to the Jews by his sermon in Acts 2, and to the Gentiles by his sermon in Acts 8. Once the gospel was opened to the Jews and the Gentiles it did not need to be opened again. There is no need for apostolic succession to redo what has already been done.

2) When Christ said he would build his church upon the rock, he was not referring to Peter. In the original Greek the word for Peter's name is "Petros," which is a masculine name meaning small rock. The word translated "rock" here is "petra" which is a feminine word and not a name at all. It means "massive bedrock" — the kind of foundation that you build a house on if you want it to last. You don't build a house on a small rock, but you do build it on bedrock. So what does the "bedrock" represent, since it clearly doesn't represent Peter? Protestants believe that it represents Christ, for the Bible says, "No other foundation can anyone lay than that which is laid, which is Jesus Christ." (1 Cor. 3:11). 1 Cor. 10:4 says "that rock was Christ." The Greek uses the same word as Matt. 16:19 ("petra" and not "Petros.") Therefore the church is not built on Peter, but on Christ.

3) Several church fathers agreed that this scripture does not refer to Peter: Chrysostom, in his 55th Homily on Matthew, said, "On this rock I will build my church. That is to say, on the faith of your confession. And what was the confession of the Apostle? Here it is: 'Thou art the Christ, the Son of the living God.'" Cyril spoke similarly in his Book IV on the Trinity: "I believe that by the rock you ought to understand the unchanging faith of the apostles."

4) The chain of apostolic succession has been broken. Church history shows that many false church leaders were appointed by kings, communists, czars or dictators who wanted someone whom they could control. These leaders were often not Christians, as can be shown in their lives and the histories of the churches. If an unbroken chain of succession is needed to guarantee the validity of church leaders, there would be none. The chain was broken every time ungodly leaders worked their way into the church, which has happened many times in the last 2,000 years. This tendency of ungodly men to take positions of church authority was noted as early as 390 A.D. in the *Apostolic Constitutions*: "If any bishop, or even a presbyter or deacon, obtains that office through money, let him and the person who ordained him be deprived. And let him be entirely cut off from communion...If any bishop uses the rulers of this world and by their means comes to be a bishop of a church, let him be deprived and suspended...."[4] Specific examples of when this "chain" of apostolic succession was broken include:

• The abolishing of the Russian patriarchate in 1700 by Peter the Great, and naming of a synod to lead the church, appointed by the czar. This government-appointed leadership endured for 200 years until the Russian revolution. All bishops and priests appointed by this non-church leadership therefore would have questionable "apostolic succession" and so would all ordained by them and their successors up to the present day.

• Communist interference with church leadership occurred throughout Eastern Europe in the 20th century, in Catholic, Protestant and Orthodox denominations. Many of the original Christian leaders were arrested, tortured or shot, and those acceptable to the party were put in their places.

• Certain Catholic popes were not Christians, as is evident from their lives. These included Alexander the VI (1431-1503), who *Encyclopedia Britannica* calls "corrupt, worldly and ambitious". He fathered several illegitimate children and was involved with several assassinations. Another was Urban VI, who had "some of his unbending cardinals tortured to death."[6]

• The establishment of three different popes in 1409: the French pope at Avignon, the Italian pope in Rome, and the pope elected by the Council of Pisa (Alexander V).[7]

In these cases and in many others, it can be shown that those ordained by such men would not have received any apostolic succession, nor would any who were ordained by their successors in the coming centuries.

5) The Bible shows that people can be used of God without apostolic succession. In Gal. 1:1 it says, "Paul, an apostle, sent not from men nor by man, but by Jesus Christ and God the father."

Paul explains further in Gal. 1:15: "But when God, who set me apart from birth and called me by his grace, was pleased to reveal his Son in me so that I might preach him among the Gentiles, I did not consult any man, nor did I go up to Jerusalem to see those who were apostles before I was, but I went immediately into Arabia and later returned to Damascus. Then after three years, I went up to Jerusalem to get acquainted with Peter and stayed with him fifteen days. I saw none of the other apostles, only James the Lord's brother."

Jesus addressed apostolic succession in Mark 9:38-39. (See also Luke 9:50.)   "'Teacher,' said John, 'we saw a man driving out demons in your name and we told him to stop, because he was not one of us.' 'Do not stop him,' Jesus said. 'No-one who does a miracle in my name can in the next moment say anything bad about me, for whoever is not against us is for us.'"

It is clear that the apostles had not ordained or authorized this man to serve as a minister, but Jesus did not stop him, despite the complaints of the apostles.

King David is another example where God used people as priests and ministers who had no right to that ministry, according to the rules.

David offered sacrifices to God even though he was not a priest and not of the tribe of Levi — he was from the tribe of Judah. 2 Samuel 24:25 says "David built an altar to the LORD there and sacrificed burnt offerings and fellowship offerings. Then the LORD answered prayer on behalf of the land, and the plague on Israel was stopped."

Only priests from the tribe of Levi had the right to offer sacrifices, as the Lord said to Aaron in Numbers 18:6-7: " I myself have selected your fellow Levites ... to do the work at the tent of meeting. But only you and your sons may serve as priests in connection with everything at the altar and inside the curtain." Lev. 17:3-4 adds: "Any Israelite who sacrifices an ox, a lamb or a goat in the camp or outside of it instead of bringing it to the entrance to the tent of meeting to present it as an offering to the LORD in front of the tabernacle of the LORD— that man shall be considered guilty of bloodshed; he has shed blood and must be cut off from his people." These verses seem contradictory. In one, David, who is not a priest nor from the tribe of Levi, offers a sacrifice that is pleasing to God. In the others, God says that only a priest from the tribe of Levi can offer a sacrifice.

These verses show the difference between the old covenant of priests and human succession, and the new covenant of the Holy Spirit whereby God chooses men and anoints them with the Holy Spirit, apart from any human succession. Christ himself is a symbol of that, in that he is our high priest, although he was never of the tribe of Levi, but was a descendant of David from the tribe of Judah. Heb. 7:14 says, "For it is clear that our Lord descended from Judah, and in regard to that tribe Moses said nothing about priests."

Heb. 7:16 says the call of God to ministry is not based on concepts such as apostolic succession, but on holiness: "One who has become a priest not on the basis of a regulation as to his ancestry but on the basis of the power of an indestructible life."

Heb. 5:4 says, "No one takes this honor upon himself; he must be called by God, just as Aaron was." It is this call of God on a person's life that qualifies him to be a priest or minister, not the approval of a human authority. The Holy Spirit chooses those who are to minister.

If, however, apostolic succession can't show which leaders are from God, how can we find out which ones are?

Jesus said we would know them by their fruit (the good or bad that they do): "Watch out for false prophets...By their fruit you will recognize them.

Do people pick grapes from thornbushes, or figs from thistles?...Not everyone who says to me 'Lord, Lord' will enter the Kingdom of Heaven, but only he who does the will of my father who is in heaven" (Matt. 7:15, 16, 21).

A true Christian will walk in the fruit of the spirit: "The fruit of the spirit is love, joy, peace, patience, kindness, goodness, faithfulness, gentleness and self-control" (Gal. 5:22-23).

In addition, as mentioned above, true Christian leaders must speak in accordance with the Bible (Isaiah 8:20, Matt. 15:3,6).

6) Apostolic succession adds a condition to salvation. Since Orthodoxy and Catholicism teach that salvation without the sacraments is not possible, and since the sacraments cannot be administered without a bishop with apostolic succession, the theory adds a condition to salvation that is contrary to scripture. Biola University's report states: "Orthodoxy's strong position on apostolic succession and the place of the bishop as the 'fountain of all the sacraments' entails that the ecclesiastical hierarchy is a necessary instrument in transmitting ...salvation." [5]

7) The hierarchy implied in apostolic succession is absent in scripture. For example, Peter, who is held to be the founder of apostolic succession, was not the leader of the church council in Acts 15 — James was. Peter was also publicly rebuked by Paul in Gal. 2:11 — not the kind of treatment you would expect of a man who was supposedly the main leader of the church. "When Peter came to Antioch, I opposed him to his face, because he was clearly in the wrong."

Paul referred to three leaders in Gal. 2:9, and Peter was listed second: "James, Peter and John, those reputed to be pillars, gave me and Barnabas the right hand of fellowship when they recognized the grace given to me. They agreed that we should go to the Gentiles, and they to the Jews."

Paul disdained the idea of hierarchical leadership in Gal. 2:6: "As for those who seemed to be important—whatever they were makes no difference to me; God does not judge by external appearance—those men added nothing to my message."

The hierarchical system created by the theory of apostolic succession is also not supported by the writings of the early church. Church members had the right to remove ungodly leaders, and leave churches ruled by ungodly leaders. This was a more democratic form of church government than is practiced today in churches holding to apostolic succession. Cyprian, writing in 250 A.D., said "....People...should separate themselves from a sinful prelate. They should not associate themselves with the sacrifices of a sacrilegious priest. This is especially so since they themselves have the power of either choosing worthy priests or of rejecting unworthy ones." [6]

8) Many churches can claim apostolic succession. Ordaining of elders by the laying on of hands was initiated by the apostles in Acts 6:6. Since that time many thousands or perhaps millions have been ordained into the ministry. It has spread far beyond the boundaries of any one church; no single church or denomination can claim that only its elders have had hands laid on them in link with the apostles. Apostolic succession is claimed by the Catholic churches, the Orthodox churches, the Episcopalian/Anglican churches and the Lutheran churches.

9) Laying on of hands has no relation to the theory of apostolic succession. There is a spiritual blessing to the laying on of hands, but that blessing is from the Holy Spirit, and has nothing to do with the theory of apostolic succession. Laying on of hands is used to transmit the power of the Holy Spirit for healing (Mark 6:5, 8:23, 16:18, Luke 4:40, 13:13), for the baptism of the Holy Spirit (Acts 8:17, 19:6), gifts of the Holy Spirit (1 Tim. 4:14, 2 Tim. 1:6), for deliverance (Luke 13:11-13), for blessing (Matt. 19:13) and for ordination (Acts 6:6, 13:3, 1 Tim. 5:22).

Scripture does not require that ordination should be done by bishops or apostles: Paul received an appointing as a missionary in Acts 13:1-3 that was not by the apostles: "In the church at Antioch there were prophets and teachers: Barnabas, Simeon called Niger, Lucius of Cyrene, Manaen (who had been brought up with Herod the tetrarch) and Saul. While they were worshiping the Lord and fasting, the Holy Spirit said, 'Set apart for me Barnabas and Saul for the work to which I have called them.' So after they had fasted and prayed, they placed their hands on them and sent them off."

---

1) *A Dictionary of Orthodox Terminology*, Part 1, Fotios K. Litsas, Ph.D., from http://www.goarch.org/en/ourfaith/articles/article8049.asp
2) Bulgakov, Sergius, *The Orthodox Church*, p. 43-44
3) *Against the Heresies*, Book 4, chap. 26.1, p. 1026 (CD), Ante-Nicene Fathers
4) *Ecclesiastical Canons of the Holy Apostles*, Book 8, 47.30, Ante-Nicene Fathers
5) *Eastern Orthodox Teachings in Comparison with The Doctrinal Position of Biola University*
6) *Eerdmanns' Handbook to the History of Christianity.*", p. 329
7) Ibid
8) *Epistles of Cyprian*, 67.3, p. 802 (CD), Ante-Nicene Fathers

29. PRIESTS:
Can they forgive sins?

Should Christian ministers be pastors or priests? And can priests forgive sins? These questions divide Protestants on the one hand and Catholics and Orthodox on the other.

Catholic/Orthodox teaching says that Christian leaders should be priests — meaning they have the power to forgive sins, perform transubstantiation, and serve as mediators between God and man.

Protestants believe that ministers have none of these powers, but primarily serve as preachers of the gospel and leaders of the churches.

Catholic/Orthodox doctrine says priests should be called father and wear special clothes. Evangelical Protestants say ministers should not be called father or even priest, and don't need special clothes.

Catholic priests must never marry. This is also forbidden to all Orthodox bishops and monks, and to some priests as well. Protestants ministers are allowed to marry. *(See the chapter on celibacy.)* Clearly the three churches have major differences about the role of Christian ministers.

The Catholic viewpoint

Catholic leaders say Christ established a New Testament priesthood when he implemented communion as a church ritual:

The Catholic *Catechism* (611, 1337) says "By doing so, the Lord institutes his apostles as priests of the New Covenant: 'For their sakes I sanctify myself, so that they also may be sanctified in truth'" (John 17:19).

The Catholic Council of Trent ruled that when Christ commanded the apostles to observe communion until his return he "constituted them priests of the New Testament."

Catholic doctrine teaches that only priests can serve communion (*Cat-*

echism 1411): "Only validly ordained priests can preside at the Eucharist and consecrate the bread and the wine so that they become the body and blood of the Lord." Only priests can forgive sins in Christ's name, or give the sacrament for healing of the sick — last rites (*Catechism* 1495, 1530).

Priests have tremendous power according to this teaching: "Priests have received from God a power that he has given neither to angels nor to archangels... God above confirms what priests do here below" (*Catechism*, 983). "Bishops and priests...have the power to forgive all sins...." "In danger of death, any priest....can absolve from every sin and excommunication" (*Catechism* 1461,1463).

The *Catechism* (1493) also says that priests are essential for forgiveness of sins: "One who desires to obtain reconciliation with God and with the Church, must confess to a priest all the unconfessed grave sins he remembers after having carefully examined his conscience."

(It should be noted that the *Catechism* (903) states that lay persons (non-priests) can in unusual circumstances administer baptism and communion: "When the necessity of the church warrants it, and when ministers are lacking, lay persons, even if they are not lectors or acolytes, can also supply for certain of their offices, namely, to exercise the ministry of the word [preach], to preside over liturgical prayers, to confer baptism, and to distribute holy communion in accord with the prescriptions of law.")

The Orthodox viewpoint

Orthodox teaching is not as uniform as Catholic teaching when it comes to forgiveness of sins by a priest. Some, like respected Orthodox church father John Chrysostom, say that the priest actually forgives sins. Others take care to say that it is God who forgives the person, and the priest is only a witness. These differences are shown in the somewhat different statements used by Russian and Greek Orthodox priests for absolution.

In the Russian version, the priest says, "May our Lord...forgive you... all your transgressions, and I, an unworthy priest, by the power that is given to me by him, forgive and absolve you from all your sins in the name of the Father, and of the Son and of the Holy Spirit."

In the Greek version, the priest says, "May God....through me a sinner, pardon you everything in this world and cause you to stand uncondemned before his awful tribunal."

Writing in the fourth century, Chrysostom strongly supported the theory that priests can forgive sins:[1] "...What priests do here below God ratifies above, and the Master confirms the sentence of his servants. ...He says, "Whose sins ye remit they are remitted, and whose sins ye retain they are retained." What authority could be greater than this,...without which it is not possible to obtain ... our own salvation......Our priests have received authority to deal, ...with ...spiritual uncleanness — not to pronounce it removed after examination, but actually and absolutely to take it away."

Some modern Orthodox leaders also believe it is impossible to be saved without a priest: "The most important thing in salvation is the presence of a pastor, a priest. Without a priest, the salvation of a man is impossible. When Christ, following his resurrection, appeared to the disciples behind closed doors, he said, 'Peace to you.' then he breathed on them and said, 'Receive the Holy Spirit. To whom you forgive sins, they are forgiven' (John 20:22-23)...In that moment, the Lord gave his church by means of the 12 apostles the authority to forgive and remove sins, which is to complete all sacraments."[2]

Confession to a priest is considered essential to salvation by some Orthodox leaders: "If your confession was not read or heard, it means that your sins remain on you," according to Russian Orthodox Archimandrite Amvrosi.[3]

Orthodox writer Fr. Mikhail Shpolyanski similarly notes: "Some ask, 'But why is it necessary to confess in front of a priest, specifically in the setting of a church sacrament?'...To wash away uncleanness, it is necessary to have an external source of clean water, and the cleansing water for the soul is the grace of God, and the source of that water is the Church of Christ, and the process of cleansing is the sacrament of confession."[4]

Other Orthodox writers, like Fr. Paul O'Callaghan, do not put the authority of the priest on such a high level: "...The Orthodox Church does not view the priest as the minister of confession. The confession is made TO GOD, and GOD alone grants forgiveness....Christ exercises his ministry to the Church through the ministry of the priesthood....He absolves and remits sins through the absolution of the priest...It is not the priest exercising an autonomous power he has received from God, but Christ exercising his ministry through the priest."[5]

Besides John 20:23, Catholic and Orthodox leaders support priestly absolution from Jesus' comment to Peter giving him the keys of the kingdom of heaven: "And I tell you that you are Peter... I will give you the keys of the kingdom of heaven..." (Matt. 16:18-19). This authority, it is held, has been passed down for centuries to subsequent bishops and priests. *(See the chapter on apostolic succession.)*

The Protestant viewpoint

Protestants do not accept the priesthood for seven reasons:

1) God has abolished the Old Testament high priesthood and replaced it with the high priesthood of Jesus.

2) Under the new covenant all Christians serve as priests to God, offering him sacrifices of praise and prayers.

3) No one has the power to forgive sins except God.

4) Christians have no spiritual fathers, teachers or masters except God.

5) Baptism, communion and confession are not exclusive powers of priests. Any godly Christian can perform them.

6) A priest has no special powers to mediate between others and God.

7) Christians can minister to others without apostolic succession, since this theory is not in the Bible.

First of all, Protestants say there are no human high priests anymore,

because God has abolished that priesthood and replaced it with the eternal high priesthood of Jesus. Heb. 7:11 says, "If perfection could have been attained through the Levitical priesthood...why was there still need for another priest to come — one in the order of Melchizedek, not in the order of Aaron?"

The new priest in the order of Melchizedek, of course, is Christ (Heb. 5:6-7). The abolition of the old priesthood is shown as follows: "For when there is a change of the priesthood, there must also be a change of the law" (Heb. 7:12). "The former regulation is set aside because it was weak and useless, for the law made nothing perfect, and a better hope is introduced, by which we draw near to God" (Heb. 7:18-19). "When he said, 'A new covenant,' he has made the first obsolete..." (Heb. 8:19).

The abolition of a special class of priests is also shown in other New Testament passages. For instance, priests are not listed in 1 Cor. 12:28-30:

"And in the church God has appointed first of all apostles, second prophets, third teachers, then workers of miracles, also those having gifts of healing, those able to help others, those with gifts of administration, and those speaking in different kinds of tongues...."

Similarly, in the list of different types of church leaders in Eph. 4:11-12 there is no mention of priests: "It was he who gave some to be apostles, some to be prophets, some to be evangelists, and some to be pastors and teachers...."

The temporary nature of the Old Testament covenant and the priesthood is shown also in Heb. 9:9-10: "This is an illustration for the present time, indicating that the gifts and sacrifices being offered were not able to clear the conscience of the worshiper. They are only a matter of food and drink and various ceremonial washings— external regulations applying until the time of the new order."

As if to emphasize this new order, the Lord had the temple destroyed 40 years after Christ was crucified and resurrected, and it has never been rebuilt. The offerings that priests made there are no longer possible. A Muslim mosque now sits on the site.

Second, Protestants believe that under the new covenant all Christians serve as priests to God and each other.

The apostle Peter wrote to the early church: "You ...are ... a holy priesthood, offering spiritual sacrifices acceptable to God through Jesus Christ" (1 Peter 2:5). "But you are ...a royal priesthood..." (1 Peter 2:9).

Other scriptures also show this priesthood of all believers: "You have made them to be a kingdom and priests to serve our God, and they will reign on the earth" (Rev. 5:10). "Blessed and holy are those who have part in the first resurrection.... They will be priests of God and of Christ and will reign with him for a thousand years" (Rev. 20:6).

This change in the priesthood was prophesied in the Old Testament: "You will be for me a kingdom of priests and a holy nation" (Ex. 19:6).

"And you will be called priests of the LORD, you will be named ministers of our God" (Is. 61:6). Protestant theologian Robert Brown notes that the priesthood of the believer "does not mean that 'every man is his own priest.' It means the opposite: 'every man is priest to every other man.' ... It is sometimes charged that the Reformers dragged the priesthood down to the level of the laity...Actually... they raised the laity up to the level of the priesthood, and ... restored the long-neglected New Testament conception of 'the priesthood of all believers.'"[6]

Third, Protestants do not believe priests have the power to forgive sins — only God does. Christians confess their sins to God, and so are forgiven: "Then I acknowledged my sin to you and did not cover up my iniquity. I said, 'I will confess my transgressions to the LORD' — and you forgave the guilt of my sin" (Ps 32:5).[7]

What then, did Jesus mean in John 20:23 when he said that the disciples could forgive sins?

First Protestants note that this verse was addressed to all the disciples, not just the apostles, priests or ministers. In Luke 24:33 the parallel passage spoke of "the Eleven and those with them," meaning everyone there received this power. All Christians today have the same Holy Spirit as they received then.

Second, the unique wording in this passage means we as Christians don't forgive or retain others' sins, we just confirm what God has done already.

Since all Christians serve as priests to God, they can do this with the help of the Holy Spirit.

To illustrate, in the Old Testament (Lev. 13) when a person was healed of leprosy (i.e., symbolizing spiritual uncleanness or sin) he was to go to the priest who would examine him and then pronounce him clean, if he was. The priest did not make the man clean or unclean – he simply confirmed what God had already done or not done.

In the same way the literal wording used by Jesus in John 20:23 implies confirmation of forgiveness, not the granting of it. In the original Greek, Jesus did not say, "If you forgive anyone his sins, God WILL forgive them." He said instead, "If you forgive the sins of any, they HAVE BEEN forgiven (NASB)."[8] In other words, a believer confirms something that already exists. They are forgiven (or not forgiven) already. Priests do not force God to forgive the person. This distinction is important, for without it, man would be in the position of being God, and God would be our servant, like a magical genie fulfilling our every command. Certainly this is not right. Note that before Jesus gave this power of confirming forgiveness, he gave the Holy Spirit.

In the same way, Christians today are priests of God who examine people, and with the confirmation given them by the Holy Spirit as priests of God, say if they have or have not been forgiven. Just as the priest looked for healthy flesh, they look for the evidence of a healthy life – sincere repentance, faith, and a love for God, and finding that with the witness of the Holy Spirit, they pronounce the person forgiven.

This is well illustrated when the prophet Nathan pronounced David forgiven: "Then David said to Nathan, 'I have sinned against the LORD.' Nathan replied, 'The LORD has taken away your sin. You are not going to die'" (2 Samuel 12:13). Nathan did not forgive David — God did. But Nathan sensed through the Holy Spirit that David had sincerely repented and that God had already forgiven him, so he told him so.

Note also the case of Peter's comments to Simon the magician (Acts 8:22): "Repent of this wickedness and pray to the Lord. Perhaps he will forgive you for having such a thought in your heart."

If the apostles had the power to forgive sins, then Peter's statement to Simon the magician makes no sense – Peter could have just said, "I forgive you." Instead he said, "Perhaps (God) will forgive you."   This is because believers can only confirm forgiveness that God has already granted.

Any believer can do this with the Holy Spirit's help. If only priests could do it, one would expect that the Bible would say that we should go to priests for this. However, there is no place in scripture where Christians are commanded to confess their sins to priests. James 5:16 says, "Confess your sins to each other..."

Jesus confirmed that only God can forgive sins when he healed the paralytic in Luke 5:20-25:

"When Jesus saw their faith, he said, 'Friend, your sins are forgiven.' The Pharisees and the teachers of the law began thinking to themselves, 'Who is this fellow who speaks blasphemy? Who can forgive sins but God alone?' Jesus knew what they were thinking and asked, 'Why are you thinking these things in your hearts? Which is easier: to say, 'Your sins are forgiven,' or to say, 'Get up and walk'? But that you may know that the Son of Man has authority on earth to forgive sins....' he said to the paralyzed man, 'I tell you, get up, take your mat and go home.' Immediately he stood up in front of them, took what he had been lying on and went home praising God."

By this healing Jesus proved that he had the power to forgive sins. This therefore proved that he was God to the Jews, as they knew (and had just said) that only God can forgive sins.

Fourth, Christians have no spiritual fathers, priests, or masters except God. Jesus said: "But you are not to be called 'Rabbi,' for you have only one Master and you are all brothers. And do not call anyone on earth 'father,' for you have one Father, and he is in heaven. Nor are you to be called 'teacher,' for you have one Teacher, the Christ. The greatest among you will be your servant" (Matt. 23:8-11).

Note that this is not a prohibition against using the word father, as it is used several times in the New Testament, nor does it prohibit us from calling someone teacher or master. Jesus is only saying not to make of any man our spiritual master, father or teacher, taking the place of God.

However, one might ask how that can be, since Heb. 13:17 says, "Obey your leaders and submit to their authority"?

The Bible establishes human authority, but limits that authority.

For instance, the apostles in Acts 5:27-29 rebelled and disobeyed the legal and spiritual authority of the nation, the Sanhedrin council.

Note that the Sanhedrin was filled with priests and other highly educated spiritual leaders, and was led by the high priest. One would think that the apostles would have to submit to such a group. But Peter and the apostles told them: "We must obey God rather than men!"

Here Peter sets up a higher authority than that of spiritual leaders – God himself. And obviously, Peter and the apostles reserved to themselves the right to determine God's will. They didn't give this right to the Sanhedrin, and didn't submit to their authority, even though they were leaders. Instead, they obeyed Jesus' command to make no man (or men) their spiritual masters, teachers or fathers.

In addition, the definition of leaders in the Bible is much broader than the priesthood (1 Cor. 16:15-16): "You know that the household of Stephanas were the first converts in Achaia, and they have devoted themselves to the service of the saints. I urge you, brothers, to submit to such as these and to everyone who joins in the work, and labors at it."

Note here that the submission is not to priests. (The word priests is not used of Christian leaders in the New Testament at all.) The word says to submit to "everyone who joins in the work."

A leader, therefore, is anyone who "joins in the work, and labors at it." In this case, it refers to everyone in the family of Stephanas. This very likely included women and young people. Obviously this is far from what some consider priests.

Therefore this submission has nothing to do with the theory of apostolic succession or the priesthood. It simply means that we should give deference to those who are working in the gospel, and do what they say as long as it does not violate our consciences or the word of God.

The independence of each believer, the right to discern the truth as he or she sees fit, is a scriptural principle. Theologian Albert Barnes (*Barnes Notes on the New Testament*, 1872, New York) in his commentary on Acts 5:27-29, says believers should submit to their leaders in, first, "those things which God has positively commanded—which are always to be obeyed," and secondly, those things "which have been agreed on by the society as needful for its welfare...unless they violate the rights of conscience" and lastly, submit when there is no violation of an "express Divine command" in "matters of convenience; things that tend to the order and harmony of the community."

Many Protestants believe that official Orthodox and Catholic doctrine inadvertently sets up priests to be spiritual masters over other Christians. Things essential to eternal life in Orthodox/Catholic teaching like the eucharist, confession and baptism are all controlled by priests. *(See the chapters on communion and baptism.)* Priests, therefore, under this system theoretically can control the salvation of others by denying communion, baptism or forgiveness.

Fifth, any godly believer can baptize, serve communion or hear confession. For instance, the Ethiopian eunuch was baptized by Philip, who was only a deacon, and not an apostle, elder, pastor or priest (Acts 6:5, 8:1, 8:38).

The apostle Paul was baptized by Ananias, who the Bible simply calls a man, not a priest, elder, pastor or deacon (Acts. 9:10-18). Jesus never baptized anyone (John 4:2), and the apostle Paul rarely baptized others (1 Cor. 1:14, 17), apparently leaving this job to other believers. There is no scripture showing that baptism must be performed by priests or pastors.

In the same way, there is no scripture saying that communion can only be offered by certain leaders. There is also no scripture saying that only priests or pastors can hear confession.

James 5:16 says each believer should hear the confessions of other believers: "Therefore confess your sins to each other and pray for each other so that you may be healed.."

Church father Gregory Nazianzen, writing in the fourth century, said that anyone can baptize (40th Oration, 26, p. 715): "...And so anyone can be your baptizer; for though one may excel another in his life, yet the grace of baptism is the same, and any one may be your consecrator who is formed in the same faith."

Sixth, Protestants feel a priest has no special powers to mediate between others and God.

There is no longer a need for a priest to intercede for us in the Holy of Holies, as Christ has opened the way to us to God by his sacrificial death. That is why the veil of the temple was torn in two by God at the moment when Christ died: "With a loud cry, Jesus breathed his last. The curtain of the temple was torn in two from top to bottom" (Mark 15:37-38).

The removal of this separating curtain between us and God is also why Heb. 4:15-16 says we can come "boldly" before God's throne to ask things of him – the blood of Jesus the high priest has made atonement for us.

There is no longer a need for priests to mediate between God and man – Christ our high priest has done that and is continually doing that.

The idea of two classes of Christians, one of priests, and the other of laymen, is against what Christ said when he said "you are all brothers" (Matt. 23:8).

Matthew Henry commented that: "Christ only is our Master, ministers are but ushers in the school....School fellows are brethren, and, as such, should help one another in getting their lesson; but it will by no means be allowed that one of the scholars step into the master's seat, and give law to the school."

Priests are not a special class of Christian who control the destiny of others, nor does God listen to priests or ministers more carefully than to other men.

Of course, if a minister/priest is living a life especially full of faith, he can believe God for more than can a man who is full of doubt. This, however, has nothing to do with his being a priest — any Christian can do the same.

In the sense of praying for others, we are all like mediators. There is no special power of mediation to priests. But in the sense of satisfying the justice of God, there is only one possible mediator — Christ. 1 Tim. 2:5

says, "For there is one God and one mediator between God and men, the man Christ Jesus." Only he, by his own blood, could satisfy the justice of God. No other mediator could. And on that basis "he always lives to intercede for" Christians (Heb. 7:25).

The unique mediation of Christ means that there is no one else who can bring peace to this situation — no one else can satisfy the justice of God. No good deed we do, nor any good deed by others, is good enough to mediate between God and man. All intercession for others to God, therefore, has its basis in the one unique mediation of Christ. We all must go through him. No priest or pastor has any way of interceding for us if it is not in the name of Christ, who said, "I am the way, the truth and the life. No one comes to the Father except by me" (John 14:6).

Seventh, Christians can minister to others without apostolic succession, since this theory is not in the Bible. *(See the chapter on apostolic succession.)*

---

1) *The Priesthood,* book 3, part five (p. 80), N&PNF, p. 80

2) *O vere i spasenii* (About Faith and Salvation)", p. 95, Archimandrite Amvrosi (Yurasov)

3) Ibid, p. 153

4) p. 24-25, *Kak pregotovitsa k ispovedi* (How to prepare for confession)," Fr. Mikhail Shpolyanski, publisher "Otchi Dom," Moscow (2001)

5) "The Cathedral Messenger", by V. Rev. Paul O'Callaghan, published by St. George Antiochian Christian Cathedral, 7515 E. Thirteenth St., Wichita, KS 67206-1223, 2001, and also at www.stgeorgecathedral.net/article_0901.html, accessed Nov. 1, 2015.

6) Brown, Robert McAfee, *The Spirit of Protestantism,* Oxford University Press, New York, 1965, page 97-98

7) Other scriptures showing only God can forgive sins are: Is. 43:25, Is. 44:22, Mic. 7:18, Mark 2:7, Luke 5:21, Luke 7:49.

8) Most modern translations of the Bible read "have been forgiven" or "are forgiven" including 22 of 24 English translations, and the Bishop Cassian (Bezobrazov) Russian translation of the New Testament (British and Foreign Bible Society, 1970). The Russian Synodal Translation, however, shows the phrase as "will be forgiven."

30. CELIBACY:
Should priests or ministers marry?

Should priests, monks and pastors be permitted to marry?

In Catholic churches, all priests, bishops and monks are forbidden to be married. Protestant ministers are usually married, but may be single as well. For the Orthodox churches, bishops and monks must be unmarried, while priests may be married. However, if they become priests before marrying, they are not permitted to marry afterwards.

The Catholic custom of unmarried priests was established in the 12th century, but not without dispute, according to Hassell:[1]

"The marriage of priests continued during the twelfth century in Hungary, Ireland, Denmark, Iceland and Sweden, notwithstanding papal anathemas."

What the Bible says about married priests and ministers

In examining this requirement from a biblical perspective, 1 Cor. 7:7-8 shows that the Apostle Paul was single, and, of course, so was Jesus. On the other hand, the apostle Peter was married, for in Mark 1:30-31 Jesus healed Peter's mother-in-law. Of course, it is not possible to have a mother-in-law without a wife.

In 1 Cor. 9:5, the apostle Paul writes, "Don't we have the right to take a believing wife along with us, as do the other apostles and the Lord's brothers and Cephas?"

It is clear from this verse, in particular, that the majority of the apostles were also married. The apostles were regularly taking their wives with them on trips.

In 1 Tim. 3:2, the apostle Paul says that a church overseer (equivalent to a priest or a minister) "should be the husband of but one wife." This shows that marriage of a priest or pastor was normal in the early church. Another verse bearing on this issue is 1 Tim. 4:2-3, where the apostle Paul warns against those "who forbid marriage."

Obviously forbidding something to someone who has need of it puts an extra burden on them, and hinders their desire to serve God by forcing them to choose between marriage and a life of service to God.

The many priests who have fallen into sin sexually seems to show the danger of forbidding marriage, Protestants believe. Paul advocated marriage in order to avoid this problem: "It is better to marry than to burn" (1 Cor. 7:9). Since at least Paul and Jesus never married, and many apostles were married, Protestants believe it wouldn't be appropriate to make a rule either requiring or forbidding marriage for church leaders.

The fact that there is a gift of celibacy that varies from person to person is shown in 1 Cor. 7:7, where, speaking about marriage, the apostle says: "But each man has his own gift from God: one has this gift, another has that."

History of priestly celibacy

From these passages, it seems that in the first century church, married priests, bishops and ministers were the normal practice. There is also evidence from the church fathers that priests were married as late as the fourth century. For instance, early church leader Gregory Nazianzen's father was a priest who was married "...The conclusion remains unshaken... that he was at any rate born during the priesthood of his father." [2] Church father and priest Hilary of Poitiers was also married.[3]

The doctrine developed slowly until celibacy was seen as a mark of holiness. By the fourth century, marriage after ordination was restricted. "The Council of Ancyra, about 315, declared that deacons had to choose between marriage and celibacy before ordination, and could not marry afterwards; the Council of Neocaesarea, about 320, ruled that presbyters [elders] who married after ordination were to be deposed." [4]

The *Apostolic Consitutions*, completed about 390 A.D., allowed married bishops, priests (presbyters) and deacons: "...A bishop, a presbyter, and a deacon [cannot] marry a second time, but to be content with that wife which they had when they came to ordination...But if they entered into the clergy before they were married, we permit them to marry, if they have an inclination thereto, lest they sin and incur punishment." [5]

The Eastern Orthodox church position was set at the Quinisext Council in 692, and is the same as it is today: bishops can't marry, but other clergy may continue already established marriages.

Pope Gregory VII (1073-85) made celibacy the rule of the Catholic church for all priests and bishops in the 11th century. All debate on the subject was further ended after the first and second Lateral Councils (1123 and 1129) ruled that marriage in any form was incompatible for priests and bishops. [6]

The importance of understanding celibacy and marriage

But why is this important today? For three reasons:

1) Denying a bishop or priest or minister the right to be married may result in fewer ministers than are needed, as those who do not have the gift of celibacy or who are already married will probably choose not to serve. In fact, at the present time there is a serious shortage of priests in the Catholic church.

2) Ministers, bishops or priests who must remain single when they do not have the gift of celibacy are tempted to sin sexually. Statistics in the Catholic church show this to be a very serious problem. Recent scandals in the Orthodox church, such as the exposing of Ukrainian Metropolitan Filaret's mistress and children, show it is also a problem there.

This is not to say that married priests and ministers will not sin, but allowing ministers to marry will likely reduce the problem, as it says in 1 Cor. 7:2 and 7:5: "But since there is so much immorality, each man should have his own wife, and each woman her own husband....Do not deprive each other except by mutual consent and for a time, so that you may devote yourselves to prayer. Then come together again so that Satan will not tempt you because of your lack of self control."

3) When we impose rules that are not in the Bible we are going against the will of God. As Paul said, "Do not go beyond what is written" (1 Cor. 4:6).

1) Hassell, *History of the Church of God*, ch.16
2) *Prolegomena: The Life*, Division 1, p. 371 (CD), Nicene and Post Nicene Fathers
3) *Eerdmanns' Handbook to the History of Christianity*, p. 215
4) Ibid
5) *Matrimonial Precepts Concerning Clergymen, Book* 6, sect. 3-17, p. 935, Ante-Nicene Fathers
6) *Encyclopedia Brittanica*, vol. 3, p. 12

31. THE OLD TESTAMENT:
Two points of view

Another surprising difference between the Catholic, Orthodox and Protestant churches is the influence of the Old Testament.

The Old Testament has many rituals and practices that are not found in the New Testament, like animal sacrifice and special holidays. While Catholic and Orthodox leaders give priority to the New Testament, they are much more influenced by Old Testament practices than Protestants.

Catholics and Orthodox, for instance, call their ministers "priests," which is what they were called in the Old Testament. Protestants note that no ministers are called priests in the New Testament. Therefore most call their ministers by other names like pastor or reverend.

Catholic and Orthodox leaders use Old Testament practices like holy water, as is seen in Num. 8:7 "To purify them, do this: Sprinkle the water of cleansing on them…" Protestants do not use holy water since it is not found in the New Testament.

Catholic and Orthodox leaders teach believers to confess their sins to priests since they are mediators between God and man, as is shown in Lev. 5:13 (RSV): "Thus the priest shall make atonement for him for the sin which he has committed in any one of these things, and he shall be forgiven."

Protestants, however, follow the New Testament pattern in which believers confess their sins to each other. James 5:16 says: "Therefore confess your sins to each other and pray for each other so that you may be healed. The prayer of a righteous man is powerful and effective."

Catholics and Orthodox use incense in their services, as is done in the Old Testament: "Make an altar of acacia wood for burning incense….Aaron must burn fragrant incense on the altar every morning when he tends the lamps…." (Ex. 30:1,7). Protestants usually do not use incense, because the New Testament does not mention it as a practice of the church.*

Catholic and Orthodox leaders observe special dates and holidays, as is done in the Old Testament (Lev. 23:1): "The LORD said to Moses, 'Speak to the Israelites and say to them: 'These are my appointed feasts, the appointed feasts of the LORD, which you are to proclaim as sacred assemblies.'" Catholic/Orthodox holidays include the Ascension, the Annunciation, the Transfiguration, and All Saints among others.

Protestants observe just a few holidays, such as Christmas and Easter. They also put significantly less emphasis on them, due to the comment of the apostle Paul: "…You are observing special days and months and seasons

and years! I fear for you, that somehow I have wasted my efforts on you."
(Gal. 4:9-11) Regarding holy days, Rom. 14:5 says, "One man considers one
day more sacred than another; another man considers every day alike. Each
one should be fully convinced in his own mind." Similarly, Col. 2:16-17
says: "Therefore do not let anyone judge you by what you eat or drink, or
with regard to a religious festival, a New Moon celebration or a Sabbath day.
These are a shadow of the things that were to come; the reality, however, is
found in Christ."

Catholics and Orthodox also use special clothing for priests, as is shown
in the Old Testament (Ex. 28:4): "These are the garments they are to make: a
breastpiece, an ephod, a robe, a woven tunic, a turban and a sash. They are to
make these sacred garments for your brother Aaron and his sons, so that they
may serve me as priests."

Most Protestants do not have special clothes for their ministers since this
is not mentioned in the New Testament.

Catholic and Orthodox leaders stress the importance if the seven
sacraments to justify us to God, similar to the importance of rituals in the
Old Testament (*see the chapter on Salvation*). Protestants follow the New
Testament pattern of justification by faith rather than by ritual. Evangelical
Protestants therefore use only two ordinances — communion and baptism.

The bread of the presence is an Old Testament concept as seen in
Exodus 25:30: "Put the bread of the Presence on this table to be before me
at all times." This is echoed in the Orthodox church ritual regarding bread
(prosphora). Catholics and Protestants do not have a similar ritual.

The Old Testament stresses the importance of holy places like the Holy of
Holies and the burning bush, which were holy ground. In the same way the
Catholic and Orthodox leaders consider certain places as holy — like the area
behind the iconostasis, Lourdes in France and other places of pilgrimage in
the world.

Most Protestants consider all places equally valid for worship, noting how
Jesus de-emphasized holy places in the New Testament (John 4:21-23): "A
time is coming when you will worship the Father neither on this mountain
nor in Jerusalem…. The true worshippers will worship the Father in spirit and
truth, for they are the kind of worshippers the Father seeks."

Orthodox refer to their church buildings as temples, echoing the Old
Testament concept.

Protestants prefer the New Testament concept in which God's temple is
now the heart of every believer instead of a building of stone. 1 Cor. 6:19
says: "Do you not know that your body is a temple of the Holy Spirit, who is
in you, whom you have received from God?"

Lastly, only Orthodox priests and deacons can go behind the iconostasis.
This is similar to the Old Testament rule allowing only the high priest into the
Holy of Holies (Lev. 16:17, Heb. 9:7): "But only the high priest entered the
inner room…"

Protestants, however, believe in the priesthood of all believers and so they
don't have special places reserved only for the clergy.

Summary of the Protestant viewpoint

Protestants see a danger in the excessive influence of the Old Testament law upon believers, as the apostle Paul noted in Gal. 5:4: "You who are trying to be justified by law have been alienated from Christ; you have fallen away from grace."

Some Protestants, however, note the important symbolism of Old Testament practices, and sometimes will have a Jewish seder meal, for example, as a way of illustrating the New Covenant using the symbolism of the Old Covenant. The New Testament notes that the Old Covenant is full of hidden symbols of Christ and the New Covenant.

Paul, for instance, notes in 1 Cor. 9:9-10 that the Old Testament passage regarding oxen is intended as a symbolic message for the New Testament church: "For it is written in the Law of Moses: 'Do not muzzle an ox while it is treading out the grain.' Is it about oxen that God is concerned? Surely he says this for us, doesn't he?"

Col. 2:17 says the Old Testament practices are symbolic: "These are a shadow of the things that were to come; the reality, however, is found in Christ." Heb. 8:5 and 10:1 say the same thing: "They serve at a sanctuary that is a copy and shadow of what is in heaven.... The law is only a shadow of the good things that are coming -- not the realities themselves."

---

* Incense is mentioned in the New Testament in the following scriptures, but never as a practice of the New Testament believers. It is shown instead as connected with the Old Testament temple in Luke 1:9, Heb. 9:4, as a gift to the Christ child (Matt. 2:11) and being used in the temple in heaven: Rev. 5:8, 8:3-4, 18:13).

32. OTHER DIFFERENCES:
Various

The Filioque controversy

The filioque controversy is what finally split the Catholic and Orthodox churches, and why they remain separated today.

The controversy began when the Catholic (western) churches wanted to add one word to the Christian confession of faith known as the Nicene Creed. The Orthodox (eastern) churches did not agree. The addition was a matter of controversy for many centuries, which culminated in 1054 A.D. when the western, largely Latin-speaking churches separated themselves from the eastern, largely

Greek-speaking churches, when the Pope and the Patriarch of Constantinople excommunicated each other.

The Nicene Creed was adopted in 325 A.D. by the early church as a statement of faith — a short summary of what Christians believe.

The additional clause says that the Holy Spirit precedes not only from the Father, but also from Jesus the Son. Orthodox say the Holy Spirit precedes only from the Father, although he may be sent through the Son.

Catholics say the Holy Spirit is sent by either the Father or the Son. Protestants, while generally accepting the addition of the clause in their version of the Nicene creed, are not strongly for one position or the other. Indeed, most Protestants don't know anything about it. Scripturally, verses show the Holy Spirit being sent by Jesus (John 15:26, 16:7), and some showing the Holy Spirit sent by the Father (John 14:16,17:26, Acts 2:33).

This issue may be one of those the apostle Paul warned about in the following verses: "Don't have anything to do with foolish and stupid arguments, because you know they produce quarrels" (2 Tim. 2:23).

"But avoid foolish controversies and genealogies and arguments and quarrels about the law, because these are unprofitable and useless" (Tit. 3:9).

"Warn them before God against quarrelling about words; it is of no value, and only ruins those who listen" (2 Tim. 2:14).

Sign of the Cross: Important?

The sign of the cross is made by Catholics and Orthodox and some Protestants. It involves tracing the image of the cross from head to abdomen and to both shoulders. It also sometimes involves making the sign of the cross on the forehead.

The origin of this custom is unknown, but it may have arisen from the scripture in which God orders a mark on the foreheads of those who were grieved over sin (Ezek. 9:4): "Go throughout the city of Jerusalem and put a mark on the foreheads of those who grieve and lament over all the detestable things that are done in it."

An angel also put a similar mark on the foreheads of Christians in Rev. 7:2-3 (See also 9:4 and 14:1): "Then I saw another angel coming up from the east, having the seal of the living God. He called out in a loud voice to the four angels who had been given power to harm the land and the sea: 'Do not harm the land or the sea or the trees until we put a seal on the foreheads of the servants of our God.'"

The difference, of course, is that in the scripture these marks were done by God, and the sign of the cross is done by man.

God's marks were intended to set apart Christians so they would not suffer under God's judgments, similar to the mark of blood on the doors of Jews on Passover night in Egypt. The sign of the cross, however, is not to avoid judgment, but to bring blessing, and protection against evil forces. God's marks on the forehead were visible, while the sign of the cross is invisible.

The sign of the cross is not found in the Bible, so it is assumed to have arisen after the apostles. This is why most Protestants do not teach this, although they are not usually opposed to it.

Church father Tertullian was the first to mention the practice. Writing approximately 200 years after the birth of Christ, he said the purpose of the sign is that, "the soul too may be fortified."[1] Writing 50 years later, Cyprian said the sign of the cross keeps the believer "safe and unharmed."[2] Lactantius, writing 300 years after Christ, said it will chase away demons.[3]

The references of the church fathers is to a sign on the forehead, but most today make the sign on the whole body, although even this is made differently by various groups. There are four main differences.

Catholics and Armenian believers and some others make the sign of the cross with three fingers, representing the trinity, ending with a movement from left shoulder to right. Orthodox believers usually make the sign of the cross with three fingers ending with a movement from right shoulder to left. Old Believers (a breakaway Orthodox group) make the sign of the cross with two fingers, representing the dual nature of Christ. Lastly, some believers make the sign of the cross on the forehead, often in addition to making

the full sign of the cross on the body. The history of the sign of the cross
is marked by one tragic event. In 1653, Russian Orthodox Patriarch Nikon
ordered several changes, one of which was that the sign of the cross be made
by three fingers (two was the traditional number). This split the country
and, over the next decade, led to the deaths of thousands of Russians. Many
were imprisoned and tortured in church-run prisons. Many chose to commit
suicide rather than risk giving in under torture and accepting the change in the
ritual. [4]

The leader of the movement to oppose the change, Archpriest Avvakum,
was burned alive at the stake after several years of imprisonment. The church
that split off from the Orthodox Church at that time is called Old Believers,
and still exists in many countries of the world.

Candles: Do they do any good?

It is a common tradition in Orthodox and Catholic churches to light
candles and place them in front of icon paintings (for the Orthodox) or statues
(for Catholics). This is usually done when a special need or request is made
of the saint represented by the icon or statue. Some Protestant churches also
use candles as an aid to prayer. Most Protestants, especially evangelicals,
don't do this, however.

In defending this practice, Catholic/Orthodox leaders point out that Christ
is the light of the world. These lights represent Christ, they say. Further they
argue that the use of lights is shown in the Old Testament, where a seven-
branched candelabra (the menorah) was used to light the temple.

Lastly, they say that use of candles before icons was established by the
seventh ecumenical council, held in 787 A.D. The report of the bishops said
that "incense and lights may be offered according to ancient pious custom" to
icons, the cross and the Bible.[5]

Theologically, however, there is really not a lot written about candle usage in most Orthodox and Catholic publications, even though candles are sold
and used every day in their churches worldwide. Most Protestants do not use
candles as part of their prayers for several reasons.

First of all, there is no example in scripture of anyone lighting candles as
a means of prayer. Jesus, when he taught the disciples to pray, did not mention candles (Matthew 6, Luke 11).

Secondly, candles cannot pray for us. At best they are a symbol of our
intercession, and are beautiful, but by themselves are just wax and a wick, and
have no power to intercede for us. Reliance upon candles, therefore, is a false
hope.

Thirdly, the earliest references to candles of the church fathers were
against them. Lactantius, writing in the third century, said this:

"Or if they would contemplate that heavenly light which we call the sun,
they will at once perceive how God has no need of their candles, who has
Himself given so clear and bright a light for the use of man. ... Is that man,
therefore, to be thought in his senses, who presents the light of candles and
torches as an offering to him who is the author and giver of light?... But their

gods, because they are of the earth, stand in need of lights, that they may not be in darkness."[6]

The fact that Lactantius was writing to pagans and told them that God did not need candles shows at once two things:

First, that Christian churches at that time (around 300 A.D.) were not in the habit of lighting candles to God, and second, that pagan religions were. So the tradition of lighting candles to God in Christian churches started after this, and was apparently adopted from pagan religions.

Fourthly, the Bible says the basic purpose of the candelabra in the temple was to provide light, and to symbolize the temple in heaven — it was never something that prayed to God for us. Ex. 25:37 says: "Then make its seven lamps and set them up on it so that they light the space in front of it." Heb 8:5 says: "They serve at a sanctuary that is a copy and shadow of what is in heaven...."

Lastly, as to the reference to the use of candles by the seventh ecumenical council, Protestants reject the seventh ecumenical councils' rulings as a whole (see the chapter on the ecumenical councils), as being politically motivated and uninspired.

Nonetheless, the fact that the council affirmed the use of candles or lights at that time (787 A.D.) and the fact that Lactantius implied that they were not used by Christians in approximately 300 A.D., does give us information that the practice took root sometime between 300 A.D. and 787 A.D. This shows that it was not a tradition of the apostles, but came later.

Monasteries/Convents: A good idea?

The practice of some Christians of living apart from the world in church-run homes or communities is a very old one. It is practiced by Catholics, Orthodox and some Protestants.

The non-Christian Essenes, who lived near the time of Christ, ran such a community near the Dead Sea, and are credited by some with writing the Dead Sea scrolls.

Such a community might be referred to in the Old Testament where a school of the prophets had been apparently established by the prophet Elijah (2 Kings 2:3). They built their own center for meeting (2 Kings 6:1-2). This, however, may have been more a training center than a permanent retreat from the world, since it is called a school.

Some Protestants oppose the practice of monasteries and convents as one that hinders the church from evangelizing the world, in that it removes Christians from contact with the lost. Christ, they note, said: "Go into all the world and preach the good news to all creation" (Mark 16:15).

Holy fools: Scriptural?

Another doctrine that is uniquely Orthodox is that of the holy fool, and the closely related "starets." A holy fool can be described as a prophet who appears insane but who nonetheless speaks profound wisdom. Perhaps the most famous in Russia is St. Basil, partly in honor of whom Ivan the Terrible built St. Basil's Cathedral in Red Square; the most well-known church in Russia.

St. Basil would sometimes go about Moscow naked, but his actions and statements were often profound and he was greatly respected. Holy fools often practice asceticism and poverty, and are often homeless.

Orthodox Bishop Timothy Ware remarks: "...He renounces not only material possessions but also what others regard as his sanity and mental balance. Yet thereby he becomes a channel for the higher wisdom of the Spirit.... He combines audacity with humility.... Like the fool Nicolas of Pskov, who put into the hands of Tsar Ivan the Terrible a piece of meat dripping with blood, he can rebuke the powerful of this world with a boldness that others lack. He is the living conscience of society." [7]

The starets (in Russian) or elder is similar in that they are often unshaven and unwashed. The most infamous starets was Rasputin, the most holy and beloved Sergei Radonezh, who founded the most famous Russian monastery in Sergeiov Posad, north of Moscow, in the 14th century.

These men may be described as wandering hermits or ascetics. They do not act as fools but are respected for their piety and self-sacrifice.

Biblically, there are several men of God who did things that shocked people. Ezekiel dug through a wall with his hands (Ezek. 12:7), laid on his side for more than a year (4:9), and shaved his head with a sword (5:1). Hosea the prophet similarly married a prostitute at God's command (Hos. 1:2, 3:1-3), while Jesus attacked the money changers at the temple and talked about people eating his flesh and drinking his blood (John 2:15, 6:54).

John the Baptist was similar to a starets, living off honey and locusts, wearing rough clothes and living in the wilderness. He was also, like Nicholas of Pskov, not afraid to rebuke authorities, telling Herod he was living in sin, for which he was executed.

The Pope: Head of the church?

The Catholic church believes that there should be only one head of the church, called the pope, who is infallible. The Orthodox and Protestant churches do not believe this.

Catholic leaders base their belief on Jesus' statement to Peter, "You are Peter, and on this rock I will build my church" and "I will give you the keys to the kingdom of heaven" (Matt. 16:18-19). They believe that Peter's successors are the popes, who have the authority of Christ. Catholic doctrine states the pope is infallible when he speaks "ex cathedra," which is to say when he makes official church announcements. The Catholic church approved the doctrine of papal infallibility at Vatican I in 1870. The church ruled that those who reject the doctrine will not be allowed in heaven: "...Should anyone... have the temerity to reject this definition of ours: let him be anathema." [8]

The Catholic church has also formally stated that submission to the pope is "altogether necessary to salvation" (*Unum Sanctam*, 1302 A.D., Boniface VIII). The first reference to the Roman pope as the head of the church was made in 250 A.D. by the North African bishop Cyprian, who was opposed to the idea: "Peter — whom the Lord chose first and upon whom he built his church — did not insolently claim anything to himself. Nor did he arrogantly assume anything when Paul later disputed with him about circumcision. He did not say that he held the primacy and that he needed to be obeyed by novices and those lately come!" [9]

Pope Leo the Great began aggressively promoting the bishop of Rome as the head of the church at the Council of Chalcedon (451 A.D.). Pope Gregory renewed this claim in 588 A.D., and it was gradually accepted over western Europe, but not by the churches of the east, nor at first by the Celtic churches.[10]

Protestants believe that the historical record shown above shows that the papacy was not a tradition of the early apostles, but something that developed over centuries, from its first mention in 250 A.D., to its general approval in the west in 588 A.D. It is still not accepted by Eastern Orthodox or Protestants.

As to the infallibility of the pope, Protestants note that Peter was rebuked by Paul for error (Gal. 2:11-14), and Peter appeared subject to the authority of James in Jerusalem (Acts 15). These passages imply, accordingly, that if Peter was the first pope, he was not supreme in authority nor was he infallible. Further, the fact that infallibility was not officially approved until nearly 2,000 years after Christ is evidence that this was not a teaching of the early church, but something that arose much later.

Protestants also note the lack of a "succession clause" establishing a series of popes, or any verse in the Bible stating that one man should lead the church. The passage where Jesus speaks to Peter is about establishing the church on Christ, not on Peter. The keys which Jesus gave to Peter were used by him, and there is no longer any need for these "doors" to be opened. *(See the chapter on apostolic succession.)* Jesus used the singular pronoun with Peter and not a plural pronoun, indicating this promise was for him alone.

Christ is the head of the church, not any man: "God placed all things under his feet and appointed him to be head over everything for the church." (Eph. 1:22-23). As Peter himself wrote, Christ (and therefore not the pope), is the chief shepherd and overseer of our souls (1 Peter 2:24, 5:4).

In the Old Testament God's people sought a king, something to which God was opposed, because he was their king (1 Sam. 12:12,17): "But when you saw that Nahash king of the Ammonites was moving against you, you said to me, 'No, we want a king to rule over us'—even though the LORD your God was your king....you will realize what an evil thing you did in the eyes of the LORD when you asked for a king."

Protestants accordingly believe we should not depend on human leadership, but on Christ.

Iconostasis: Is it useful?

The iconostasis is a wall covered with icon paintings in most Orthodox churches. It separates the people from the altar on which the priest prepares communion (the Eucharist). There are usually three doors to an iconostasis.

Only the priests and deacons are allowed behind the iconostasis. No woman is ever allowed behind it.

The iconostasis was originally a curtain, and began to be used to separate the altar from the congregation in the fourth century. Protestants and Catholics do not use iconostases. Protestants do not do so for three reasons:

1) When Christ died, the veil separating the Holy of Holies was torn in two, symbolizing free access to God through the blood of Christ. The iconostasis, however, erects a barrier where there should be none, making believers feel distant from God and unworthy.

2) God does not dwell behind the iconostasis and does not live in a building made with hands. His temple is the human heart of those who love him.

3) The fact that only the priests and deacons can go behind the screen establishes a hierarchy of believers — some with more access to God than others. The forbidding of women to go behind the screen is also wrong, Protestants believe. There are not two tiers of believers — all are equal before God: This equality is shown in the following scriptures:

Gal. 3:28: "There is neither Jew nor Greek, slave nor free, male nor female, for you are all one in Christ Jesus."

Col. 3:11: "Here there is no Greek or Jew, circumcised or uncircumcised, barbarian, Scythian, slave or free, but Christ is all, and is in all."

Rom. 10:12-13: "For there is no difference between Jew and Gentile— the same Lord is Lord of all...."

Eph. 2:13-19 seems to speak directly against the separation caused by an iconostasis: "But now in Christ Jesus you who once were far away have been brought near through the blood of Christ. For he himself is our peace, who has made the two one and has destroyed the barrier, the dividing wall of hostility, by abolishing in his flesh the law with its commandments and regulations. ...Consequently, you are no longer foreigners and aliens, but fellow-citizens with God's people and members of God's household."

Calendars and Holy Days: Do they matter?

Catholics, Protestants and Orthodox use two different calendars for religious observances, and different methods for calculating religious holidays.

Catholics and Protestants and most Greek Orthodox use the Gregorian calendar, developed in 1582 by the Catholic Church to correct errors in the Julian calendar. Most other Orthodox Christians worldwide (in Russia, Serbia, Jerusalem) use the Julian calendar for religious observances, but use the Gregorian calendar for daily life.

Some Orthodox, mostly in Greece but also in the United States, Romania and Bulgaria, have broken off from Orthodox who use the Gregorian calendar, feeling it is evidence of compromise with the world (ecumenicism). These breakaway groups are called "Old Calendarists."

The Julian calendar was adopted in 46 B.C. by the Roman empire.. It is 13 days behind the Gregorian calendar in most holidays. For instance Christmas is observed on Jan. 7th in Orthodox countries, and on Dec. 25 in most other countries.

Another difference in holidays is because all Christians use a lunar calendar to determine the dates for Easter, Ash Wednesday, Palm Sunday and other holidays, and therefore their dates change from year to year. The Orthodox, further, use a different lunar method to calculate Easter, and accordingly their Easter often differs from the dates observed by Catholics and Protestants.

The importance of observing religious holidays varies from Orthodox to Catholic to Protestant, with Protestants generally feeling such holidays are helpful but not essential for a Christian to observe. Observing religious holidays is part of the old covenant, and is not binding on Christians today.

Protestants believe the apostle Paul made a particular criticism of the Galatians for observing special days and seasons (Gal. 4:9-11): "...How is it that you are turning back to those weak and miserable principles? Do you wish to be enslaved by them all over again? You are observing special days and months and seasons and years! I fear for you, that somehow I have wasted my efforts on you."

John Calvin noted that Paul's comment is not meant to say that holidays are wrong — only that observing them is not something we are required to do by God. "No condemnation is here given to the observance of dates in the arrangements of civil society. ...Of what nature, then, was the observation which Paul reproves? It was that which would bind the conscience, by religious considerations, as if it were necessary to the worship of God..."

John Gill, in his commentary on this passage, said "these Galatians are blamed...because they were taught to observe them, in order to obtain eternal life..." However, Paul's statement in Gal. 4 against religious holidays seems to contradict Rom. 14:1-6, where he says we can observe religious holidays: "Accept him whose faith is weak, without passing judgment on disputable matters... One man considers one day more sacred than another; another man considers every day alike. Each one should be fully convinced in his own mind. He who regards one day as special, does so to the Lord."

But rather than contradicting himself, Paul is only asking us to tolerate minor differences. Christians can disagree on the importance of religious holidays, and still remain in fellowship. He is not saying that observing religious holidays make us more acceptable to God.

Paul also defended the rights of believers to observe or not observe religious holidays in Col. 2:16: "Do not let anyone judge you by what you eat or drink, or with regard to a religious festival, a New Moon celebration or a Sabbath day."

Divorce: Wide differences

The Catholic church does not allow divorce, but permits marriages to be annulled in certain cases. Divorced Catholics who remarry others are denied communion, which is a serious matter in Catholic theology *(See the chapter on communion, and the Catholic* Catechism, 1650).

The Orthodox churches permit divorce and remarriage, but believe the first marriage is the greatest in the eyes of God. A person can be married no more than three times in most Orthodox churches. Some base this openness to divorce on the Russian Synodal Translation of Mal. 2:16, which says about divorce: "If you hate her, let her go." This translation, however, contradicts the preceding two verses which oppose divorce, as well as other Bible verses (1 Cor. 7:10-13, Matt. 19:9) and also two other Russian Bible translations (Agape Biblia and the "Vsemirni Bibliski Perivodheski Tsentr"), as well as most other foreign translations of the Bible.

Protestant churches have different opinions on this subject — some allow divorce for any reason, while others only allow it in cases of adultery or abandonment, and some feel it is wrong in all cases.

Evangelical Protestant churches that allow divorce in some cases base this on Jesus' comment in Matt. 19: 9: "I tell you that anyone who divorces his wife, except for marital unfaithfulness, and marries another woman commits adultery." Accordingly, they believe divorce is permitted only when one partner is guilty of marital unfaithfulness (adultery).

Some Protestants also believe that divorce and remarriage are permitted when a person is abandoned by their spouse, based on the apostle Paul's comments in 1 Cor. 7:15: "But if the unbeliever leaves, let him do so. A believing man or woman is not bound in such circumstances..."

Some interpret the phrase "not bound" to mean they are free from their marital commitments to marry another.

Abortion: general agreement

The Catholic Church consistently opposes abortion and excommunicates those who have had abortions or helped in obtaining them (*Catechism* 2270-2275).   The Orthodox Church "very clearly and absolutely condemns it as an act of murder in every case....In regard to all of the very difficult cases, such as a young girl being raped or a mother who is certain to die, the consensus of Orthodox opinion would be that a decision for abortion might possibly be made, but that it can in no way be easily justified as morally righteous, and that persons making such a decision must repent of it and count on the mercy of God." [11]

Most evangelical Protestants are against abortion, and work with pro-life Catholics and Orthodox to stop it. Most liberal Protestants, however, are supporters of abortion rights.

Birth control: significant differences

The Catholic Church is opposed to all forms of birth control (except for methods that involve abstinence). Pope Paul VI outlined the church's position in his *Humanae Vitae* letter in 1968. Catholic leaders point to the writings of the church fathers as support for this; they consistently opposed birth control. Some point to the case of Onan, killed by God, as scriptural proof that birth control is wrong (see Gen. 38:8-10). The Orthodox Church, while opposing birth control, says "married people practicing birth control are not necessarily deprived of Holy Communion, if in conscience before God and with the blessing of their spiritual father, they are convinced that their motives are not entirely unworthy." [12]

Most Protestant churches allow birth control, although a few do not. Some cite the following words of Jesus: "...there be eunuchs, which have made themselves eunuchs for the kingdom of heaven's sake." (Matt. 19:12 KJV). This has traditionally been interpreted to mean celibacy, but some Protestants argue it can mean birth control. Gen. 9:1 is also cited by Protestants: "Then God blessed Noah and his sons, saying to them, 'Be fruitful and increase in number and fill the earth.'" The earth, they say, has been filled. As to the case of Onan, previously mentioned, Protestants believe that his punishment was due to his selfishness in wanting to deny children to his brother, rather than to birth control.

Homosexuality: The three agree that it's wrong

The Catholic Church, the Orthodox churches and the evangelical Protestant churches all consider homosexual acts to be sinful. A few liberal Protestant churches, however, perform wedding ceremonies for homosexuals and ordain practicing homosexuals, as the Episcopalian church has done. The official Catholic view is stated in the *Catechism* (2357): "Basing itself on Sacred Scripture, which always presents homosexual acts as acts of grave depravity, tradition has always declared that homosexual acts are intrinsically disordered." The Orthodox churches say that "homosexuality and any form of abusive sexual behavior are considered immoral and inappropriate forms of behavior in and of themselves, and also because they attack the institution of marriage and the family." [13]

Evangelical Protestants base their views on the following scriptures: "Do you not know that the wicked will not inherit the kingdom of God? Do not be deceived: Neither the sexually immoral nor idolaters nor adulterers nor male prostitutes nor homosexual offenders ... will inherit the kingdom of God" (1 Cor. 6:9-10). "Do not lie with a man as one lies with a woman; that is detestable" (Lev. 18:22). "Because of this, God gave them over to shameful lusts. Even their women exchanged natural relations for unnatural ones. In the same way the men also abandoned natural relations with women and were inflamed with lust for one another. Men committed indecent acts with other men, and received in themselves the due penalty for their perversion" (Rom. 1:26-27). "...Sodom and Gomorrah and the surrounding towns gave themselves up to sexual immorality and perversion. They serve as an example of those who suffer the punishment of eternal fire" (Jude 7).

Scapulars/Medals

These are bits of wool cloth hung over the shoulders by some Catholics as a form of devotion to God, either under or over the clothes. For monks they can be large, but for laymen as small as a postage stamp. They must be worn day and night. These are believed to bless those who wear them.

Indulgences are granted for their use (i.e., less time in purgatory). Neither Protestants nor Orthodox use scapulars, which arose from Catholic monasticism in the Middle Ages. Orthodox monks wear a garment similar to a large scapular, but there is no theological relation between it and the Catholic scapular. Medals blessed by a priest can replace scapulars, according to a ruling of the Catholic church in 1910.

Medals in general (even those not replacing scapulars) are seen as bringing a blessing (e.g. sacramentals).

Holy Fire

Holy Fire refers to a reputed miracle that occurs every year at the Church of the Holy Sepulchre in Jerusalem. There, the day before Easter, an Orthodox bishop or patriarch holds a lamp of olive oil which allegedly lights itself on fire while he is alone in the tomb. The bishop then lights other candles with the lamp, and the fire is carried to other countries. The ceremony is often carried live on Greek and Russian television. The Holy Fire was first mentioned in the fourth century. An account by a Russian traveler dates from the 12th century. However, excerpts from the diaries of Orthodox Bishop Porphyrius (Uspensky) (1804-1885) indicate that the Holy Fire was fake.. Porphyrius was sent by the Russian Orthodox Church to Jerusalem in the late 19th century. His account of the trip (Kniga bytija moego -- The book of my being. vol. 1, p. 671) states: "A hierodeacon who penetrated into the shrine of the Tomb at the time when, as everyone believes, the holy fire descends, saw with horror that the fire is ignited from a mere icon-lamp which never goes out, and thus the holy fire isn't a miracle. He himself told me about this today" [14]

Porphyrius said the fire is lit from an icon-lamp which is hidden behind the marble icon of Christ's Resurrection behind the burial couch. (vol. 3, pp. 299-301). Other cynics say the fire may be due to white phosphorous, which can spontaneously ignite when in contact with the air (see http://www.greatlie.com/en/). The Orthodox tradition of Holy Fire is not mentioned in the Bible, and is not recognized by Protestants or Catholics.

---

1) *On the resurrection of the flesh*, chap. 8, p. 1025 (CD), Ante-Nicene Fathers

2) *Treatises of Cyprian*, 5.22, p. 997 (CD), Ante-Nicene Fathers

3) *True Wisdom and Religion* (Book 4), chap. 26-27, p. 267 (CD), Ante-Nicene Fathers

4) *Archpriest Avvakum: The Life Written by Himself*, p. 20-23

5) *Decree of the Ecumenical Synod*, Seventh Ecumenical Council, p. 1326 (CD), Ante-Nicene Fathers

6) *Of True Worship*, chap. 2, The Divine Institutes, p. 337 (CD), Ante-Nicene Fathers

7) Ware, Timothy, *The Orthodox Way*, p. 131, St. Vladimir's Seminary Press, 1993

8) http://www.ewtn.com/library/COUNCILS/V1.HTM#6, accessed Nov. 1, 2015.

9) *Epistles of Cyprian* 70.3, p. 817 (CD), Ante-Nicene Fathers

10) *The Story of The Church*, p. 65

11) Orthodox Church in America official web site: http://oca.org/the-hub/the-church-on-current-issues/orthodox-christians-and-abortion, accessed Nov. 1, 2015

12) Ibid

13) Greek Orthodox Church official web site: http://www.goarch.org/ourfaith/controversialissues, accessed Nov. 1, 2015.

14) http://medlibrary.org/medwiki/Holy_Fire, accessed Nov. 1, 2015.

33. CONCLUSION:
Historical trends

Most churches agree that Christianity today is far from what it was in the first century of Christ and the apostles. Exactly in which areas it is deficient, of course, varies with the point of view of each denomination.

A natural question is how did the church get so far from what Christ intended? Some of the forces that affect us may include:

1) Demonic influence
2) Incrementalism
3) Influence of unredeemed society
4) Inertia of tradition
5) Syncretism
6) Human nature.

Demonic influence

The first of these, demonic influence, is shown by the apostle Paul in 1 Tim. 4:1, where he warned about "doctrines of demons."

This phrase literally means beliefs prepared and promoted by demons. These demons are intelligent beings who have their own agenda that is at odds with God's will. They create doctrines that will ultimately destroy people. Notice also in the following scripture (1 Tim. 4:3) what doctrines they are developing — "they forbid people to marry and order them to abstain from certain foods..." In other words, they are interested in being more strict and more religious than necessary.

Col. 2:23 echoes this: "Such regulations indeed have an appearance of wisdom, with their self-imposed worship, their false humility and their harsh treatment of the body, but they lack any value in restraining sensual indulgence." The Pharisees were the most strict sect of their day, and they led the opposition to Jesus. They judged and hated Jesus, accusing him of not being strict enough. This is a true demonic religious spirit, as is seen in Rom. 2:1: "Who are you, oh man, who judge another, for you who judge do the same things?" The great harlot Babylon of Rev. 17 will be, many think, a church in the end times that will be deeply influenced demonically, promoting blasphemies and persecuting true Christians. (*See the end of this chapter.*)

Incrementalism

A gradual drifting away from the truth of the gospel is usually much more often the cause of spiritual disaster than sudden collapse. The gradual drift of Christianity away from the faith of the apostles is a generally accepted observation among Christians. Heb. 2:1 warns against this tendency: "We must pay more careful attention, therefore, to what we have heard, so that we do not drift away." Deut. 4:9 says: "Only be careful, and watch yourselves closely so that you do not forget the things your eyes have seen or let them slip from your heart as long as you live."

Influence of unredeemed society

The church lives in the midst of a world that is not redeemed. Jesus said in Matt. 7 that most people will not be saved ("many" by the broad way, "few" by the narrow). Accordingly, true Christians will always be in the minority. The influence of the majority on the children of God is shown in Ex. 32, where the ungodly masses prevailed on God's anointed, Aaron, to the point that he helped them fashion an idol for false worship:

"When the people saw that Moses was so long in coming down from the mountain, they gathered round Aaron and said, 'Come, make us gods who will go before us. As for this fellow Moses who brought us up out of Egypt, we don't know what has happened to him.' Aaron answered them, 'Take off the gold earrings that your wives, your sons and your daughters are wearing, and bring them to me.'...He took what they handed him and made it into an idol cast in the shape of a calf...Then they said, 'These are your gods, O Israel, who brought you up out of Egypt.'"

Inertia of tradition

Once a tradition has been established, properly or improperly, it is extremely hard to change it. Note that in the 16th century when the Russian Orthodox Church tried to change how many fingers were used in making the sign of the cross, it resulted in a civil war and the deaths of thousands. Jesus greatly offended the Pharisees by not keeping their traditions about the Sabbath or washing of hands.

The traditions in many churches — Protestant, Catholic and Orthodox — may contradict the word of God, but changing those traditions is often so difficult that it is easier to keep the tradition and ignore scripture.

Syncretism

The blending of the gospel with worldly traditions is well-established. Sometimes this is harmless, such as when early Christians decided to celebrate Christ's birth on the same date as a pagan holiday (Dec. 25th).

In some cultures, fertility symbols from pagan religions have worked their way into Christianity, such as the egg and the rabbit, which are used as symbols of Easter. Even the word Easter is the name of an ancient fertility goddess, Eostre. Many of these symbols are harmless, and the name of Easter does not mean people worship a fertility goddess.

When, however, this syncretism occurs with foundational doctrines, the result is more serious. This is especially the case when Christianity is adopted culturally only as a veneer, and pagan beliefs continue beneath the surface. An example would be the common belief that one must do good works to earn salvation.

Human nature

Human nature is intrinsically separated from God. Its tendency is to do wrong instead of right. This is a continual hindrance to godly living and correct doctrine.

This is shown in Gen. 6:5: "The LORD saw how great man's wickedness on the earth had become, and that every inclination of the thoughts of his heart was only evil all the time."

Paul described this natural tendency to sin in Rom. 7:18: "I know that nothing good lives in me, that is, in my sinful nature. For I have the desire to do what is good, but I cannot carry it out. For what I do is not the good I want to do; no, the evil I do not want to do—this I keep on doing."

The natural nature of man to reject the things of God means a revival in one generation can be quickly cooled in the next.

A prophetic warning from the Bible

The trends seen in the history of the church are still active, and will lead many farther and farther from the truth.

Scripture warns of a great false church that will arise in the last days, called the harlot Babylon (Rev. 17).

In symbolic language, John writes that this organization will be:
- A persecutor of real Christians ("drunk with the blood of the saints").
- International ("sits on many waters").
- Rich ("glittering with gold, precious stones and pearls").
- Allied with national governments ("with her the kings of the earth committed adultery...").
- A misleader of the people, teaching what they want to hear ("the inhabitants of the earth were intoxicated with the wine of her adulteries.")
- A betrayer of the truth for money ("prostitute").
- Unfaithful to God ("She held a golden cup in her hand, filled with abominable things and the filth of her adulteries.").

Few believe this church is fully on the earth today, but the trends that will lead to its establishment seem already at work.

These include the forces described above. A desire to "be like other nations" was the Achilles heel of Israel, leading them to demand a king and wander from God. Just so many churches today desire to be politically correct. They are willing to turn from scripture in order to teach things that are popular. They are willing to sell themselves and the truth, like the great prostitute of Rev. 17, for the sake of popularity.

Followers of Christ must be careful to do what he says. As Jesus said, in John 14:24, "He who does not love me will not obey my teaching."

As Christians are buffeted by society and other influences to gradually compromise the truth of the gospel, they need to remember 1 Tim. 4:16: "Watch your life and doctrine closely. Persevere in them, because if you do, you will save both yourself and your hearers."

STUDY/DISCUSSION QUESTIONS
By Chapter

1. THE THREE CHURCHES: Compared and contrasted   (p. 6)
- Which is the largest of the three churches? Which is second?
- Is Ethiopia considered to be Catholic, Orthodox or Protestant?
- DISCUSS: How do you determine who is actually Christian?

2. THE THREE CHURCHES: Which is oldest? (p. 11)
- What is the difference between organizational antiquity and doctrinal antiquity? Which of the three churches does not claim organizational antiquity but does claim doctrinal antiquity?
- DISCUSS: How can you evaluate religious traditions to determine if they are from God or from man?

3. THE CHURCH: Can it be wrong? (p. 13)
- The Catholic Catechism says Christ gave to the church "a share in his own infallibility." Is the Catholic church infallible? Why or why not? (Rev. 2:14-24, 2 Pet. 2:1)
- What is the proper understanding of Matt. 16:18?
- DISCUSS: If churches can make mistakes, how can we know which church is right?

4. THE CHURCH: Can it be divided? (p. 15)
- Since Eph. 4:5 says there is "one faith," how can there be thousands of denominations? How can there be three great churches? Shouldn't there be just one?
- Was Christianity unified as one church until the Orthodox/Catholic split in 1054 AD? What does the New Testament show? What does history show after the New Testament was completed?
- Is the Catholic church one church, or are there divisions in it and groups that have split off of it?

5. MYSTERY: Can we understand God? (p. 22)
- Is God unknowable? Should we try to understand him?
- What is the problem with emphasizing the mystery of God? (Eph. 5:17)
- The Bible says God has made himself known. In what way?

6. THE BIBLE: More important than tradition? (p. 24)
- Define sola scriptura
- Why is 1 Cor. 4:6 important in discussing church tradition and scripture?
- What is the best scripture to use in ministering to persons who value tradition more than the Bible? Why? (Mark 7:8)
- What did Paul mean about keeping oral traditions?

7. THE BIBLE: Who has the right to interpret it? (p. 28)
- What are the 2 main scriptures we use to show that individual believers can interpret scripture without church leadership? (Acts 17:11, 1 John 2:27a). Why?
- 2 Peter 1:20 says "no prophecy of scripture is of any private interpretation." Does this mean private interpretation of scripture is wrong?

8. THE BIBLE: Who gave it to us? (p. 35)

- Shouldn't Protestants accept Catholic/Orthodox teaching since they also accept the Bible, which came from Catholic/Orthodox leaders?
- How did the early Christians know which scriptures were from God? And how can we know today?

9. BAPTISM: Does it save us? (p. 37)

- Is it a sin to be baptized twice? (Acts 19:1-7)
- Does the act of baptism save us? (Luke 23:43)
- Doesn't John 3:5 mean we must be baptized to be saved?

10. BAPTISM: Should we baptize infants? (p. 42)

- Should we baptize infants?
- Why is it important to know that John Chrysostom, Jerome, Augustine, Gregory Nazianzus and Basil the Great were baptized as adults?
- DISCUSS: Is there anything wrong with being baptized as an infant?

11. SALVATION: How do we get to heaven? (p. 51)

- Name the five main Orthodox/Catholic teachings about salvation, that differ with Protestants.
- What is the sole Biblical condition for salvation? (Eph. 2:8-9)
- Does James 2:24 mean we must do good works to be saved? - Why do Protestants have assurance of salvation? (1 John 5:13, John 5:24)
- Write the two different formulas for salvation involving faith.

12. THEOSIS: What is it? (p. 67)

- Explain theosis. Which of the three churches teaches it?
- What is wrong with combining justification with sanctification?

13. CHRISMATION & CONFIRMATION: Ritual or reality? (p. 70)

- How do the ceremonies for chrismation and confirmation differ from what we see in the New Testament?
- Can a ceremony at a certain age guarantee reception of the Holy Spirit?
- What are the advantages and disadvantages of these ceremonies?
- Can an external action make an internal change?

14. HESYCHASM: Introspection or way to God? (p. 73)

- Which of the three churches practices Hesychasm?
- What is the Philokalia?
- Define Hesychasm.
- Why are Hesychasts called naval-gazers?
- Name two problems with the Hesychasm doctrine.

15. COMMUNION: Key to eternal life? (p. 75)

- Does communion cause the forgiveness of our sins?
- Are the communion elements literally the body and blood of Jesus? How do you explain Jesus' comments in John 6 about this?
(Heb. 9:25-28, 1 Cor. 11:24)
- Should we worship the communion elements?
- Should communion be limited to only those in our church?
- Does John 6:54 mean we must take communion to be saved?

16. ICONS AND STATUES: Help or hindrance? (p. 82)

- Are icons windows to heaven or idol worship?
- Is it okay to have icons but not statues?
- Why don't Protestants use icons?
- If Jesus was the image of God the Father, and people were allowed to see him, why is it wrong to pray to a painting of him?
- What is the significance of Peter in Acts and the angels in Revelation refusing veneration of themselves?
- How would you answer someone who says a relative or friend was genuinely, miraculously healed after praying before an icon or a holy relic of a saint? (Matt. 9:22)
- Orthodox say that to reject the veneration of icons is to deny the incarnation of Christ. Why? How would you answer them?
- DISCUSS: The seventh ecumenical council says those that do not pray before images will be condemned to hell. Was this a valid council? If so, will we truly go to hell if we do not pray before images?

17. RELICS: Do they have supernatural power? (p. 94)

- The Bible shows that when a dead man's body touched the bones of Elisha, the dead man was raised from the dead. (2Kings 13:21). Why don't Protestants accept this particular example as proof of the power of relics to do miracles?
- All Catholic churches and Orthodox churches have something special in or under the altar. What is it?

18. THE APOCRYPHA: Should it be part of the Bible? (p. 100)

- List a verse reference from the apocrypha that shows you can give money and have your sins forgiven.
- What one Protestant church includes the apocrypha and believes in transubstantiation?
- Why don't Protestants accept the apocrypha?
- Are there different versions of the apocrypha? Explain.

19. PRAYER TO SAINTS: Right or wrong? (p. 110)

- Are there any examples of someone praying to a saint in the Bible?
- State one of the 3 verses that shed some light on praying to saints or Mary. (Matt. 6:9, Deut. 18:10-12, 1 Chron. 10:13-14)
- DISCUSS: Catholics and Orthodox say asking a saint to pray for us is no different than asking a friend here on earth, as we are united with those in heaven. Your opinion?

20. MARY: Sinless intercessor? (p. 114)

- Did Mary ever sin? Explain your answer. Why is that important?
- What is the most prayed prayer in Catholicism?
- After Jesus, who does the Bible say was the greatest person in history?
- List some scriptures that are useful regarding devotion to Mary (Luke 11:27-28, Mark 3:20-21, 31-35, Matt. 11;11, Matt. 1:25, Ps. 69:8, Matt. 13:55-56, Rom. 3:23, Gal. 2:16, 1 Kings 8:46)
- Did Jesus ever refuse to listen to his mother in the New Testament?
- Is Mary more understanding of our sins than God?
- Is there any danger in devotion to Mary?

21. PURGATORY: Does it exist? (p. 125)
- What is the danger in believing in purgatory?
- What scripture is used to support belief in purgatory? How do protestants interpret that scripture?
- How did many church fathers feel about purgatory?
- Explain how Luke 23:43 and Luke 16 speak against the idea of purgatory.

22. PRAYING FOR THE DEAD: Does it do any good? (p. 131)
- Should Christians pray for the dead? (Luke 16:26)
- Is paying money for the dead something the Bible supports? (Ps. 49:7, 1 Pet. 1:18-19, Acts 8:20)
- The Bible says the opportunity to repent is a gift from God. Does that mean we can put off repentance until we feel like it? Explain.

23. THE LITURGY: Is this how we should worship? (p. 138)
- Some liturgies are in languages many do not understand (Latin, Old Church Slavonic, etc.) What did the apostle Paul say about speaking languages others do not understand in church?
- DISCUSS: What are the pluses and minuses of a written formal church service?

24. THE 7 CHURCH COUNCILS: Were they infallible? (p. 142)
- Given the precedent of a church council in Acts, why don't Protestants accept the seven ecumenical councils as infallible? (James 3:2)
- Give examples of councils that contradicted each other.
- Why don't Protestants accept the seventh ecumenical council, but the Catholic and Orthodox churches do?

25. THE CHURCH FATHERS: Did they agree? (p. 148)
- Why don't most Protestants put much faith in the writings of the church fathers?
- Why is it significant that the church fathers disagreed on many things?
- DISCUSS: Catholics and Orthodox say that since the church fathers lived closer to the time of Christ and the apostles that we should heed what they wrote.

27. HOLY AND UNHOLY PLACES: Where should we meet? (p. 151)
- DISCUSS: Are there some places more holy than others?
- Jesus addressed the issue of holy places in his conversation with the woman at the well. What did he say?
- DISCUSS: Did the destruction of the Jewish temple 2,000 years ago send a message to us about holy places?
- 2 Cor. 6:16 describes God's temple today. What is it?

28. APOSTOLIC SUCCESSION: Is there such a thing? (p. 153)
- What is apostolic succession and why don't most Protestants accept it? (Mark 9:38-29, Gal. 1:1)
- Since Christ gave Peter the keys to heaven, does this mean the church has the right to keep people out? Why or why not? (Rev. 1:18).
- Catholics and Orthodox say that Christ founded the church on Peter. How do protestants respond to this argument? (1 Cor. 3:11)

29. PRIESTS: Can they forgive sins? (p. 159)
- Are all priests closer to God with special authority, or are all Christians equal?

- Does John 20:23 mean that priests and ministers have the power to forgive sins?
Explain.

30. CELIBACY: Should priests or ministers marry? (p. 168)
- Were some of the apostles married?
- Since Jesus and Paul were both celibate, should we not follow their example?
- What scriptures explain Christian celibacy?
- DISCUSS: What are the advantages and disadvantages of celibacy?

31. THE OLD TESTAMENT: Two points of view (p. 171)
- What is significant about the fact that Catholics and Orthodox are closer to the Old
Testament in practice than protestants?
- DISCUSS: How does the book of Galatians relate to the tendency of some churches
to return to an Old Testament style of worship?

32. VARIOUS DIFFERENCES (p. 174)
- What caused the Catholic and Orthodox churches to split in 1054 AD?
- What is holy fire? DISCUSS: Is it a true miracle of God?
- Is the sign of the cross something all Christians must do? Why or why not?
- What do most Protestants think about monasteries and convents?
- What is a holy fool?

33. CONCLUSION: Historical trends (p. 185)
- The Pharisees were the most religious of the Jews in the first century, and they were
the ones who resisted Jesus the most. What does this say about the roots of a religious
spirit?
- What is incrementalism and how has it affected Christians over the centuries?
- Paul says in 1 Tim. 4:3 that some strict religious practices are not from God, but from
other creatures. Who?

SELECT BIBLIOGRAPHY

Avvakum, *Archpriest Avvakum: The Life, written by Himself*, Michigan Slavic Publications, Dept. of Slavic Languages and Literature, The University of Michigan, Ann Arbor , ISBN 0-930042-33-6 (1979).

Bercot, David W., Editor, *A Dictionary of Early Christian Beliefs*, Hendrikson Publishers, P.O. Box 3473, Peabody, MA 01961-3473, ISBN 1-56563-357-1 (1998).

Meyendorff, John, *Byzantine Theology*, New York: Fordham Univ. Press, 1979.

Catechism of the Catholic Church, Image Books, published by Doubleday, 1540 Broadway, New York, NY 10036, ISBN 0-385-47967-0 (1995).

Robert L. Saucy, Th.D., John Coe, Ph.D., Alan W. Gomes, Ph.D. . *Eastern Orthodox Teaching in Comparison with The Doctrinal Position of Biola University* , Biola University, (1998).

Eerdmanns' Handbook to the History of Christianity, Lion Publishing, 121 High Street, Berkhamsted, Herts, England, ISBN 0-8028-3450-7 (1977)

Stephanou, Eusebius, *The Challenge of the Ecumenical Movement for the Orthodox Church* (booklet).

Fairbairn, Donald, *Eastern Orthodoxy through Western Eyes*, Louisville, London, Westminster John Knox Press, ISBN 0-664-22497-0 (2002)

Karmiris, John., "Concerning the Sacraments" Chapter in *Eastern Orthodox Theology: A Contemporary Reader,* edited by Daniel B. Clendenin. Grand Rapids: Baker, 1995.

McCarthy, James G. , *The Gospel According to Rome: Comparing Catholic Tradition and the Word of God*, Harvest House Publishers, Eugene, Oregon 97402, ISBN 1-56507-107-7 (1995).

Nicene and Post-Nicene Fathers, Philip Schaff, editor (1889), Sage Digital Library (1996), Volumes 1-4, Master Christian Library (CD), P.O. Box 1926, Albany, Oregon USA 97321-0509.

Renwick, A.M., *The Story of the Church* , InterVarsity Fellowship, 39 Bedford Sq., London W.C.1. (1962).

Unger's Bible Dictionary, The Moody Bible Institute of Chicago, Moody Press, c/o MLM, Chicago IL 60610, ISBN: 0-8024-9035—2 (1977).

Ware, Timothy (Kallistos), *How are we saved? The Understanding of Salvation in the Orthodox Tradition* , Light and Life Publishing, P.O. Box 26421, Minneapolis, Minnesota 55426-0421 USA, ISBN 1-880971-22-4 (1996)

Ware, Timothy (Kallistos), *The Orthodox Church*, Penguin Books USA Inc., 375 Hudson St., New York, NY 10014, ISBN 0-14-014656-3, (1963, 1993).

Slepenin, Konstantine, *Azi Pravoslaviya* (Fundamentals of Orthodoxy), Satis, St. Petersburg, Russia. ISBN 5-7868-0001-6 (2002).

U Boga Vse Zhivi (With God Everyone Lives), Blagovestnik, 129090, Moscow, Russia, Sergeiovoi Lavra, Svatoi Troitskoi Periulok 6/9, ISBN 5-89083-028-7 (2001).

INDEX